DON'T BLOW IT
with
GOD

MW00469434

Praise for
Don't Blow It with **God**

In golf as in life, bogeys happen. Every golfer makes them as does every person in life. To be successful on the golf course, you must have a plan in order before you start your round to prepare for the inevitable trouble that will come your way. Jack has written a tremendous book that will help every person as they venture through life. "Don't Blow It with God" is a "hole in one" reading experience!

RUSS HOLDEN
PGA Professional/Founder, *Caddy For A Cure*

Jack Levine allows us to peek into a very powerful and personal journey with God. God takes Jack from the "fast track" to the "faith track" as he learns the lessons one can only discover seeking God in the spiritual "waiting room" of life. A great read, especially for someone feeling a little stuck or stagnant on the pathway to God's best."

DAVID HUGHES
Senior Pastor, Church By The Glades

In tennis, there are two ways to learn something, by trial and error or being coached on how to obtain the most successful result. Jack Levine is serving up aces using his life's experiences and spiritually tough life coaching that will save you years of mistakes and wasted time. "Don't Blow It with God" shares (coaches) with you in a fun and encouraging way.

SCOTT WILLIAMS
Tennis Professional/Author of *Serious Tennis* & *Spiritually Tough Tennis* DVD
Founder/President of Match Point Ministries, Inc.
www.matchpointministries.com

We are put on this earth for many reasons, one of which is to help others navigate their way. Jack accomplishes this by sharing with us his life's journey as navigated by God's 'illuminating light.' Jack's is a stirring and thought-provoking story that every reader will benefit from, no matter where they are in their search for the proverbial light.

STEVE ROM
3-time cancer survivor/co-author of
Centered by a Miracle: A True Story of Friendship,Football and Life,
written with former Super Bowl champion, Rod Payne.

Jack's unique style of communicating God's plan for an abundant life is a must read for all Christians. This book knocks it out of the park. Jack not only talks the talk but he walks the walk. If you've been striking out and want your life to be the perfect game for God then you need to read this book. Great stories, real talk and real life applications that create a road map to a successful life and relationship with God.

CHRIS HAMMOND
Major League Baseball pitcher

Don't Blow It with God is a terrific read. It will challenge your faith, stimulate you to grow closer to Christ and help you to rethink your Christian priorities. The book is a fast read that is filled with great stories and insights from Jack's life which brings this work to reality. We heartily recommend this book. Go out and get a copy now; Don't Blow It!

WAYNE and SHARON GILL
Founders: *Oasis Compassion Agency*

Lights, Camera, Action! *Don't Blow It with God* is your blueprint for Christian living. What a great gift from Jack, a jet-setting Madison Avenue executive and successful television production owner. He grew up Jewish then battled the demons of drugs and life's temptations, and now has peace and happiness for YOU and everyone that reads this dynamic book.

CARL 'THE FOSS' FOSTER
Good Sports Magazine Radio/TV Show Host; *Reach FM* Sports Director;
Board Member of the *Fellowship of Christian Athletes (FCA),*
DeVos-Blum YMCA and *Match Point Ministries*

DON'T BLOW IT

with GOD

Your Road Map to the Ultimate Life

JACK ALAN LEVINE

DON'T BLOW IT WITH GOD
By Jack Alan Levine

Published by Great Hope Publishing, Coconut Creek, FL
www.DontBlowItWithGod.com
www.JackAlanLevine.com
www.GreatHopePublishing.com

© 2010 Jack Alan Levine. All Rights Reserved. Printed in the United States of America. Excerpt as permitted under the United States Copyright Act of 1976, no part of this publication may be reproduced or distributed in any form, or by any means, or stored in a database retrieval system, without the prior written permission of the copyright holder, except by a reviewer, who may quote brief passages in review.

Neither the publisher nor the author is engaged in rendering advice or services to the individual reader. Neither the authors nor the publisher shall be liable or responsible for any loss, injury, or damage allegedly arising from any information or suggestion in this book. The opinions expressed in this book represent the personal views of the author and not of the publisher, and are for informational purposes only.

Many of the various stories of people in this book draw from real life experience, at certain points involving a composite of stories. In some instances people's names have been changed in these stories to protect privacy.

ISBN 978-0-9825526-0-5
Library of Congress Control Number: 2009937131

Printed in Korea

Scripture taken from the HOLY BIBLE, NEW INTERNATIONAL VERSION®. Copyright © 1973, 1978, 1984 Biblica. Used by permission of Zondervan. All rights reserved.

Scripture taken from the New King James Version. Copyright © 1982 by Thomas Nelson, Inc. Used by permission. All rights reserved.

Scripture taken from the NEW AMERICAN STANDARD BIBLE®, Copyright © 1960, 1962, 1963, 1968, 1971, 1972, 1973, 1975, 1977, 1995 by The Lockman Foundation. Used by permission.

Scripture taken from The Message. Copyright © 1993, 1994, 1995, 1996, 2000, 2001, 2002. Used by permission of NavPress Publishing Group.

Dedication

To my wonderful wife Beth and my three children, Ricky, Jackson and Talia. To my mom and dad (Marcia and Jerry); my brother Mike and sister-in-law, Leslie; and my favorite nephews in the whole world, Zachary and Dylan. I used to think that perhaps, just maybe, I was the luckiest man in the world ... because of all of you, I am now sure of it. I thank God for you every day.

Table of Contents

Foreword

If there is any being you don't want to blow it with, it certainly is our God, and Jack shows you the way, even if you THINK you have blown it!

I have learned that the most important spiritual principle to a life filled with enrichment, is living by and acting upon what I refer to as life's great "Tap Moments." I see how God has "tapped" Jack to deliver the word of God with the ability to relate to each of us on how to live an abundant Christian lifestyle each day, and experience true joy, peace and prosperity.

When writing my first spiritual bestseller, "The Tap," I was inspired by the biblical passage from Luke 12:48 "from those to whom much is entrusted, much will be expected." Jack certainly lives by this most important life mantra.

Wealth is found in the responsible stewardship as I'm blessed daily by the smiling faces and completed villages in Haiti built through our Caring House Project Foundation (www.frank-mckinney.com). Jack has dedicated his life, from a successful Madison Avenue executive and television production company owner, to acting on God's "Tap," calling on his heart to use a similar spiritual practice on this test of endurance for the ultimate prize, our soul.

When you read this book, you'll notice something different right away, and that's because Jack Alan Levine is having a conversation with YOU rather than simply 'writing at you.'

If you met Jack tomorrow, you'd know him by the sound of his voice in the pages to come.

He's real. He's direct. He's loving.

And his writing style doesn't try to sound holier-than-thou because Jack doesn't live that way. Christians often point out that God meets people when they are experiencing challenging circumstances in life, and Jack's words do the same thing; they meet you right where you are.

Whether you're a seeker, believer or a season saint, *Jack Alan Levine* proves by living God's Great Commandments and Great Commission that there is great hope in using this roadmap to the ultimate life.

I know you will thoroughly enjoy *"Don't Blow It with God!"* Be sure to share these wonderful insights with your family and friends too.

Frank McKinney
5-Time Bestselling Author, including "The Tap" (www.The-Tap.com)

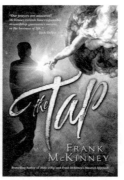

Introduction

I wrote this book because I believe it offers a road map to the ultimate Christian life, one filled with the joy of the Lord and the peace of the Lord, a peace that transcends all understanding. I wish someone had written it for me so I wouldn't have wasted so much time trying to "do life" my own way.

I also wrote it so that you and I will never be able to say, "I blew it because I didn't know what to do." I believe God has laid it out very clearly through His words in this book.

Over the last several years, many people have asked me why I am so happy and how I stay so calm in many pressure-packed situations. The answer is in this book. I believe God has provided us a way by which we can live not the ordinary Christian life or the plain old Christian life, but the ULTIMATE CHRISTIAN LIFE. But like any other map, if you don't follow it, you'll get lost. So, this is for all of you who want to make sure you are heading in the right direction and want to make sure you get to the right destination. What a shame to take a long trip and get to the wrong place.

I am so grateful to God that He has shown me the way to live the ultimate Christian life, and it breaks my heart to see many Christian friends and believers losing the battle. They suffer in anguish, fear, despair, and discouragement, overcome and overwhelmed by the circumstances and happenings of this life. It need not be so.

In theory, we shouldn't need anything more than God and His word (the Bible) to serve as our illuminating lights to the joy of our lives. And we really don't. Yet I believe God has inspired this book and has allowed me the privilege of sharing its message with you based on my experience with God and my life. I share these with you joyfully and believe they will benefit you tremendously and will literally change your life in a way you never imagined possible. You might see a few verses mentioned more than once throughout the book. Take note of them... it is because they are so important!

Wishing you all of God's best, which is exactly what He wants to give you always. And a reminder... Don't Blow It With God!

Love,
Jack

Live the Life You Imagined

Some years back, I was having dinner with a friend of mine who was going through a divorce. Of course, I told him that God's will for his life was that he wouldn't get divorced, but he was past that point, unfortunately. He had a few children, and as he talked about his wife and the divorce settlement, he looked me dead in the eye and said, "I have to have my kids, Jack. I just have to have my kids." The most important thing to him in the whole world was his children, and at that moment, it hit me. I stopped him and said, "Phil, that's exactly what God must think about us."

God must be looking down at us and saying. "I have to have my kids." It's a great comfort to know that God loves us and is our protective father, a father who is watching out for us through every storm in our life, a father who has to have us, who will do anything to get us, and has done everything to get us. The question is whether we have accepted His effort and embraced Him as our heavenly Father. It's a big question.

As I thought about Phil's approaching divorce and the storms it was causing in his heart – storms that were going to rip at every part of his life and would probably destroy some things that were most important to him – I couldn't help comparing that to a coming hurricane. It's not unusual to think of the troubles we face as storms, but this conversation with Phil took place in 2004, which was a very busy hurricane season for south Florida. We'd been in storm-warning mode several times. For the first time in my 20-plus years of living in Florida, these threatening weather events became all too real, with names such as Frances and Jean. In later years, we'd have other killer hurricanes named Charlie and Wilma.

And while I'm glad to have checked hurricanes off my to do list of life's adventures, I don't care to repeat the process. For the inexperienced, there can be a feeling of excitement and adventure from the idea of toughing it out and braving the elements, but believe me, the romance wears off as soon as the power goes off, the sewage backs up, and the food rots in the warm fridge. What has been interesting for me is to see how the thought process of a person's response to a storm forecast and its arrival is so similar to a person's spiritual condition.

It all starts with the warnings. We were forewarned these hurricanes were coming. We were told in advance how they were developing and what would likely happen, unlike my cousin in California who does not have that privilege because his earthquakes hit without warning. The ground just explodes under your feet or under your car. If you're out walking or driving, you could easily wind up dead, but it's not as if you could have prepared. The only way to prepare for earthquakes is not to live where they are prone to happen. Hurricanes last longer, but at least we get warnings – at every hour of the day, on every television station, every radio station, and every place you could possibly look for information. We are inundated with warnings that a storm is coming. And not just any storm, but a bad storm!

If you were smart, they all said, and if you wanted to save your life and your possessions, you would board up for the storms. You would take the necessary precautions. You would get bottled water and other supplies, so you could survive the storm. Naturally, being intelligent and wanting to keep your possessions and your life and the other things that were important to you, you did just that – you and half a million other people at the same time, certainly adding to the stress level. Sometimes, it seemed the storms first hit in the checkout lines before they ever hit the coast.

In truth, nobody could say they weren't warned. They could say they chose not to believe the newscasters, the politicians, neighbors, friends, and family members giving the warnings, which meant by default that they were choosing to suffer the consequences of being unprepared. Ah, but they could never truthfully say they didn't know what was coming. It was obvious, judging from the sheer number of people that paid attention to warnings from the newscasters and the weather people, that we were giving those people a lot of credibility. We were taking them and all their predictions and analyses to heart and acting on them.

What amazes me, though, is that so many believers in Jesus Christ don't give Jesus the same credibility that we give newscasters, politicians, friends, and neighbors. God warns us very specifically that there is a storm coming, that there is trouble ahead, and that we need to be prepared. So, how is it that, immediately upon hearing the warnings of weather forecasters and politicians, we scurry to buy every bottle of water, every piece of plywood, and all the batteries within a hundred-mile radius of our homes. We do everything the newscasters, weather people, and politicians tell us to do. However, when it comes to our God who loves us, our father who has to have His kids – who wants us to have His peace, His love, His mercy, forgiveness, grace, and joy every single day – how is it when our God gives us a warning, we don't heed it?

All I can think is that we just don't believe God, because in my mind, there is no other explanation for not heeding his warning. If God is God, then why wouldn't we do everything He says? Are we simply calling Him "our Lord" in words only? Here's a warning: Don't do that. In Luke 6:46, Jesus specifically calls people to account for doing that: "Why do you call me 'Lord, Lord' and not do what I say?" If we believe God is God, and we call on His name, then we should do what He says. Why?

Because God is trying to prepare you and me for some bad weather ahead, and trust me, God loves us a whole lot more than all those newscasters and politicians. He is not just relaying weather conditions and exaggerating them to drum up ratings. He loves us because we are His children, and He wants to protect us. Our God tells us exactly what to do when the storms come. He warns us that there will be two different kinds of storms: the ultimate one that's already been named, called Judgment Day, and then there are the seasonal storms of life. I want to look at those life storms first and see how we are to deal with them. So here we go!

Now, insanity has been defined as "doing the same thing over and over and expecting a different result." Sometimes, the cure for our "life of insanity" can only come from a breakthrough that's rough enough to knock you off your same old hamster wheel you call life. Believe me, I know what I'm talking about.

You could say I went through a period of such insanity because my life consisted of a continuous spin cycle of partying, drugs, gambling, and fast-track living. I was caught in the proverbial hamster wheel, thinking, believing, and desperately hoping that somewhere in all this stuff I was doing, there had to be something that would make me feel satisfied and fulfilled. I was living a rerun and expecting a different result. How crazy is that?

Most people I talk to can relate on some level. We all have a hamster wheel or two with different labels on them. What's yours? Career? Image? Alcohol? Porn? Drugs? Sex? Money? Fame? How's that working for you? Are you satisfied with your relationships, your job, your finances? Are you satisfied with your life? Are you satisfied spiritually?

Or, do you feel as if something is missing, as if you're doing everything you know how to do, and life is still not what it could be? You're working hard and playing hard and getting nowhere.

"Nowhere" is easy to get to and hard to escape. I know because I landed in nowhere by putting my car through a fence during a drug-induced blackout. When I regained some semblance of consciousness and sobriety, I had to face an ugly realization – at age 36, this was neither the life I had imagined for myself nor the life I wanted to be living.

Looking back, I see that I had to nearly lose that life (one that wasn't what I had imagined or hoped for) to get to this one (one that is better than I could ever have imagined and more than I could ever have hoped for), which I wouldn't trade for anything.

Being an ad agency executive is in my blood. I can't help but go around the house, singing advertising slogans, and one of my all-time favorites is, "You'll look better in a sweater washed in Woolite." (Hey, maybe it will come up in a trivia game one day, and then you'll be glad I told you.) My wife always wants to fast forward over the commercials when we watch TV, and I want to fast forward to them.

Some slogans originate from unexpected sources. For example, Henry David Thoreau was not an advertising executive; he was a poet. He came up with a catchy slogan, anyway, which I saw used a while back in an ad for a large insurance company. The headline of the ad was "Live the life you imagined." I want to ask you something.

Are you living the life you imagined?

Think about this for a minute. When we were kids, we all used to imagine what our lives would be like when we grew up. In our imaginations, our grown-up life was exciting and fulfilling. No kid dreams about someday mowing lawns or working as a janitor in an office building. Kids dream about being astronauts, athletes, scientists, rock stars, the President, firefighters, or police officers. Why? Because they imagine that life is going to be exciting. As they grow, their dreams might change. They might decide that, instead of being an astronaut, they want to be a doctor, teacher, or a lawyer, but they still think it will be exciting, fulfilling, and satisfying.

When I was growing up, I used to imagine myself as a baseball player for the New York Yankees. I'd picture thousands of people screaming for me from the stands, baseball cards with my picture on them, people asking for my autograph, and the joy of playing on a field that has seen the likes of Mickey Mantle, Joe DiMaggio, and Babe Ruth. What could be more exciting than that? As I got older, I knew that it was probably never going to happen because I grew up in New York, and we could only play baseball for three or four months a year. It's tough to compete with the kids from Arizona, California, and Florida, where they can play year-round, but it was thrilling to think about. I imagined my future life being exciting!

So, let me again ask the question: Are you living the life you imagined? Is this truly what you thought it would be? Do you find your life satisfying and fulfilling? Or, like most, has real life turned out to be significantly less than you always hoped for? Do you come home numb, with every day blending into every other, wondering what you're accomplishing, if anything at all, and wanting something more?

Most of us are not living the life we imagined, and that's because we are not living God's plan for our lives. God has a perfect plan for each of us, and it's always better than the one we imagine or devise, but until we deal with God, we can't get the benefits of that plan. We will keep running on our frustrating, disappointing hamster wheel, wondering if this is all there is. Why?

I'm a huge baseball fan, so let me explain it in baseball terms and see if it makes sense. Picture yourself as a player at bat. You get ready to swing, and every time the pitcher throws the ball, you hold the bat up above your head, swing it straight down like an axe, and bang it on home plate. The balls keep zooming past you. Maybe you actually do connect with one, but because of the way you're swinging the bat, anytime you hit one, the ball simply goes straight down and hits the ground. Are you ever going to hit well and get base hits? No! You'll never have success. Why? Because you're doing it wrong! Whether it's swinging the bat or trying to live the life you imagined, it won't matter how much time you spend doing it or how hard you try, concentrate, or repeat self-esteem slogans to yourself. If you're doing it wrong and if you're not willing to consider that there might be a better way, then you will never get the results you want. Does that capture how your life seems to be going?

If so, examine yourself. Are you doing the same things over and over and getting nowhere? No wonder you're feeling crazy!

What do I mean? It's the second part of the God thing.

The first part was to make sure you were saved by accepting Jesus Christ as your Savior, so you could access all that God has for you. The second part is growing in that relationship. Hear me clearly: This is not something you "do" to get more brownie points with God. You can't earn favor with Him; you can't "work harder" to make Him give you more and to "renew" your spot in heaven or to make God love you more. You are saved. It's a done deal, but the more you commit yourself to growing spiritually – getting to know God through prayer, reading the Bible, and obeying – the more you access God's perfect plan for your life. However, you can be saved and still not grow, you can be saved and stay on your "hamster wheels," and most likely, nothing will change. That's what happened to me at first. I was saved at 33 and didn't commit to growing my relationship with God. I didn't change what I was doing. I just stayed on my "hamster wheel" on my trip to nowhere for three years.

And you say, "Hey, Jack, why would I want to get saved if you got saved and ended up crashing, literally and figuratively?"

Let me hit that issue head on. Lots of people think that if they believe in Jesus, they should never have problems in their lives. Get real. Being saved from hell isn't a free ticket to do stupid stuff and not have any consequences. It's not a bubble that surrounds you, so you're free of any problems. The Bible says, in James and in 1 Peter, that we will have trials and tribulations of many kinds, but God uses them to strengthen us and mature us so that we are perfect and complete and lacking nothing.

Romans 8:28 is a verse we all need to get familiar with. I paraphrase it this way, "All things work together for the good of those that believe." Get this in your mind. You're driving home, and you get a speeding ticket. You're mad at yourself and at the cop; you're going to get points on your license; and you have to pay a triple fine – 200 bucks. The day is ruined! Are you sure? How do you know? Perhaps, if you hadn't been stopped, you would have died in a car accident. You don't know. As a believer in Jesus, you are to put your faith in Him and His promises. God says all things – not some things, not a few, not most – but "all things work together for the good of those that believe," even the things that seem lousy at the time. If you trust God, then that will be the case.

Keep focused on God, and believe that all things work together for the good of those that believe. How could that be true? Examples abound. In 1812, at the age of three, Louis Braille lost his eyesight when he accidentally stabbed himself – a tragedy that would have put any child into a state of despair and hopelessness. However, by the age of fifteen, Braille had finished creating the system of raised dots that have become what the world knows as the Braille alphabet, and multitudes have benefited.

Gianna Jessen was supposed to be aborted. By God's providence, she was born alive before the abortionist arrived at the clinic to make sure that things were running "as planned." A staff nurse called 911, and newborn Gianna was transported to a hospital, where she spent three months in ICU. She is now a young adult who has overcome incredible obstacles, including cerebral palsy brought on by the saline abortion procedure, and she speaks on behalf of the unborn. How many babies have been kept from abortion because of Gianna's willingness to allow God to use her problems to help others?

Many other famous cases, such as Joni Eareckson Tada and Dave

Dravecky, have turned what the world sees as a tragedy into something God can use to bless others.

Let me share with you God's great promises for believers. In Revelation 2:11b, God speaks and says, "... He who overcomes ..." Overcomes what? You have to overcome Satan's attacks. You have to overcome the storm by sticking with Christ and living your life focused on Him. God says, "He who overcomes will not be hurt at all by the second death." You won't be hurt by the final storm of judgment because you will be in heaven with God.

He promises, "To him who overcomes and does my will to the end [not halfway but all the way to the end], I will give authority over the nations" (Revelation 2:26). Authority over the nations! Can you imagine you and Jesus having authority over the nations, ruling together with your brother Christ, ruling your father's empire? This has to be the greatest thing ever. And to him who overcomes, Revelation 3:5b, "... I will never blot out his name from the book of life, but will acknowledge his name before my Father and his angels."

He further promises in Revelation 3:21, that "To him who overcomes, I will give the right to sit with me on my throne, just as I overcame and sat down with my Father on his throne." Jesus promised that we are heirs to the throne of heaven!

Last, in Revelation 21:6–7, He says, "...To him who is thirsty I will give to drink without cost from the spring of the water of life. He who overcomes will inherit all this, and I will be his God and he will be my son."

Why does He make that promise? Because of His love for His children. The most famous verse in the Bible is probably John 3:16: "For God so loved the world that he gave his one and only son, that whoever believes in him shall not perish but have eternal life." Because He loved us – before we even knew about Him, by the way – He made a way for us to spend eternity with Him. That was as far away from my background as anyone's, so in case you're wondering about the rest of my story, here it is.

I was brought up Jewish. I was Bar Mitzvahed when I was 13, but it was like a fake one. I never went to Hebrew school, so my father donated some money to the temple, and they let me say some lines in English to make my grandmother happy. My parents were middle-class. We grew up in Yonkers, New York, but fortunately, for me, my father and mother spoiled my brother and me pretty well. They were wonderful parents and gave us everything. After high school, I went to Syracuse University in Syracuse, New York, where I majored in advertising. Given my lifestyle, it was a miracle I graduated with two degrees: one in advertising and one in sociology.

My education took an interesting turn. I did a lot of drugs, way too many, starting in high school. I continued using in Syracuse and took that habit, a habit that would nearly kill me, with me to my career on Madison Avenue. (I have that under control now. I can't say that I will ever be completely free from the desire to do drugs, but God has now given me the grace to deal with it and have victory over it.) After graduating from Syracuse, I went to live my new dream life on Madison Avenue, where I worked for some of the largest ad agencies in the country on some of the most famous ad campaigns such as AT&T's "Reach Out and Touch Someone" and the U.S. Army's "Be All You Can Be." That carried a lot of prestige, and I was on the fast track. I was the poster boy of a "hot shot" rising executive.

For years, I wasn't satisfied with anything or by anything, but you wouldn't know it by looking at me. Outwardly, anyone would have decided that Jack had a pretty good life – young, fast-tracking in a top New York ad agency on Madison Avenue, and with lots of friends. I was a nice, educated, articulate guy with a loving family. Jack must be very satisfied with how things are shaping up for him.

The truth was quite the opposite. I was never satisfied, and believe me, I tried many artificial ways to make myself happy. Prestige, power, money, drugs, sex, gambling. I tried all that and more, but when my head hit the pillow at night, I was still miserable. I would literally say to myself, "My life stinks. There has to be more than this. Is this the way my life is supposed to be? Is this why I was born? Was I really just born to do all these drugs that are now killing me and no longer giving me pleasure?" That's the thing about drugs. They're fun in the beginning, and then the fun ends, and it gets miserable. It's the same with alcohol. For a while it's fun, but then it's about hangovers and stupid behavior and trying to get through the day, so you can have that next drink.

I realized my plan to make myself happy was not working. I didn't know why I was alive. Even back then, before I accepted Jesus as my Lord and Savior, I was trying to talk to God, saying, "Hey, God, there has to be more than going out to play baseball. There has to be more than going to the racetrack, having sex, and making money. There has to be more than this, right? Why am I here? What is the purpose of my life? You think there is some way that you and I can communicate, God?"

Can you relate to that feeling of dissatisfaction in the midst of your life now – in the midst of all the stuff you do and all the stuff you have? And how come all that "stuff" can't satisfy?

Satisfaction is hard to find and hard to keep because of doubt and fear. We don't know what the future is going to be; we don't know what our lives are supposed to be about or why we are here. We don't have to ask ourselves those exact questions out loud, but the fact that we are constantly looking for the next thing to make us "happy" proves that the questions are there in our soul. Where is all this life leading?

Looking back, I can say that I probably would have continued to do that for the rest of my life, except in 1987, God gave me a "lifectomy" in the form of back surgery. It put me flat on my back for about six months. No getting out of bed, no walking, nothing. Drove me nuts. At the time, I viewed it as a tragedy, but I now consider it a tremendous blessing. Why the change?

God used that time not to shorten my life or take away from it, but to enhance it and enlarge it. It got me thinking. And I had plenty of time to do that.

The thinking led to this revelation: I had been surgically removed from the fast track of my life (the hamster wheel), and I had a choice to make. I could continue with my life as usual once I healed from this surgery, or I could change it. It just hit me that I had been taken off the "hamster wheel." God had pulled me out of the rat race and put me on the bench, so I could look in and see. And all I could say was, God, my life stinks. This life is horrible, people might think it's great and awesome, but this is not what it's about. I didn't know why I was, who I was, what my purpose in life was. It took three more years and a move to Florida before I came to know Jesus Christ.

Like a lot of people who move to Florida, I was trying to get away from something. For me, it was the drug problem. I left my job on Madison Avenue and decided that if I didn't get away from my usual circle of friends who partied their brains out every day, I would end up dead or destitute. I needed a new start. I remember telling my father. (He was an old school guy. I mean he had no clue what was going on.) I told him the truth about what was happening, and he, as always wanting to protect my mom, said, "Go ahead, go to Florida, but don't tell your mother the real reason." So, I didn't.

I came down to Florida and still partied a little too much, but God was knocking on my heart. One day, after I had broken up with this girl that I was living with, I walked into a church, looking for a place to pray. I remember it was a Tuesday, and I asked the secretary if I could pray there. She said sure. I was in the sanctuary for a couple of hours, talking to God, and when I came out, the pastor asked if I would like to know about Jesus Christ. I said no, I just wanted to pray.

"Here's a Bible," he said. "You never have to come to church again. It would be a good thing if you did, but coming to church is not a requirement for having a relationship with Jesus Christ. Everything you need to know is in this Bible."

I was intrigued, took it home, started to read it, had questions, highlighted them, circled them, called the pastor up, met with him a few times, and a few months later, after running out of questions and objections about God, I was saved. That was at age 33.

At age 36, God had me in the gutter, where I needed to be, with my drug problem. I had blacked out and put my car through a fence. It was truly a miracle that I didn't die. That's when I finally said, "Lord, I have to give this over to you. I can't stop on my own." Of course, I had to go into rehab because of that event, and the gig was up. My secret was out, but I got the help I needed. And God was waiting for me, where He had been all along, still loving me.

It was then that he put a Bible verse into my life. Matthew 6:33 says, "But seek first his kingdom and his righteousness, and all these things will be given to you as well." By "things," it means your needs will be met. So, I put God first. I remember saying to God, "I don't care if You want me shining shoes on the street corner for the rest of my life. It's good enough for me."

That's my story. Since putting God first, I have been growing in my relationship with God; my life has changed in so many ways for the positive, and I can't imagine not "going there" with Jesus. But remember, it's this second thing, this commitment to that relationship, that has made the difference. God is always ready for us to go deeper into that relationship with Him, but unfortunately, we are the ones who tend to wander off or to treat it lightly.

Putting God first means making a relationship with Him a priority. Real relationships take time, effort, and commitment. Don't tell me that your definition of a love relationship is "I'll see you for an hour a week because I have to, and oh, by the way, God, if I am ever broke and need money or get sick, I'll call you to help me." Is that how someone expresses love to you? That doesn't sound like somebody I love. Somebody I love is somebody I want to be with all the time – someone I want to share my heart and soul with. That someone wants to help me, come to me for guidance, teach me, and love me, and I want to share everything – my happiness or my sadness and tears – with him or her,. God wants that relationship with you. He's always ready; He's just waiting for you.

Are you now part of God's family – one of His children? God loves His kids. It's not about how smart we are or what we do. The stronger our relationship with Him, the more peace and satisfaction we will have in life, regardless of what's going on around us. In 1 Peter 1:8, it says, "Though you have not seen him, you love him; and even though you do not see him now, you believe in him and are filled with an inexpressible and glorious joy..." Have you ever longed for your life to be filled with inexpressible and glorious joy?

If you're already a Christian, and you aren't living the spiritual life you imagined, I really want you to remember the story of the prodigal son (Luke 15:11–31). I want you to go back, read it, pray on it, and just remember how that father embraced his son when he turned back. It didn't matter that the son had squandered everything his father had given him. The son came to his senses and went home, and his father welcomed him with open arms, expressed his love for him, and celebrated.

That's how God feels about you today. Turn back to Him. Admit you've wandered off. Tell Him, "God I'm back. I don't know where we are going. I am going to let your Holy Spirit take me and guide me, and I want to be with You. I don't want to live like this anymore because living life my way stinks."

Get off your "hamster wheel." Go with God, the creator of the universe and the creator of you, and start living the life that He imagined for you!

What are you waiting for – another storm warning?

Yet When It Grows 2

Once in a while you just need to stop your life and realize what's important. And sometimes, God hits the "pause" button with your name on it until you learn what's important to him.

God hit the "pause Jack's life" button on me in 2002 by calling me to leave a television production company I had founded and operated for over nine years. Here's what I was thinking back when this happened.

I knew that, at some point, God would lead me to the next phase of my working life and that it wouldn't happen instantaneously. A new career or ministry opportunity, like anything else, will have to start with a seed and will take time to grow.

I was learning many things since I sold that business to pursue ministry and charity work – things such as if I don't stop my life and pay closer attention, then God, as my ultimate Father, would make sure I did. And I was learning how to put God and family first and to really find joy in the simplest of things. I was especially learning how much He wants and expects His children to grow up.

I was looking at my infant son, Jackson. He sleeps in his crib every night, but we bring him into our bed in the morning. I'm looking at how much he's grown in just a few months. He can crawl now, and when we put him in our bed, he tries to crawl off the edge. He tries to get away and thinks he can just crawl off the edge of the bed and keep going forward.

I let him get close to the edge, and then I grab his legs and pull him back. I'm laughing at him because as soon as I let him go, he crawls off again toward the edge. He would keep going and fall – if I let him. We have a high bed, and he'd take a pretty good tumble for a guy his size. But every time he gets to the edge, I pull him back and laugh because his efforts are futile. I know that one day, not long from now, he'll have grown enough that he'll understand, and instead of crawling to the edge and blindly falling off, he'll find another way, a better way, to get down. Then, my job will be to pull him back from the edge of other things in his life that can harm him. But for now, his efforts are futile; he just doesn't know it. So, he cries because I won't let him keep going and because he's not getting what he wants. For him, it seems like a perfectly good idea to keep crawling, but the thing he doesn't know and can't understand is that if he keeps going, he will fall to the floor and break his neck.

Now, I'm his father. I love him. I grab him before he falls. Am I being mean? No, I'm protecting him. I won't let him do what he wants because it's not in his best interest. But he cries, anyway, because I'm stopping him.

I'm watching all this, realizing that God is the same way with His own kids – us. Me. God must be sitting there laughing at me sometimes, shaking His head, saying, "Jack, you just have no clue what's in your best interest. You're running off the side of the bed (or to the next job or career) crying over and over, "God, this is what I want to do; this is what I want to do. Why won't You let me do this? You must not love me if You're stopping me."

God just pulls me back away from the edge and says, "No, no, no, I stop you because I love you, because I'm your Father, and I can see where you're headed, and it's not a good idea."

Like Jackson, I've done some growing, but I'm nowhere near as grown up, spiritually, as my Father, God, wants or expects me to be.

It's been about two-and-a-half months since God called me out of the television production business. I'm a guy who likes to be busy, and I have to tell you I have not been busy. Well, I've been busy doing *stuff*.

I don't know how I ever had time to work. I have more stuff to do now that I am not working, but I'm ready for the next stage of my life.

I've been seeking God's face, attempting to humble myself before Him, to turn from my wicked ways, and I've really been thinking about that and looking for what's next. I knew I was supposed to leave that company. I felt God calling me out of there to do some kind of ministry work, so I knew it was time to go, but nothing has really happened since. I have the desire to preach, and a few things happened in that area, but nothing concrete. It's not as if I'm on the road to a new career. If you're a guy, you know that's a frustrating place to be parked.

God and I talk regularly about this – I, by praying, and God, by responding through the prompting of His Holy Spirit living inside me. I'm praying; we're going back and forth; and God finally reveals to me the reason he took me out of the business world was to show me how evil and wicked my flesh is. I have to confess that if I had not gotten out of the rat race I was in (and you don't have to live in New York City to be in that race), if I had not been stopped so I could really look at things, I might have missed God's blessings. He showed me things that I needed to get rid of, things that scripture calls "the wickedness of the flesh." What's that, you ask? Stuff like anger, rage, jealousy, evil, slander, malice – in one degree or another, I saw all that in me. And man, I hated it. I hated that these things were all in me, and I hated that I'd never noticed before. God had to take me out of the race and hit the "pause Jack" button, so I could really see just how bad it was. Now, I realize that when you're working, and you're busy just living, you don't see it. You can't see it until you sit there, without distractions, and focus.

I said, "Okay, Lord, I understand now. I understand what Your motivation was and why it has to be that way, why I had to leave the business world, stop my life, and make some changes." I'm glad, truly glad, that God pulled me out of the business world and gave me time to see the things He wants me to deal with, so I can grow up spiritually. Most of us have things that happen to us, and we can't understand why God is allowing them to happen, just as Jackson couldn't understand why I kept pulling him back to me, but we need to trust that God loves us and is acting in our best interest at all times, even when we can't figure out why. One of the first blessings I got out of being "between careers," so to speak, is that God keeps pulling me back to Him, and the closer I am to Him, the more of His protection and love I feel. Do you need to feel that too? Maybe that tough time you're going through, or have been through, was really God trying to pull you back to Him. So, I wonder, is there something you keep wanting to do, some place you keep trying to get to or thing you keep reaching for that God seems to be keeping away from you? Maybe He is keeping you away from it because He sees that if you keep going, you're going to fall off the edge and hurt yourself, your marriage, your family, or your health.

The downside, at least temporarily, of being pulled closer to God is that the closer we get to our holy God, the more we see how unholy we are. It's one of those times when you have to face the truth of that old saying that things will get worse before they get better. God wants us to have joyful lives, but sometimes, He has to show us things about ourselves that are standing in the way of our joy and need to be removed – kind of like cutting branches off a tree to prune it, so it grows bigger and stronger. The good news is that He shows us these things and gives us a way to deal with them, so we can find more joy.

So, I saw all this crud in myself, and for a while, I felt like such a wretch. I really got bummed out and miserable. I said, "God, now that I'm not working, I'm looking at myself and starting to see these things about who I am, and I am just the worst."

God says, "That's right, and that's exactly why Jesus had to die for your sins. But Jack, I don't want you to be defeated by that thought. I don't want you to be defeated by your flesh; I don't want you to be defeated when your heart condemns you." See, God knows us through and through, and He knows that our hearts will condemn us. He knows we can be really critical of ourselves and how we act. God is letting you know that your heart is going to condemn you from time to time and so will your friends and so will Satan. You are going to be condemned, not just by those outside sources, but also by inside ones – your flesh, your mind, your own heart will condemn you, and then what are you going to do? Sink and dissipate into this level of torment and despair and depression and run away from God? Have a permanent pity party?

No, no, no. God says we don't have to live that way. He wants us to run *to* Him and not be afraid. He wants us to relax in His presence, rather than fearing we're going to get whacked and be tempted to run.

In 1 John 3:18–20, He tells us how to live our lives, so we don't get condemned: "Dear children, let us not love with words or tongue but with actions and in truth. This then is how we know that we belong to the truth, and how we set our hearts at rest in his presence whenever our hearts condemn us. For God is greater than our hearts, and he knows everything." According to God, it doesn't matter what your tongue says and it doesn't matter what your words say. He says the only way that you are supposed to love, the only way you are supposed to live, is with actions and in truth. If I do that, I can set my heart at rest in His presence, even if my heart wants to condemn me or torment me. So, while my heart was bummed out and condemning me for the anger, rage, jealousy, evil, slander, and malice that I was finally seeing, my words about myself didn't matter. What mattered was what I did about those things.

So, I confessed them and repented. I don't have to stay bummed out if I take action according to what God's truth tells me to do. By repenting of them, I change the way I live around, and act with, others. I don't have to feel miserable or wretched, and neither do you. If you're feeling that way about yourself, then get into the Word. In 1 John 3:21–22, it goes on to say, "Dear friends, if our hearts do not condemn us, we have confidence before God and receive from him anything we ask, because we obey his commands and do what pleases him." The reverse of that is if our hearts *do* condemn us, if we disobey His commands, and we don't do what pleases Him, then we can't go before God with confidence, and we can't get what we ask.

As a Christian, this is a no-brainer. Of course, I want to go before God with confidence. Of course, I want to get what I ask, which is His blessing in my life, and to do that, I will live by actions and truth. Is it gonna be tough? Yes. Am I gonna want to quit or give in to that pity and the condemnation? Yes, but God has given us a way out of that. In 2 Peter 1:3–4, it says: "His divine power has given us everything we need for life and godliness through our knowledge of him who called us by his own glory and goodness. Through these he has given us his very great and precious promises, so that through them you may participate in the divine nature and *escape* (emphasis mine) the corruption in the world caused by evil desires."

God has given us a way out, a way to escape that crud we still see in our hearts when we finally stop to see it. Our way out is by accessing His divine power, a power that has given us everything we need for life and godliness. How do we get it? Through our knowledge of Him who called us by His own glory and goodness. But guess what? If you don't have knowledge of Him, you can't access His divine power. We need to get that knowledge and grow it.

So, I'm learning. I'm getting knowledge from scripture, and I'm putting it into practice during this free time I have now, which is turning out to be a busy place for me, spiritually speaking.

One of the first places I'm relearning how to live in truth and action is with my family. Oddly enough, being out of the rat race is teaching me how to enjoy life; I mean really enjoy it. Some of you are probably thinking, yeah, hit the golf course or spend the day fishing, let the wife deal with the kids. Who wants to go back to work? But that's not it. I'm learning how to focus on the little things and really getting a lot of joy out of them, like spending time with my family. For example, I was supposed to fly to Boston to drive in a harness race. I do some amateur harness racing (it's a great hobby). Five o'clock in the morning, I wake up, and I can't get peace about the trip. I have my plane ticket; I'm packed; I'm listed in the program as driving the horse; and I can't get peace about the trip. I start thinking, okay – I'm tired; it's five in the morning. What do I expect? I have a cup of tea, and now, it's a quarter after five. I go, whoa, something ain't right here. So, I sit there and pray for a few minutes. I go, "God what's the deal here?" I still can't get peace about it. I go back into the bedroom. My wife Beth is sleeping with Jackson next to her. I'm thinking, man, I just want to be back in bed. I just want to be hugging Beth, hugging Jackson. I thought about it, prayed about it, and God gave me the peace to change plans.

I called the horse's trainer, a friend of mine who is also a driver. I said, "I'm not coming."

He said, "No problem. I'll drive the horse; no big deal."

And it wasn't a big deal. I'd thought it was, until I got peace from God, but once I got that, no problem. I got back into bed and had the most peaceful, joyful feeling. My wife and kid were sleeping, and I was hugging them. Later that day, Beth asked me, "Why are you so happy today? You're giggling and laughing, and you haven't been giggling or laughing for a month."

I had to say it was because I had God's peace. I'd spent time with Him to find out what was important for that moment, and it was my family, not my hobby. I'm not saying that I wasn't supposed to be on that plane or that I would have been hurt in the horse race; I don't know. What I am saying is that God and family are the two most important things, and when I live that way, when I act that way, I have joy that I didn't have in the rat race.

Here's another newfound joy that almost sounds silly. Sometimes I sit in McDonald's in the morning having an egg-and-cheese biscuit and a cup of tea, and I can't tell you how wonderful it is to take the time to relax and enjoy some food and have a peaceful moment without the world crashing in on me. Have you done that lately? If not, I urge you to try it. Just sit there, even if it's five or ten minutes, so you understand about the little things. It's not having great accomplishments that is so important. I wouldn't have said that back when I was in television production because there, in that role, I focused only on producing millions of dollars a year in revenues for the company. Accomplishments are nice and wonderful, but I'm learning, because God is showing me, that in the little things, in the everyday living, second by second, I can experience a joy I've never known before. Climbing back into bed with my wife and kid. Sitting at McDonald's and being glad I'm alive. Or having a cup of tea. They're such simple things, such inexpensive things, and yet I'm grateful to have them.

However, I will also be grateful when I start working again. Not working full time can really challenge your faith. Waiting on God's timing always does that, yet He always finds little ways to encourage me, like with my monthly Promise Keepers newsletter that talked about the mid-life crisis in men. This line got my attention: "Being unemployed right now is part of God's purpose for your life. Like Churchill's election defeat, it may be hard to see what the plan is, but you must trust him with your life." I'm thinking what a great message for me right now – unemployed, looking not necessarily for the next job, but looking for the next stage of my life, which will definitely include work. I plan to be working, and I'm anxious and excited about the future. I said in the beginning that I'm not a sit-still guy, and everybody who knows me knows that. Lately, those business wheels have started spinning in my head.

Since I've been out of the television production business, I've come up with five or six different ideas that I was ready to do, each one a business idea that I thought would be something Godly. I prayed about them and I felt the Holy Spirit of God speaking to me very clearly in the deepest parts of my soul.

With the first one, God says, "No, don't do that."

"No, God? Okay, you know it sounded good to me, but okay."

With the second one, He says, "No, don't do that."

By idea four or five, I'm still getting NG'd, which means "no good." I'm getting NG'd by God on all these ideas, and I'm going, "Hey, God, what's going on here?"

He says, "Absolutely, under no circumstances are you to go back into business right now."

I wonder if God thinks I'm looking like Jackson crawling for all I'm worth to the edge of the bed, about to take a fall, and He has to keep pulling me back to Him. "Okay, God, then what am I going to do? I want to preach, but the opportunities are slow in coming. If you want me to do something else in ministry, then please tell me what it is because I'll do it. It doesn't have to be my plan. Preaching is the desire of my heart; at least it's what I think I want. I guess until I really do it more often, I won't know, but, Lord, if you have a different plan, if you want me to do something else in ministry, please let me know."

But I'm still not working full time, so I guess God isn't ready to let me know the plan yet, or else I'm not yet ready for the plan. This is a good time to continue in the Word and to be doing everything I can to be ready for whatever God has for me. You see, I know that God is saying, "wait," not "goof off."

Fortunately for me God had given me enough financial resources at that time to take up to 6 months off to think about what I wanted to do next and to pray about God's direction for my life. Obviously, I know it is my responsibility, and that of every Christian man, to be working, to function as head of the household and not rely on my wife or anyone else to feed and provide for my family. The waiting place is more an emotional place then a physical place. Being in the waiting room doesn't mean you are not working, it just means you are striving to listen to God and focused on hearing what God would say to you.

If you've listened to a variety of pastors or spent much time in church, you'll know "what sets some men apart to be used by God while others aren't" is a familiar topic for sermon messages, but at my stage of life, it got my attention in a fresh way. I couldn't help but wonder, what sets some men apart to be used by God while others aren't? I'm an ordinary guy, and I want to be used by God, so I spent some time reading the book of Ezra. Ezra was an Old Testament prophet who wanted to rebuild Jerusalem. He is often used as an example of a man being set apart by God, and three times in Ezra, Chapter 7, he is described as a man who had God's hand on him. I wondered, how do you get God's hand on you? Do you have to be special? I found my answer in Ezra 7:10, where it says that "... Ezra had prepared his heart to seek the way of the Lord and to do it ..." (NKJV).

Can we say the same thing? Don't be too quick to answer. Did you catch the last few words, "and do it"? I think most of us seek the law of the Lord and even study it, but the "and do it" part somehow gets overlooked.

I cannot honestly say that I act on every single thing I read in my Bible. I feel stupid for not being able to say that. I feel embarrassed for not being able to say that. I should be able to say that. I know what's in the Bible is truth, so why wouldn't I act on the truth? If I want to be described as a man with God's hand on him, then I have to also be described as a man like Ezra – one who is totally sold out to understanding and living God's word.

I have no excuse. I can go to God, just like Ezra, and ask for help understanding what it says so that I can do it. Ezra 8:21 says, "Then I proclaimed a fast ... that we might humble ourselves before our God, to seek from Him the right way for us and our little ones and all our possessions" (NKJV). Now, because I'm an ordinary guy, I can say with confidence that, at some point, you, too, a fellow human being, are going to need direction, help making a decision, or clarity in a situation. Are you following Ezra's example by seeking God? I figure if God's own Son, Jesus, did that, then so can I.

When Jesus wanted to speak to God for clarity on something important, He prayed and fasted. Why didn't He just say, "Hey, Dad, what's the deal? What's going to happen. What's this? What's that?" No. No, Jesus never did that because He knew that God was holy, and in order to communicate with God, His own Father, He needed clarity. He needed to focus only on God. He needed to get the distractions of the world away from Him. So, He fasted and prayed, as did Moses and Elijah and other prophets of old. They did not just casually accept an idea or a thought as having been a word from God. They fasted and prayed, and when they were sure it was from God, they went and acted on it.

Do we do that? Do we spend time fasting, praying, and seeking God's wisdom and his answers? Then, when we hear from Him, do we act on it? What if we get an answer that wasn't quite what we'd hoped for? Do we trade our intention to act for a lame response like, "Um, well, I'm not sure which voice I heard. Maybe that wasn't God?"

Not a good idea.

The Bible tells us "the hand of our God is upon all them for good that seek him, but his wrath is against all of them that forsake him." This is another thing that sets a man apart – when we are seeking to do good for God rather than forsaking Him, we will have His hand upon us. And there is a promise here as well – that the Lord extends His touch to those who are determined to seek Him. If you want God in your life, and you really want to see the hand of God, you need to be attuned to God for real, not just with your words, but with the way you live your life. Your actions will tell you and the rest of the world if your words are true.

Ezra sought God with all his heart, devoted himself to studying God's Word, and chose to live his life by those words. Because of that, God's hand was on him, and he got to be a significant player in God's history. I am seeking God with all my heart. I am devoting myself to studying His Word and to living by what it says. I have to tell you, though, that sometimes I feel as if this is taking forever, like I'm taking all this information in, I'm praying, I'm fasting, but I'm not necessarily seeing results. Ever feel like that?

But I'm not quitting. I'm not goofing off in the waiting room. I'm reading Matthew 13:31–32, which is a well-known verse. It's the parable of the mustard seed. Jesus says, "... the kingdom of heaven is like a mustard seed, which a man took and planted in his field. Though it is the smallest of all your seeds, yet when it grows, it is the largest of garden plants and becomes a tree, so that the birds of the air come and perch on its branches."

I must have read this verse, I don't know, maybe a thousand times in my life. And I'm reading it again and wondering, hey, I have faith at least the size of a mustard seed. And I've set my heart to seeking God. And I am praying, and I am fasting. So, what's going on here? What is God trying to say to me? Is there something more than prayer and fasting for my faith? Those are critical, sure, but I was stuck on this verse with the mustard seed, and finally, it hit me. I said, stop, Jack, here's the whole point: *yet when it grows.*

It's not until it grows that the mustard seed becomes the largest of garden plants, not until it grows can it become a place of rest for other creatures. Nothing happens until it grows and unless it grows. Our faith is a seed. Each of us, every Christian, has the seed of faith planted inside him or her when born of God. And just like the mustard seed, it's only when the seed of faith grows that anything happens in our lives. So many Christians are walking around complaining that God is not working in their lives.

Have you grown your seed? Have you grown your faith? God said it has to grow.

But how do we make that happen?

Just like anybody makes any seed grow.

The first thing we do (and God talks about it a little bit in the parable of the sower, Matthew 13) is plant it in good soil. Are you planted in good soil? None of us, if we had flower seeds, would take them, throw them on cement, and really expect them to grow. You say, "That's right, Jack, I wouldn't do that." But is the faith seed in your life planted on good fertile soil, or did you toss it on the cement of thievery? Or the cement of adultery, anger, jealousy, pornography, rage, or maybe malice, slander, drugs, alcohol or sexual immorality? By this, I mean, where are you planted in your heart? If you plant it on cement, it can't grow, and you are never going anywhere spiritually. It has to be on good fertile soil, and if it is, that's good, that's where you need to be to grow, but you still have to do something.

You have to water it, right? What happens if you don't? It dies. How often are you going to water it? Once a week? I don't think so. I water my lawn every day and water my plants every day or every other day, not "whenever I get around to it." I water them on a schedule if I want them to grow. Or I can water them once in a while if I really don't care, and they'll still grow a little bit, but they won't grow as big as they could have, and they won't grow the way that they should. If you want your faith to grow the way that it should, you need to water it every day. And God gives us His water, His Word, to water our faith seed. God says (John 4:14), "... whoever drinks the water I give him will never thirst. Indeed, the water I give him will become in him a spring of water welling up to eternal life." Drink of God, and you will never thirst again. God never runs out of water for our faith seed.

What else do seeds need to grow? Food. So, we also have to feed the plants. We have to nourish them so they can grow, just like kids.

I'm looking at Jackson again. He's worked up an appetite with all that crawling, and he's letting Beth and me know about it. I'm smiling, watching him eat, and thanking God he has a good appetite, and we can feed him the right things, so he can keep growing right. I also ask God to help me know how to nourish my son in the Word, so he can thrive spiritually.

Who doesn't want their kid to be well-nourished? As much as you possibly can, if you have a baby, you're going to feed him right because if you don't, he'll die. That's a bad thought. Ever see photos of mal-nourished kids? It's horrible and incredibly sad. That's what happens to your faith when you don't feed your spiritual seed. You have the seed in you, don't feed it, and then you and others and God watch it starve, shrivel up, and die. Do you really want to do that to yourself? Do you really want God to look down and see his spiritual kid being starved to death?

Don't think you can get away with eating junk food, either. No filling up on empty calories and artificial ingredients. It's not just enough to feed your spirit; you have to feed it good food. We know that feeding babies and kids junk food is bad, but people do it. Are you feeding yourself junk that's poisoning your soul – the poison of the world? Or are you feasting on the good food? Jesus said, "I am the bread of life. He who comes to me will never go hungry ..." (John 6:35). Eat the good stuff!

How often should you feed yourself? Once a week? Oh, man, you'd be really sick if you only ate once a week. You'd be scary skinny and have headaches all the time. Come on, that's no way to live. No, we see all the time that we should eat a few times a day. And drink. I bet you drink a lot, too, because you want to be at your peak; you want your body to feel good. If you want to grow and reach your full potential, then you have to put gas in your tank and give your body energy.

It's the same thing with our faith.

God gave us that seed of faith, and He says, "yet when it grows," it becomes the largest plant in the garden. Don't plant it in the right spot; don't water it; don't feed it; it's not gonna grow. Do two of those things, and not the third, and you will not get to where you need to go. You need to do all three of those things. Does faith always grow? No, it doesn't always grow, but every one of us has that seed in him. There is an action required of you to make it grow. You have to feed it, water it, and plant it in good soil. We all have that responsibility, and God expects us to do it. What's the point of setting our minds to knowing God's Word if we're not going to do what it says? God wants us to have all of Him and grow and flourish to our fullest potential. Look at this great example for us all in Luke 11:5–13:

> Suppose one of you has a friend and goes to him at midnight and says, "Friend, lend me three loaves of bread, because a friend of mine on a journey has come to me, and I have nothing to set before him." Then the one inside answers, "Don't bother me. The door is already locked, and my children are with me in bed. I can't get up and give you anything." I tell you, though he will not get up and give him the bread because he is his friend, yet because of the man's boldness he will get up and give him as much as he needs. So I say to you: Ask and it will be given to you; seek and you will find; knock and the door will be opened to you. For everyone who asks receives; he who seeks finds; and to him who knocks, the door will be opened. Which of you fathers, if your son asks for a fish, will give him a snake instead? Or if he asks for an egg, will give him a scorpion? If you then, though you are evil, know how to give good gifts to your children, how much more will your Father in heaven give the Holy Spirit to those who ask him!

Action.

You must want more of God. Don't just *say* you want more; go after it. God says if you want your faith to grow, then you come, you knock, you ask, you seek, and you WILL grow more than you can ask or imagine. You leave it alone; you don't come; you don't knock; you don't ask; you don't seek; you will not grow at all. God tells us to be bold, especially when we are going out and seeking spiritual knowledge, especially when we are seeking our relationship with Him. I think Ezra was bold. The guy was in a foreign country. He set his mind on God and His Word and serving God, no matter who tried to stop him. And Ezra had God's hand on him.

We can have God's hand on us, too. God is very clear. He wants us to be bold; He wants us to keep coming to Him. God loves us, and He wants our faith to grow. And for me, that's been an unemployment benefit that I didn't expect.

The last time I fasted, which wasn't too long ago, I was fasting specifically to get an answer from God on the future.

"God," I said, "I know you called me out of television production. I believe you have some ministry work for me to do. Tell me what it is. Let's get going. I want to plant the seeds for a new phase in my life." So, I fasted, and in this fast, God revealed to me, not the plan for my future, not the direction to go in, but rather, He just reminded me of the simplest of all truths.

He said, "Jack, your sins are forgiven."

I said, "Yeah, God, I know my sins are forgiven. That's why you died on the cross."

He said, "Jack, your sins are forgiven." And He gave me the tale of the paralytic in Matthew 9:5–7, in which a paralytic is lowered through the roof, and Jesus says, "Which is easier: to say, 'Your sins are forgiven,' or to say 'Get up and walk?' But that you may know that the Son of Man has authority on earth to forgive sins… get up, take your mat and go home."

Sometimes, we take it for granted that our sins are forgiven, and sometimes, we forget it. Sometimes, Satan, the outside world, my heart, my mind, or my flesh will condemn me. As I told you in the beginning of this chapter, I was looking at myself and seeing how ugly I was, compared to Jesus, and I mean spiritually ugly. God said, "No, Jack, your sins are forgiven."

I was so grateful for that simple, beautiful reminder, and it is yet another unexpected unemployment benefit to remember how to rejoice over the simple things that God has given me. Yeah, our hearts are going to condemn us, but God showed us the way out. He showed us how to grow our faith. He told us to come and ask and seek and knock and find Him. It's up to us to act.

You have to do it. It's not an option, not if you want the full blessings of God in your life.

Besides, if you don't do it, He just might have to push the pause button with your name on it!

All Is Forgiven, or Is It?

My dad always loved Dixieland jazz music. When I was a little kid, he used to take me to jazz clubs in New York City – places such as Eddie Condon's and Your Father's Moustache. He'd take me all over with him to listen to the music he loved. It was one of the special father and son things we did together, and thinking about it was always a comforting memory. I also came to really love that music very much, not just because of its great sound, but also because of my father's willingness and desire to expose me to it by taking me with him to those clubs.

During my time at college in Syracuse, New York, they had a Dixieland jazz club there called Dinkler's, which I used to visit occasionally to experience what my dad and I had enjoyed so much together. It was a pricey place, though, and because college kids don't have much money to begin with (and because I was making rotten financial decisions), I could rarely go.

Unfortunately, finances weren't the only subject where I was making rotten decisions.

I was really screwed up in college. I got involved in a lot of bad stuff and made some horrible decisions.

At one point, I had wrecked my car for probably the 10th time. I was blowing money left and right, spending it very unwisely and illicitly (mostly on gambling and drugs). I had gotten to the point where I had nothing left, and I desperately needed money. Bad choice after bad choice had piled on, until I was in a huge jam. I had put myself in a spot where I had to do something I didn't want to do – I had to go home and ask my father for a bunch of money. To make matters worse, it seemed as if it was the 100th time I was asking him for cash to bail me out of trouble, and this time it was a very significant amount, something like 1,500 dollars, which these days is still a lot of money.

Dad was pretty disgusted with me, and I couldn't blame him. I was so far over the line. I gave him my half-hearted, feeble excuses of why I needed the money. And he gave it to me, all of it, though I could tell just by looking at his face how fed up he was with me. I just knew that after all he had done for me and how far I had pressed him this time, there was no way I could possibly go back to my father and ask for anything else ever again. I was embarrassed and humiliated and angry with myself for having blown it so badly.

I returned to Syracuse, grateful for my father's willingness to bail me out but saddened and depressed at the thought of how greatly I had disappointed my father, who had always been so good to me. It was a bleak time, to say the least.

About a week and a half after I returned, I got a letter in the mail. It was from my father. I stared at the envelope, wondering what would be inside. My heart started thumping. I was almost afraid to open it after I had disappointed my dad so deeply only a few days before. The envelope shook, as I slowly opened it and took out the contents – a hundred dollar bill and a note that said, "Dinner at Dinkler's and all that jazz."

That is unconditional love – a love I didn't deserve. Just when I had screwed it up the worst, just when I had imposed on my father beyond any reasonable expectation, my dad gave me grace and unconditional love. He blessed me when I least deserved it. And you know something? That's a picture of God. That's true for each one of us. Just when we had blown it, blown our finances, our relationships, or our integrity, screwed up beyond repair by rebelling against our perfect, all-loving, all-good God, He loved us and blessed us anyway.

Bob Dylan once wrote, "Do you ever wonder just what God requires? You think he is just an errand boy to satisfy your wandering desires."

God is not our errand boy. He has requirements. And one of them is that we forgive people.

Errands. Short stops on the way to some place else. From a spiritual perspective, our lives on Earth are like errands. They're really just a short time compared to eternity, the ultimate destination for everyone.

Imagine, if you will, I'm headed to the store with you, and I say, look, I have a few errands to run, so I'm going to drop you off at Sports Authority. I'll be back in fifteen minutes. You think, hey, no big deal; you'll go in, look around, swing some bats, look at some tennis rackets, and kill some time. Fifteen minutes, no problem.

Fifteen minutes. That's exactly how God looks at our lives. In his timetable, our lives and existence are like fifteen minutes, like a snap of the fingers. Gone, that fast. Compared to eternity, where we are going to spend the rest of our time, this time here is nothing. It wouldn't seem to me like such a big burden to be dropped off in a Sports Authority for fifteen minutes. I'd certainly make the best of it, and most likely, you would too. So, the challenge is to see our lives on Earth from God's perspective – it'll be gone in a flash, so why not make the best of it? It's only going to last a short time and then comes heaven and eternity for all who believe in Jesus.

Eternity is a long time. I was thinking about heaven in my quiet time recently, and I realized that I have no clue, aside from the book of Revelation, of what heaven is really going to be like. The thought crossed my mind that maybe heaven is going to be boring, up there worshipping God all day. Sure, the idea of worshipping God sounds great because I love God, and I'm psyched to worship Him, but ... all day? Come on! I want to go to a ballgame or a jazz club or something. What am I gonna do, worship God *all* the time?

You ever have one of those moments when you hear what you must sound like to the other person? Well, I heard myself "saying" that to God, and I immediately got on my knees and asked Him to forgive my lack of faith in His wonderful power and in His knowledge of His heaven. Just because I can't imagine or comprehend what it'll be like doesn't mean I won't like it. One thing I am sure of – God doesn't lie. If God says that heaven is the greatest, most wonderful time we are going to have, uninterrupted, with all happiness and no bad, then I can rest assured and trust that that's the case, and I am sure it is going to be awesome. That makes me realize how ridiculously small and misguided our sense of time and what's important down here can be.

For instance, I was talking to a friend of mine the other day, and we were arguing about the past, things that I had done and why and things that he had done and why. So, we're going back and forth, rehashing some old thing that I'd rather not go into, and I make my point about some event that happened in our past, and he says, "No, Jack, that's not the way it happened."

And I said, "You're out of your mind."

He stormed off and I stormed off, and a half hour later, I'm driving down the road thinking what an idiot he is, until it dawned on me that he was right. My mind went back to that point in time and that event, and I remembered that I really had done what he said, and I had done it for the exact motivation that he had accused me of. It was selfish; it was greedy; and he was right.

I thought, wow, this is amazing; my mind had tricked me all these years into believing my own lie. I had actually come to believe that I was right and that the story I had created was the truth. For years, I didn't want to forgive this guy for the wrongs that I perceived he had done, yet in reality, they were my fault, and it was my lack of forgiveness and my stubbornness that had prevented that relationship from going forward.

I'm not the only one who has these odd lapses of truth or forgets the reason for a decades-old feud. A more famous one than mine involved Dean Martin and Jerry Lewis, a great comedy team back in the 1940s and 1950s, the ancient days of film and TV. They were incredible together, but at some point, they had a fight about something and went their separate ways, and for decades, they never spoke. Dean Martin went on to do other movies and a TV show, and Jerry Lewis did other movies and hosted the Muscular Dystrophy Telethons for years. At different times, each was interviewed, and neither could remember what started the fight that ripped them apart. One of them said, "I just know I hate him; I don't remember why."

It sounds so tragic to me, as an outsider, to hear something like that. But am I really such an outsider to the same dilemma?

Absolutely not. I was thinking about my first marriage and subsequent divorce many years ago. I remember at one point I hated my wife. Yeah, that's a strong word; but you know, it's a real human emotion that we all have to deal with. I hated her, and now, I don't remember why. I know we had differences, and I understand why we got divorced, but if you ask me now what was so traumatic that this divorce happened, I couldn't tell you.

The point is that time will often dull our memories. It can even take away our recollection of what was so critical at that moment that we got so angry and so upset that we couldn't forgive, as if whatever happened were the ultimate crime against us. The irony is that years go by, the memory fades, something else becomes more important, and time takes that memory away. Is that biblical?

I think not. Letting time fade the thing is not the same as forgiving, and God wants us to practice forgiveness. Why? Because He said so in the Bible, the instruction manual he gave us for our lives. Not only does he want us to forgive, but he also wants us to practice forgiveness *immediately*, so nothing will hinder our relationship with Him (Matthew 6:14). Throughout the New Testament, Jesus tells us to forgive, and He is giving us examples of forgiveness. As a matter of fact He is the ultimate forgiver, because He bought God's forgiveness for us all (because we all need it) by His death on the cross. He did it because He loved us and wanted us to be with Him in eternity. If Jesus were a superhero, He could be called "The Ultimate Forgiver" because He has forgiven us more than we deserve.

Well, you say, of course, He can forgive everyone, He's God, but it's not so easy for me; I'm only human.

Yeah, you're right. You and I are only human, but when we entered into a relationship with Jesus Christ, we gained an inheritance from God, which included his power and strength to enable us to obey Him. In Ephesians 1:18–20, Paul states, "I pray also that the eyes of your heart may be enlightened in order that you may *know* the hope to which he has called you, the riches of his glorious inheritance in the saints, and *his incomparably great power for us who believe.* That power is like the working of his mighty strength, which he exerted in Christ when he raised him from the dead and seated him at the right hand of the heavenly realms ..." (emphasis mine). Paul is stressing that the incredible divine power God used to raise Christ from the dead is also at work in and through all those who believe.

This means we have in us the same power that raised Christ from the dead. We don't need a drug to get it; we don't need a drink to get it. But we still have to access it and use it; we are still required to take action. So, there is no excuse that we don't have the power to forgive. We do have the power. We have the same power in us that Christ had in Him. Christ had the ability to forgive, and we have his power to forgive.

Why does it matter whether we forgive or not?

First, we are called to obey God, and God specifically wants us to forgive. If we don't forgive, we are sinning, and sinning interrupts our relationship with God. God has given us instructions on how to live our lives. He literally spells it out for us in Matthew 6:14–15, where He says, "For if you forgive men when they sin against you, your heavenly Father will also forgive you. But if you do not forgive men their sins, your Father will not forgive your sins."

Is anything about that not clear? If you forgive people when they sin against you, God will forgive your sins. If you don't forgive others for their sins, God won't forgive you your sins. It might seem like a big deal to forgive someone who has hurt you, but the big deal is that God forgave you in the first place. Anything other than that is insignificant. God wants us to forgive because it offers bigger benefits to us than *not* forgiving.

Next, it matters because the Bible says we "... are being built into a spiritual house to be a holy priesthood, offering spiritual sacrifices acceptable to God through Jesus Christ" (1 Peter 2:5). In Old Testament times, priests offered animal sacrifices to atone for sin. We don't have to offer physical sacrifices like those that they did, but we are to offer *spiritual* sacrifices by being obedient to God's will and His Word. God asks us to be forgiving, so obeying God means sacrificing (giving up) something we want (such as carrying a grudge) to please God. Why should we make these spiritual sacrifices to God? So that we can continue to be built into a holy priesthood of God, as God desires us to be, and so that, by being obedient to God's will, we can receive his full blessings. As parents, we can appreciate that there are full blessings we can give to our obedient children, and there are blessings we must withhold from children who are disobedient.

Forgiving is not easy. It might even be one of those things we have to learn how to do by practicing it. Scripture gives some instructions in Ephesians 4:1–3: "As a prisoner for the Lord, then, I urge you to live a life worthy of the calling you have received. Be completely humble and gentle; be patient, bearing with one another in love. Make every effort to keep the unity of the Spirit through the bond of peace." In order to live a life worthy of the calling we have received, we have to be COMPLETELY humble – not a little humble, not a good amount of humble, but COMPLETELY humble. By being completely humble, gentle, and patient, we let go of selfish tendencies and our "need" to not forgive someone else, and by bearing with one another in love, forgiveness comes very easily. Forgiveness will be a natural extension of these things.

Another reason forgiveness matters is that we can grieve the Holy Spirit, and that causes a rift in our connection with God. We can interrupt God's plan for our lives by being disobedient and saying "no" to God. Oh, we'll still go to heaven because we've accepted Jesus, but we can still ruin or interrupt the perfect plan God has for our lives. The Bible says, "And do not grieve the Holy Spirit of God, with whom you were sealed for the day of redemption. Get rid of all bitterness, rage and anger, brawling and slander, along with every form of malice. Be kind and compassionate to one another, forgiving each other, just as in Christ God forgave you" (Ephesians 4:30–32).

If you do not forgive, you are grieving the Holy Spirit of God.

Do you ever have a fight with your wife, your kid, or best friend? Not very pleasant, is it? How do you feel? Cruddy, even if you were right and, especially, if you were wrong because you have separated yourself from the love of someone you care for deeply, even for a temporary period. When we don't forgive, when we grieve the Holy Spirit of God, we are fighting with God. We are separated from him at that point in time. Trust me; you don't want to be grieving the Holy Spirit of God in your life unless you want things to keep going downhill. If you want to fix things, you have to use God's instruction manual, and that's "the Bible."

God's instruction manual is so clear. Think about it this way. If you were part of a bomb squad, and I told you to disable a bomb that's about to blow up and kill everybody, you'd go in and take it apart. Certainly, you wouldn't want to do it without the instruction manual because you would probably blow yourself and everyone else around you sky high! Bomb squads have instruction manuals on how to disable bombs so they don't blow up and kill you and everyone else around you.

God has forgiven us so much, and we should be grateful. Let's look at some examples we can relate to. If I had a knife to your throat, and I said, "I'm gonna kill you, but if you hand over the keys to your car, I'll let you live," what would you do? It would be a no-brainer. You would give me the car keys.

If you were lying in a hospital bed dying of heart failure, and the doctor said, "I have a new heart that I can use to replace yours, and you can live a long, healthy life, but there's an artery in your leg that I want to take out and give to the guy in the bed next to you because he needs one." You have a choice. You don't have to give up the artery, but if you don't, you don't get the new heart, and you're going to die. Would anybody not go along with the doctor's suggestion?

If you owed a bookie $50,000, and he was coming to get you, and I said, "I'll pay that $50,000 debt, but that hundred bucks that your neighbor down the street owes you, I want you to forget about it." Is there anybody that wouldn't forget about it? Of course not.

In each example, we give up something relatively small in order to get the bigger benefit. God wants to remind us that he forgave our sins when we accepted his son, Jesus Christ, as our Lord and Savior. By accepting that offer, that free gift, we should agree to do what God wants us to do because we believe and trust that God, our Father, knows what's best for us and has our best interests at heart at all times. It doesn't have to be hard because, as part of the deal, He also gave us his power, remember? God wants to remind us that He didn't allow Jesus to die for us so we could just say thanks then continue merrily along our way. We can, of course; that's our choice, but we will pay the consequences of those actions. We'll interfere with God's plan for our lives here on Earth and the blessings He wants to give us. (We will never interfere with salvation if we have accepted Jesus. We are going to heaven. That's a one time transaction between you and God, as it says in Romans 11:29, "God's gift and his call are irrevocable.")

Why does God have to keep reminding us about forgiving?

Because we forget.

Because our minds trick us into believing other things. Because we end up thinking the other person is the idiot when in fact, we're the one with the problem.

And because living on Earth means we're going to have to do this forgiving thing a lot. *A lot.* And we reach the point where we want to say "Enough! I'm not going to forgive you *again.*"

Even the disciples brought this up when Peter asked Jesus in Matthew 18:21, "... 'Lord, how many times shall I forgive my brother when he sins against me? Up to seven times?'" Peter must have been thinking, come on, Lord, seven times, that's enough ... forgiving my brother three times would make me the kindest guy in the world, seven times is more than enough! But keep reading. In verse 22, it says, "Jesus answered, 'I tell you, not seven times, but seventy times seven.'" That means your job is just to keep forgiving. Don't try to get 'your pound of flesh' because that means you're judging how to deal with this person. That's not your job; it's God's, and He will deal with each person according to his or her actions (Romans 14:12). That day will come according to God's timing, and whatever he does in judgment of the person you are upset with will be far worse than anything you could ever do.

Why does it matter that we keep forgiving someone?

In my life before Christ, I would have said that continuing to forgive someone is crazy and makes you Christians look like a bunch of wimps. In my life with Christ, though, I see the benefit of forgiving. It can lead others to a saving relationship with Christ, and it can keep us from being outwitted by our enemy, the devil, Look at 2 Corinthians 2:5–11:

> If anyone has caused grief, he has not so much grieved me as he has grieved all of you...The punishment inflicted on him by the majority is sufficient for him. Now instead, you ought to forgive and comfort him, so that he will not be overwhelmed by excessive sorrow. I urge you, therefore, to reaffirm your love for him. The reason I wrote you was to see if you would stand the test and be obedient in everything. If you forgive anyone, I also forgive him. And what I have forgiven – if there was anything to forgive – I have forgiven in the sight of Christ for your sake, in order that Satan might not outwit us. For we are not unaware of his schemes.

Paul is clearly concerned that our unwillingness to forgive and comfort someone can cause him to be overwhelmed by excessive sorrow, and that can lead to more problems. I ask you, what opportunity are you giving Satan to get into your life and other people's lives by not forgiving them? Ever think of it that way? I do – now. What if I didn't forgive someone, and he walked away with guilt and sorrow, thinking he's a loser or a failure, and Satan has that opportunity to come to him? Where is God's witness? It should be the other way around. I should be forgiving that person. He should be walking around saying, "Hey, that Jack, I burned him, and he just hugged me and forgave me. Man, there's something he's got that I want. I just have to come to church and check that out."

But we have a choice. We don't have to forgive, and we can let the guy think he's a loser and get discouraged, and when we do that, we are the real idiots because we have played right into our enemy's scheme, allowing him to outwit us. If we allow him to take advantage of the person's excessive sorrow, Satan will keep that person's focus off God and will gladly keep some earthly thing between you and that person so that he will stay miserable and keep burning people because he's not going to find forgiveness, anyway. And you lose the opportunity to witness to the guy because you aren't forgiving. Satan's smart. He wants to outwit us.

Maybe so. But we have that Jesus power thing, remember? And in 1 John 4:4, God says that "... the one who is in you is greater than the one who is in the world." God's power in us is greater than Satan's is, anytime, all the time. That's what enables us to forgive others, even in the worst cases. The worst. Consider Denise Eunick-Paul, a mother whose daughter was murdered in 1998 by a 12-year-old boy named Lionel Tate. At Tate's sentencing, she told the kid who murdered her daughter, "I forgive you, Lionel. I love the Lord so much that I forgive you for murdering my daughter." Denise Eunick-Paul is a daughter of the Lord, and she behaves like it! Her heavenly reward for her faith and trust in God will be great, indeed.

This instruction to forgive others so God will forgive us is so important it even turns up in the Lord's Prayer (Matthew 6:9–13), where Jesus taught his disciples how they should pray. Remember? Near the end of the prayer, it says, "And forgive us our sins, as we forgive those who sin against us," meaning, in the same way that I forgive others, God, is how I want You to forgive me. Wow! That's a biblical spin on the old "what goes around comes around." So, we are to ask God to forgive us our sins, but there is a requirement to receiving it: We must also forgive everyone who sins against us. We are showing that to God in prayer. Forgive us our sins, Lord. But why? Because we're nice guys? Because we love others? Because we are saved? No! Forgive us our sins, Lord, because we forgive everyone who sins against us. It's a requirement, not an option.

Finally, one of the blessings of obedience to God, including obeying the command to forgive others, is that we get rewards in heaven. No one really knows when they are going to breathe their last breath, so delaying obedience to God could cost you some rewards when you end up in front of him.

So, what now? It's the end of the chapter. Don't just turn the page and close the book, and go do an errand and forget all this stuff. Do it now. Practice forgiving others *now*.

I want you to picture yourself standing in front of a wall, like a big chalkboard that divides a room. Picture the people in your life that you burned. Get specific to help you remember because we all know how easily we can forget what we did to others and how easily we can remember what they did to us.

What did you do? Did you steal something? Break someone's heart? Lie, cheat, not keep your word, bear false witness in court, lie about someone across the neighbor's fence? Did you commit adultery? Not honor your mother or father? Are you a drunkard, a homosexual, a bed-hopper? Are you bitter, angry, filled with malice and rage? All these are sins against God. Think about the very worst sins that you've committed in your lifetime and how guilty they made you feel, all the way back to childhood and up through this moment. Imagine that drunk driver that killed someone – was that you? Imagine the man or woman that wrecked someone else's marriage – was that you?

Do you remember how those sins made you feel? As a believer in Jesus Christ, do you remember how it felt to have those sins forgiven?

It doesn't mean the consequences are removed; it just means you don't have to suffer God's eternal wrath for them. In his eyes, your slate has been wiped clean.

Now, I would like you to think about God, and I want you to picture the people that have sinned against you. Picture them clearly in your mind. Maybe it was your mother or father, or sibling; a girlfriend, a wife, a child. Maybe a business partner, a Christian brother, a pastor, a boss, an employee. Did somebody rob you? Did somebody sue you? Slander you?

Picture them in your mind right now, and picture yourself writing their names on the wall in front of you. Mentally write each name and what they did. Did somebody betray you? Insult you, violate you, or commit what you perceived to be crimes against you, or your soul, or your pride? Is that imaginary chalkboard full?

Take a moment to think about the significance of those actions against you and to consider God's requirement that we forgive. When we don't forgive, we put that person between God and us. Our connection with God is interrupted. Get enough interruptions, and communication becomes next to impossible. Imagine God trying to talk to you through that wall or trying to hand you a blessing, but your wall is so full of names and events that you won't let go of, you can barely hear Him.

The only way to hear Him is to clean out the stuff that's muffling His voice.

Forgive those people, and erase the board.

It's really not that hard. If you were going to die today, if I really had that knife against your throat and said, "Look, I'm going to kill you, but if you forgive that person, you could live," would that grudge be so important anymore? Does that score have to be settled? Does that violation have to result in criminal charges and criminal sentencing? I think not. I think that with your life on the line, it would be very easy to forgive those people.

In our everyday busy-ness, we forget that our lives were on the line, and Christ paid the price so that we could have forgiveness. I want you to visualize anyone who has hurt you and, with your eyes closed, remember that God wants you to forgive them, and God wants you to give that forgiveness to Jesus Christ. If God thinks you need to have justice in this thing, He'll take care of it for you in His way and in His time.

The funny thing about all this is that you and I are that "guilty person" in someone else's life. Maybe right now, somewhere in the world, someone is reading this and picturing you or me and is erasing our name from that imaginary blackboard.

Remember, as you forgive others their sins, Jesus will forgive ALL your sins.

It doesn't get any better than that!

Letting Go

Today, I was thinking about work and about how good managers and leaders have a responsibility to address employees' weaknesses in order to guide them toward improvement, both for their own good as well as for the good of the company.

Most people can relate to the challenge of working with someone who is not performing up to the level that we expect. As the owner of a company, if my management team or other employees weren't performing up to the expected level, I would call them in and say, hey, I expected this from you, it's not quite happening, you're weak in this area, you need to kick it up a notch or two and get with the program. I expect the employees would take that information and act on it, so they could be good at their jobs, improve their lives, and improve their performance. If they didn't, I would call them in again, repeat the expectations, and eventually, if they didn't get with the program, I would have to get rid of them and find somebody else to do the jobs.

God is the same way with us – He expects us to get with the program. He's not getting rid of us, but there are times when, figuratively speaking, He calls us in and says, hey, this is the level I expect from you, it's not quite happening, you're weak in this area, get with the program, so I can give you all the benefits and blessings I have in store for you. Naturally, just as you'd expect an employee who had received that kind of evaluation to rededicate himself to being better in those areas, when God says that to me, I need to kick it up, whether it takes extra study, extra training, or extra work. I would rededicate myself to being the best I could be. Based on an experience I had not long ago that I'll share with you in a moment, I believe that the sooner I get with the program, the less God has to do to get my attention.

This rededication is not just about words; it's really about a rededication of the heart. How do we go about that?

To rededicate yourself to God, you have to let go. If the employee I described above is committed to his own success, he will have to let go of some personal preferences or bad habits (or less effective ones) and rededicate himself to doing whatever it will take to get the prize. He might prefer to work from 11 a.m. to 7 p.m., but if our business requires his presence from 8 a.m. to 5 p.m., his preferences aren't going to work. Likewise, if I want to rededicate myself to God, I need to let go of the preferences or habits I'm holding on to, so I can receive more from God. As we all know, however, letting go of things that are familiar, even if they are working against us, can be frightening.

We all have bad habits that we need to deal with, particularly if they affect our physical health, but changing those habits can be really hard. We're familiar with a way of eating (fast food, for example, or lots of processed food) that we know is unhealthy, but we're *comfortable* with it. Ask anyone who's had to switch to a low-sodium or a sugar-free diet, and they'll tell you it wasn't fun to give up the stuff they were used to, even though they knew it was harming them.

My biggest challenge in this area was dealing with my drug addiction. I knew it was bad, but it was familiar and "normal" for me, and it was ingrained in my life, making it very hard for me to change what I was doing. However, back in 1995, when I was in the thick of a serious battle with it, one specific instance of terror got my undivided attention. I recall distinctly feeling like I was hanging from a ledge over a boiling pit full of alligators, just like you see in the movies, but I was seeing it in my own mind. It was Satan's pit, and I knew that pit was my drug addiction and I knew I could no longer do anything to get myself out of it. Falling into it meant it would completely consume me, yet I didn't have the strength to pull myself up to safety.

The terror was coming face-to-face with how powerless I was to save myself. I had tried before, thought I could do it, but finally had to admit that I couldn't kick the addiction on my own. I then realized that the problem was not the drugs, but rather the drugs were just a symptom of the real problem.

The real problem was my unwillingness to let go to God, my unwillingness to turn this addiction over to Him. You see, I wanted God to take away the addiction (the control this had over me), but I didn't want to turn it over to Him (because a part of me still desired the drugs). It was almost as if I valued that addiction or the high the drugs gave me more than I valued God. But even that was no longer reality because once you cross that line into addiction, the high is no longer pleasurable. Instead, it *owns* you; it controls you. You become a slave to it, which only goes to prove what God says in His Word, that "a man is a slave to whatever has mastered him" (2 Peter 2:19). If anything has you mastered, whether it's drugs, stealing, lying, ego, pornography, or whatever, you are a slave to it. It controls your thoughts, actions, how you spend your money, what you say, where you go, and your relationships. What kind of life is that?

I knew I was enslaved to the drugs, but I also knew that nothing would change until I could honestly consider how I was going to deal with it since all my own efforts had failed. Even then, even when I was mentally hanging over that pit and absolutely terrified, I was still struggling with turning it over to God, still hesitant to value God's joy and God's love more than the familiarity of addiction. Of course, logically, that doesn't sound right. If you ask me what's more valuable, loving God and getting all God's benefits or my drug addiction, I would *say* loving God, but my actions clearly proved the opposite. I would not and could not let this go. As I hung over that pit, I heard God say, "Jack, Satan wants to sift you like wheat," just as He said to Peter (Luke 22:31–32). But God continued to tell me the same thing he told Peter, "but I have prayed for you, and when you have turned back, [not if you turn, but when you turn and you are better] strengthen your brethren [go out and share the message with your brothers]."

God was giving me a choice: Continue down my path into the pit, or choose His way, turn toward Him, get better, and share this with my brothers and sisters.

I can look back and truly say this was a life or death choice for me.

It reminds me of something from my college days. Maybe you heard the same story about a cocaine addiction test being done on lab monkeys. The monkeys had two levers – one for cocaine and one for food – and they were allowed to choose either one. Guess what? They always pulled the cocaine lever – always, that is, until they died. There was food available, and they knew it was food, but they consistently chose the cocaine, and it killed them.

While I sure don't believe that we evolved from monkeys, I can't help but see the similarity here. We have the sin lever and the God lever. Day after day, we choose sin, sin, sin. We know the God lever is over there, and we can use it to get blessings, but we don't hit it, apparently believing that the sin lever brings more joy or satisfaction than what God can give us. We have this notion that we know the God lever is there if we need it, if we have a crisis, as if it's an insurance policy stuck in a file. We know we're saved, so it's no big deal to pull the sin lever a few times. God will bail me out, right?

Well, sort of. If you are saved, if you have believed in Jesus as your Lord and Savior, then you have a guaranteed place in heaven. That is a permanent, one-time transaction, so as far as eternity goes, you are "bailed out." In the meantime, you're still here on Earth, where there are consequences for choices, including pain, trouble, and especially, missing out on some earthly blessings from God, as well as reducing or eliminating the rewards you will receive in heaven. The conclusion: The more a believer chooses disobedience (the sin lever), the fewer blessings he or she gets on Earth and the fewer rewards he or she gets in heaven. It's tempting to keep putting off the decision to pull the God lever, but the problem is we don't know when our gig will be up, and we will have to face God on Judgment Day and give an account of our lives.

God warns us (Matthew 24:36) that we don't know the hour, the time, or day that He is coming. He also talks about the guy who filled up his storehouse and said, now I'll eat, drink, and be merry. God said, "You fool! This very night your life will be demanded from you" (Luke 12:20). Time's up.

Why do we constantly hit the sin lever instead of the God lever? We have the choice; it's a life lever or a death lever, sin or God, life or death, cocaine or food. Which lever are you pulling? It's time to think about what you're really doing. Are you betting your life that you can hit this God lever one day when you think you're done sinning, and now, you want to stop, so you can make everything right again? Yeah, well, I thought I could too.

I believed I could stop using drugs. I had started using when I was 16, convinced I could stop, but one day, a lot of years later, it dawned on me that I couldn't. One day, it hit me so clearly that I was over the line, and I really couldn't stop on my own. I wasn't stabbing a needle in my arm, that wasn't my drug of choice, and I never thought I could overdose and die, as in "it'll never happen to me." But you know what? No one wakes up in the morning, looks at the multiple choice list for the day, and circles "overdose and die." While I didn't fear an overdose, I certainly knew that my life was ruined.

Has something ruined your life? Is it in the midst of falling apart? It doesn't matter what is ruining your life. What does matter is that it is separating you from God. Why? Because if you're not saved, it's condemning you to hell where you will be eternally separated from Him. And if you are saved and you are being disobedient to God, you can't get the full benefits of your relationship with Him, which means you are missing out on earthly benefits and heavenly rewards.

Stop and think. What haven't you turned over to God? Why? Do you fear that giving up the sin will be more painful and more of a loss than receiving the joy from God? Do you doubt God's power?

God has the power to set you free from that thing that enslaves you. God always had the power to remove my sin. God always had the power to change me, and God was always willing. I was the stubborn, unwilling one determined to stay where I was, even in my miserable state. But not now. If I could tell you where not to go in life, it would be where I have been. Maybe one of the reasons God allowed me to go through all that was so I could be an Anti-Travel Agent: "Don't go there, it looks fun, but it'll kill you. Really." Great travel brochure, right? Forgive me. (Sorry, sometimes the advertising guy in me just won't shut up.)

Trust me; you don't want to go where I've been. Learn this lesson without the terror. I was at a spiritual crossroads, hanging on to the ledge, staring into the pit, and this wasn't a one-second vision that I could just blink and make go away. No, God showed me where my life was going, and it was going down until it was over and dead. At that crossroads, I had a choice to make. Would I let go and hand this over to God or not? It was an awful thing, but in the big picture, the eternal perspective, it was the best thing that ever happened because it forced me to let go and really see what God wanted for my life.

Picture yourself in the water, holding on to a large rock that is weighing you down to the point that you will drown. I show up next to you in a rescue boat and say, "Let go of the rock."

"No," you say. "I have to hang on to it."

"Let go, and I'll rescue you." I can't reach down and grab it from you; you have to let it go yourself, in order for the rescuer to take hold of you.

You say, "No. I can't let it go. It's the only rock I have; it's the way I've always done things."

"But it's killing you."

"I know."

Reading that, the issue is obvious: Let go of that rock, or you're a goner. The sad thing is that most of us have rocks we won't let go of, even when we know they are ruining our lives, because we have this odd sense of security in familiar habits, even if they're bad for us. As my drug counselor reminded me more than once, "there's comfort in familiar pain." How scary is that?

Spiritually speaking, that is what we so often do. God is reaching out from the rescue boat, which might look like a spouse, a pastor, a stranger, or maybe the ambulance guy that's picking you up off the road, but we have to let go of what we are holding on to so that He can save us. So I ask you today, are you at a spiritual crossroads? One choice, the sin lever, leads to death. Is that what you are holding on to? The other choice, the God lever, leads to life. If you are like me, you have probably chosen the death lever so many times; it's a habit. I almost didn't know how to hit the God lever. I knew that's the one I should have been choosing, but when you're so used to choosing the other way, it's hard to change. There is only one way to change. You need to access God's power, and the only way you can access God's power is by letting go.

As believers, we have that power because God gave it to us. We can do all things through Him (Christ) who gives us strength. God says with Him, all things are possible (Matthew 19:26). At the point of salvation, we have a relationship with Christ, and He will give us the strength to do what He wants us to do and what He expects us to do.

One of the most basic things He expects us to do is this: "...live up to what we have already attained" (Philippians 3:16). What have we attained? We have attained salvation through God's grace. We didn't earn it, but we've attained it because God gave it to us. If we are living up to the salvation God gave us, then we are obedient to God, behaving as God wants us to and letting God work in our lives.

My employees had certain expectations to meet. As the owner of a large company, I had to live up to certain expectations. As the husbands and spiritual leaders of your houses, you have to live up to certain expectations. The President of the United States has to live up to certain expectations.

God expects us to live up to what he has given us. He made us heirs to the throne of Jesus Christ. He made us brothers with Christ. We are His sons, and He loves us, so He wants us to live up to that, and that will mean having to let go of things that will keep us from living up to what we have attained.

Remember that employee I described in the beginning of this chapter? To live up to the expectation that he would be at work between 8 and 5, he will have to let go of the notion he can stay up until the wee hours watching TV or cruising the Web. He will have to change his behavior. The question is can he do that on his own? Does he have it within him to rededicate himself to succeeding, or will he need help?

When I think about rededication and refocusing our lives to the Lord, I think about my man, Peter, who said Lord, Lord, I won't deny you, I'm with you no matter what. And Jesus said before the rooster crows, you will deny Me three times (Luke 22:34). And he did. Peter failed Jesus because he was operating on his own strength. He thought he could handle anything that came along. Later, Peter came back and understood that, while he might fail on occasion, God purposely allowed that to happen, so he could see that his own strength, his own abilities, would not be enough. He needed strength and power from God to do what God wanted him to do. The same is true for you and me. We can only succeed based on the power that God gives us and accessing that power might require us to rededicate ourselves to Him, not with words, not with our lips, but with our hearts.

Rededicating means putting God first. "But seek first his kingdom and his righteousness, and all these things [physical needs] will be given to you as well" (Matthew 6:33). This is different from accepting

Jesus Christ as your Savior; that's salvation, and that's the first step to accessing God's power. It's a one-time transaction. But being dedicated to God is different. It's seeking him first in all that you do.

It's like the difference between a wedding and a marriage. The wedding is a one-time event, but the marriage, the result of that event, is an ongoing relationship that takes dedication to last.

After being saved, we have a relationship with God based on Jesus Christ. If we're following Jesus, which means doing what He would have done, it will be obvious, just as a tree is known by its fruit. There will be changes in our behavior, our attitude, and our choices because we are obedient to God. We will not be perfect (just look at Peter), but there will be evidence things are going in the right direction because of the dedication of our heart.

If the heart isn't in it, sooner or later everyone knows. God *already* knows. Jesus gave the Pharisees, the religious leaders of His day, a warning about this in Luke 11:42: "Woe to you, Pharisees, because you give God a tenth of your mint, rue and all other kinds of garden herbs, but you neglect justice and the love of God. You should have practiced the latter without leaving the former undone." Jesus was getting on their case because they were going through the outward motions – tithing a tenth, looking good in public – but they were neglecting matters of the heart.

We need to examine ourselves. Are we serving at church, teaching Sunday school, helping in the nursery? Does everything *look* good on the outside, but on the inside, there's no love for God? Jesus tells us, just like He told the Pharisees, yes, doing those things is good and right, but don't neglect the love of God. All those acts of service should come as a result of loving God, but loving God is the first thing.

So, I ask you today, are you just going through the motions, or is love for God reflected in your outward service? If not, what is separating you from God? What haven't you given up? Whatever you are holding on to, know this – it will affect your relationship with God. Let go of the pride saying you can do it on your own. Let go of that ego that demands a lifestyle you can't afford. Let go of whatever keeps you trapped.

What are you afraid of? Jesus says, "Do not be afraid ... for your Father has been pleased to give you the kingdom" (Luke 12:32). God is pleased to give you the blessings of His kingdom, which far outweigh the short-term pleasures we get from these earthly habits, so make a commitment today to rededicate yourself to this relationship with Him.

What does it take to make a relationship work? Think about a marriage. Do you see your spouse once a month? Is she on the to do list after the golf game, the party, and the business trip? Is your husband an after-thought – second or third place after the kids, the house, and the bank account? That sounds like somebody you don't want to be with, like somebody you want to avoid, as if the relationship were a chore: "I have to be with you because you're my spouse? Well, okay, fine, I'll talk to you … if I have to." Is that how you treat God? Where is God on your list? If he's not first, what can you do to make him first?

Get to know God. I dare you to take up this challenge. Spend time with God on your own. Read the Bible. Spend quiet time with Him in the morning before the crazy schedules start. Listen to CDs, attend church, and develop friendships with other Christians. But the best thing you can do is to read God's Word on your own because, if you're a Christian, God says He'll teach you all things though His Holy Spirit (John 14:26), who is deposited inside you when you become a believer. As you read, ask God to reveal what He wants you to learn in that thing, and then give Him time to answer.

Is there a wave of resistance welling up in your heart? Why? Are you scared of what God might reveal in areas of your life? I know what it's like to be standing there in a pit when it's just God and me, and I have nothing to hide behind. As weird as it sounds, that's a *good* thing. The circumstances aren't always good, but they are ultimately for our eternal, spiritual benefit because it's in those places when God really works on us and in us and shows us how much He loves us. I promise you that once you feel that love, you will never forget it.

This is the secret to letting go and to rededicating yourself. It comes ironically enough from my days of being in counseling for drug use. My counselor used to challenge me with this line, "Hitting bottom is only half the job. The real task is staying there." Let me explain this to you. If I could wake up every morning and have that feeling that I had of clinging to the edge of the pit, of looking down and crying out to God to save me, I would be the greatest, most God-loving, wonderful guy in the world. This is because, at that point in my life, my sole focus was on God because He was the only thing that could save me.

I know that some of you reading this have had similar experiences. How do you feel today? Are you far away from the pit? Do you remember that bad time in your life? Are you thinking, hey, God got me through that catastrophe or that incident, and now, I'm back in control?

Guess what? That's absolutely the wrong place for an alcoholic, an addict, or sinner to be. The place to be is at that bottom spot, on the ground at Jesus' feet. It doesn't mean that you have to be beaten down by it; it simply means you can never forget it. Daily, if we place ourselves in a position of humbleness, in a love relationship with God, then we know we are hopeless and helpless, and we will continue to let go of whatever rocks we have accumulated, so we can keep our focus on God alone.

For you guys reading this, being on the ground and staying at Jesus' feet does not mean you're a wimp. This has nothing to do with how the world defines strength. This is all about staying in that spirit of loving God and letting go of our idea of strength so that His power can work through us.

I bring that up because I've learned that we confuse what we think is strength for what is really a locked rigidity, a locked belief, and a locked attitude that keeps us tense and prevents us from letting go. What do I mean? We build up patterns in ourselves – patterns for how to handle things, how to respond, how to control. Are you doing this? Are you so structured in your responses to life, to people, and to God that you can't let go? If so, you've mistaken your rigidity for strength, and it's holding you back from God. It's stopping you from getting the very things that God wants to give you.

Is that a promise that God will give you only money and happiness? No. It's a promise that God works out everything that happens, the crappy stuff included, for the good of those who believe – for those who have a relationship with him through Jesus (Romans 8:28). In Philippians 1:18–19, Paul says, "... I will continue to rejoice, for I know that through your prayers and the help given by the Spirit of Jesus Christ, what has happened to me will turn out for my deliverance."

Paul never doubted, through all the incredibly bad stuff that happened to him, that everything would turn out for his deliverance and benefit. I am not as famous or as great as Paul was, but I also know that Romans 8:28 is true – that everything that happens is for my good and for my deliverance. I am sure of it. I have experienced it over and over, especially through the bad times – because I let go to God and allowed him to work, rather than fighting him.

God loves you. He has your best interest at heart. He is guaranteeing you that the same thing is true in your life, which is that everything is happening for a purpose. Romans 8:28 has a sister paragraph, Ephesians 1:11, "In him we were also chosen, having been predestined according to the plan of him who works out everything in conformity with the purpose of his will ..." God works out everything in accordance with His purpose and His will. He's got the big picture, and it's for your long-term benefit.

So, what are you holding on to that is keeping you from experiencing God's plan to work everything out for your good?

Are you sinking under the weight of that "rock" you're holding on to?

Are you hanging over the edge of the cliff, staring down into a pit?

Are you ready for a change?

It's time, time to let go of that "rock" you're holding on to, time to let go of your fear, time to let go of your own strength. It's really time to experience God's love, His strength, joy, and peace. You do not have forever to do this. The clock is winding down on life, and you don't know when it will be over. Something has to change. If you are going to rededicate yourself to God, you have to let go of these areas of your life, and you know what they are. Turn them over to God, and let go of that rock drowning you.

Trust in God. He has a rescue boat with your name on it, just waiting. Are you willing? He is. Need proof?

In Mark 1:40–41, a man with leprosy walks up to Jesus, extends his shriveled hand, and says "If you are willing, you can make me clean." Jesus is filled with compassion and says, "I am willing." Jesus looks at every one of us, and he says, "I am willing." Jesus is willing to heal you, to love you, to help you.

Are you willing to receive that offer? Are you willing to let go to God? Are you willing to rededicate your life?

Don't be the monkey in the lab as I was, hitting the sin lever repeatedly until it nearly killed me. Rededicate yourself to God, starting with your heart. This time, pull the God lever, which is the lever of life, and live.

It's amazing how difficult this can be. Maybe you remember the old

TV game show called "Let's Make a Deal." Monty Hall was the host, and during a portion of the show, he'd go into the audience and make trades with them. They were easy deals. He'd say something like "If you have a paper clip on you, I'll trade you this box of delicious donuts for it." Who would turn that down? Sometimes it was amazing to see the crazy, silly things people were actually carrying around with them. So, somebody would end up with the box of donuts, and then he'd give them the opportunity to trade the donuts for whatever was inside a big box. "Okay, Monty, give me the box." Oh, there's a new microwave oven in the box! That's not bad. Monty would keep going. Then, you'd have the opportunity to trade the microwave for what's behind door 1, 2, or 3. Now, two of those doors had garbage behind them – wasted motor oil or something – but one of the doors had the grand prize, a nice, spanking-new Cadillac. If you picked right a few times, you just traded up from a paper clip to a new car. If you picked wrong, whatever you ended up with was about as worthless as your paper clip.

Fortunately, it doesn't work that way with God. God does not have multiple choice doors. There aren't two that are crummy and one that's good. There is one clearly marked door, and it has God's complete joy behind it. The true prize is right behind that door, and all we have to do is hand God this stupid box of donuts. (We treat our lives as if they were those donuts.) All we have to do is say, "Lord, here is this lousy box of donuts. I want the grand prize!" But it's so difficult for us. We're willing to settle for so much less. Believe me, I know – I've been there. We hold on to these donuts like a prize, forgetting the fact that, in a short amount of time, they'll be stale, moldy, and worthless. Why not take the opportunity to put them aside for something of lasting value?

Our lives are like those donuts. Ten out of ten people die in the end. In a short amount of time, it'll be over, but while we're here, we can make the trade with God. We can give Him our stale, moldy bodies and lives (donuts), and He will give us a guaranteed place in heaven and an abundant life now, where we can live each day with His holy spirit inside us. Now, that's a deal!

It's Not Too Late

I got a call from a friend of mine a few years ago – a guy from my "before life," way back in the past. I met him in 1985, and we became pals. We did a lot of partying and other things together, intensely, and so we knew each other from drugs, alcohol, and wild stuff I would not care to remember at this stage in my life. I found the Lord and got cleaned up, and he didn't do either, unfortunately, so I keep praying about that.

But every once in a while I get a call from him, maybe every six or eight months, and I have had the privilege of witnessing to him a little bit over the phone and sending him a CD or two of some sermons I preached, even though he didn't seem particularly responsive. At least, he knows where I stand. His calls were always asking to borrow a few bucks here and there when times got tough on his end. He's married, twice divorced, and has a couple of kids. He's still mired in alcohol and has even gone into the hospital for it, back and forth for the same problems, and when he calls, he constantly reminds me of the times in my life that he bailed me out when we were in that lifestyle together.

"Jack, remember when it was the two of us, and you couldn't get up and walk?"

And I say, "Yes, Tom, I remember. Thank you, thank you for picking me up back then." And thank God that I'm now living a different life.

I'm so grateful to God for delivering me from those days, for delivering me from myself and from what many people would say was a high-flying lifestyle. The problem with high-flying is that sooner or later, you gotta deal with gravity, so you can either land God's way, or you can crash, but either way, you're gonna deal with it. So, I'm glad those drug days are over and I know it's God's hand on me, that keeps me from backsliding.

I pray one day Tom will finally see that what he's doing is harming him and his family and could even kill him if he doesn't stop.

Maybe you can relate to this with someone in your life. You see and you know there is such potential and that life could be so much better if that person would just turn away from the thing that has a hold on him or her. Yet, you also know that until they see it for themselves and want to change, nothing's going to be different. Maybe you're thinking of someone right now that this applies to. Maybe it's you.

So, it was a Monday when I got the call from Tom, this at a time when my television production business had been really hectic, and we were focusing on very intense stuff. I'm too busy, so I tell the secretary I can't talk right now, have him call back later, or I'll call him back later. That was in the morning. About two o'clock in the afternoon, he calls back, and now, I know that he either really needs some money or something is on his mind, but I figure this is going to take some involvement on my part. I'm still busy, so again, I don't talk to him. I'm driving home in my car about 5:30, and I dial him up.

I say, "Tom, how you doing, buddy? What's up?" I'm just waiting for him to hit me with whatever he is going to hit me with.

He says, "Hey, buddy, I had to call you. I just had to call you."

My knuckles get white on the steering wheel. I'm figuring okay, here it comes. What does he need this time?

He says, "I need a favor. I need you to pray for somebody."

I nearly let go of the wheel. "What?"

"I need you to pray for somebody. I'm painting this lady's house. She is the sweetest lady in the world, and I'm painting her house today, and she finds out she has breast cancer. Jack, this can't be; this lady is so sweet. I need you to pray for her. I know God hears your prayers."

I'm thinking, wow, this is great. Not that someone has just been diagnosed with cancer, but that Tom would even think about prayer, much less take the time to call me and ask me to do it. So, of course, I told him that I would pray for her, and I did, right then on the phone. But I reminded Tom that he didn't need me to pray for her, that he could have a direct relationship with God, but that he could count on me to keep praying for her.

After we hung up, I was so joyful as I drove home, I was so grateful to God, grateful that prayer was on Tom's heart at this time when something was bad and that he'd cared about someone else's life. At least, he'd realized that God was the answer. Whether he believed that he could communicate directly was a separate issue, but he at least realized that God was the answer. Then, I thought how amazing it was that God had brought my life and Tom's to the point where at least now Tom associates me with prayer instead of alcohol and drugs, like he's finally taken down the "before" picture of the Jack he used to know and has replaced it with the "after" photo. This is a big step for most of us.

Isn't it interesting how our human nature fixates on who somebody is when we first meet them, and it's like a plumb line for the relationship? Tom and I met through wild living, and that became the connection, even after I changed. A lot of other people wanted nothing to do with me after I found God. So often, it's hard for people to deal with changes we make in our lives, whether it's change for the good or the bad, because of that plumb line. They want what's best for us, but it's normally according to *their* definition of "best," which is often based on what's best for *them*.

My giving up the high-flying lifestyle, in Tom's eyes, wasn't best for our friendship, and it had taken years for him to finally see me differently. I remember being in Lake Tahoe with my wife and four other couples, most of whom I'd met through my business partner, so I'd only known them for about five years when we went on vacation together. We were at dinner, and somehow, the story drifted to college, and I shared a story about my drug days. One of the women, a wonderfully sweet woman named Yvette, said, "Jack, I would have never imagined you to be that way or do something like that." When I went back up to my hotel room after dinner, I began to cry (by the way, I don't cry often, but it seems as if you're hearing about it a lot) because I realized that God had completely transformed me into another person over these last few years – a person who did not resemble or look like anything I used to be. I was so grateful to God and so happy that people now saw the new me – the born-again-of-Christ me.

Part of my sense of being grateful to God was that I realized Tom saw me as a source for something else – he saw me as a source for hope when he had none of his own to offer someone in need. Funny thing about Tom is that once I got saved and cleaned up my act, I never heard him say, "Jack, who are you? I don't know you anymore" the way a lot of people do when they turn away from you. So, I think, one day soon, Tom's going to make the change and get cleaned up with God's help.

The longer I'm a believer, the more I know that once we're saved, God never says, "Who are you?" or "I don't know you anymore," and he never turns away from us. Instead, he tells us over and over, "I know who you are because I created you. I knew you before you were born. I've seen everything about you. I've even counted the hairs on your head, and you can turn away from me, you can ignore me, but I still know who you are. I still love you, and I will never turn away from you."

That doesn't mean He won't deal with the things we put between Him and us, and that's anything interfering with our focus on God and our making Him first in our lives. I mean stuff such as pornography, alcohol addiction, career ambition, social status, our checkbook, our season tickets to our favorite baseball team, or all our electronic gadgets and other stuff like that. Call them whatever you want, but when they get between God and us, He calls them worthless idols, and in this chapter, we're going to take a hard, hard look at what God has to say through Jeremiah to and about his people when they let something come between Him and them.

I am still in awe when I think of all the things and all the ways God used to bring me to this point in my life, but when I look at this Old Testament book, I realize that my journey is not so different from the Israelites'. They had a history of interacting with God, but as generations went by, they drifted farther and farther from God's ways until they treated God, if they acknowledged him at all, as just another thing that they owned, or a possession they had, that had no say or input in how they lived their lives. They turned their backs on Him, thinking He was irrelevant. What they couldn't or wouldn't see was that He had all these good things waiting for them – if they would return to Him and give up the things that had made God so upset with them, so upset that He was going to send them into captivity in another country where someone else would rule over them.

When I was growing up, our family's Judaism was more cultural than theological, the same way many Americans say they are Christians, go to church twice a year, probably have a Bible somewhere, and have heard of Jesus. We did Jewish things (exchange Hanukah presents, light candles for dead relatives, have Passover supper, and take a day off for Yom Kippur), but I had no religious training or practice on which to build a faith that would lead me to the promises God had for me. That's not because it wasn't offered to me. My brother went to Hebrew school, and I could have, too, but I didn't want to go, and my parents did not force me. I wandered in the wilderness of wild living, to the point where, as Tom has often reminded me, I could not get up and walk and go home, and Tom, who wasn't in much better shape than I at any given moment, would have to help me. I knew *of* God because of my upbringing, but I wanted nothing to do *with* God in my life. So, I ignored what little I had learned along the way and ignored the warnings others gave me about my lifestyle of recreational pharmacology, until I had to face up to the fact that I was crippled by and ruled by my addictions.

When I faced the truth of what I was and the truth that I was powerless to change anything on my own, that's when I turned to God. When I did that, when I accepted Jesus as my Savior, I knew I would not have to face God's anger and wrath in the future. That didn't mean I was free from the consequences of years of bad choices or from the temptation to use drugs again. Some people, they get saved, and that desire for alcohol or cocaine, or whatever their drug of choice was, is totally gone. Yet for me, it's lurking in the background and reminds me that this is a long-term process and that I have to choose daily to turn away from that and turn to God with all my heart. Otherwise, I risk backsliding into places I don't want to go, at prices I'm not willing to pay.

So, before we go any farther, I'm giving you a warning, as a fellow believer. We all put things between God and us, and the question is do we see them for what they are. It's easy to see the drugs or the abuses in someone else and how it makes them backslide away from God, but

God wants us to see it in ourselves and repent and return to him, or else. Or else?

Yeah, or else. There won't literally be "hell to pay" because we can't lose our salvation, but we can sure lose a lot of blessings in this lifetime and a lot of rewards once we get to heaven. God wants us to hear the message He had for the people of Israel back in Jeremiah's day and relate it to our lives today.

We're gonna get blunt about our own lives and relationship with God. We'll see that the Israelites had all the promises of God available to them, but they had become trapped in a lifestyle that ignored God, that went after the things of the world, and that stubbornly refused to hear His voice, and that lifestyle cost them dearly. And yes, this is for New Testament believers because we also have God's promises available to us through Christ. Yet, even after we're saved, we can be trapped in a lifestyle that puts God second or third place, and it will cost us too. We will lose God's blessings in this lifetime, and we will lose some of our rewards in heaven if we don't keep God where He belongs, and that's first place in everything. So if it's in the Bible, God wants us to know it and apply it.

As I said, we have this human mentality that fixates on who someone is when we first meet them, but God's mentality is different because of when He knew us. God asserts his sovereignty and his authority from the get-go in Jeremiah 1:5 by saying, "Before I formed you in the womb I knew you, before you were born I set you apart." God says that to all of us today. He tells us He created everything. He created you; He knew you; and He formed you. He says He has a perfect plan for your life, and that before there was Earth, He created you, and your name is written in the Book of Life. Up in heaven, there is a place for you if you are a believer. Even if you are not a believer, God formed you and created you, and His desire is that you have a relationship with Him.

How well does God know us? In Matthew 10:30, in the New Testament, God goes so far as to say, "and even the very hairs of your head are all numbered." Pretty intense knowledge of someone, isn't it?

With everything God knows about us, he also knows our future. I'm not talking about crystal balls or palm reading, but that He absolutely knows our future. First because He has a plan for us, and second, because our future is evident to Him by the way we relate to Him and obey His Word. That means that if we pay attention to His Word, we can have a pretty good idea of what our lives will be like. God says in Jeremiah 29:11, "'For I know the plans I have for you,' declares the Lord, 'plans to prosper you and not to harm you, plans to give you hope and a future.'" Can we know what's in the future? Well, we can know some things for certain. We know that obedience brings blessings, and disobedience, at some point, will bring trouble or disaster. We know that if we get drunk and drive, we will likely get a DUI. If we sleep around, our future is likely to include a sexually transmitted disease. If we disobey God's clear instructions, we are going to be called to account. And yet we do that and other rebellious things anyway, just like the Israelites.

God was looking at their behaviors and at their relationship with Him, and he was saying, This is it. I've been patient long enough. If they don't change, there will be consequences.

So what were they doing that got Him so upset He had to give Jeremiah all these warnings to tell them? And what was it Jeremiah was telling them? Warnings about God's coming judgment on them. In Jeremiah 1:16, God is warning them, "I will pronounce my judgments on my people because of their wickedness in forsaking me, in burning incense to other gods and in worshipping what their hands have made."

What got God so upset? Forsaking him. Burning incense to other gods. Worshipping what their hands have made.

You say, "Well, Jack, I go to church. I love Jesus. I haven't forsaken God. I certainly haven't burned incense to other gods, and I haven't worshipped the work of my own hands."

Really?

You go to church. You listen to Christian radio, but do you gossip about your co-workers and put down your friends behind their backs? Are you praying to and trusting God to provide for your needs, or are you looking for the next get-rich-quick idea that you can do? And maybe you aren't worshipping a golden calf as they did in the desert, but let's take a look at that business you own. Did you create that, or did God? Did you build that house, or did God? Did you give yourself the ability to be a great athlete, or did God?

There is a lot of stuff we do that makes us so proud of our own hands. There is nothing wrong with those things individually, unless we put them ahead of God, unless God isn't our first love. It's like putting a hobby or a boss in first place ahead of our spouse. Throughout Scripture, God describes our relationship to him as a marriage. In marriage, we expect the relationship to take priority over everything and for it to be a faithful and committed relationship. So when we put something or someone before those things, it's as if we're looking for something that the marriage partner could not give, and so we "stray" and wind up having an affair. Here is God, asking this question of the people in Jeremiah 2:5, "What fault did your fathers find in me, that they strayed so far from me? They followed worthless idols and became worthless themselves. They did not ask 'Where is the Lord?'"

God has the same question for you and me, and remember, we are believers. We are saved. We have a relationship with Him in the same way the Israelites had a relationship with Him, but they strayed, and so do we. So, what fault, what lack did you find in God that you have chosen not to follow Him, that you have chosen not to do everything that He asks and, instead, to follow idols and become worthless? You say you don't follow idols. Are you sure? Would your checkbook and your calendar show you follow brand names, sports teams, and social activities more than you follow God? If so, why? Maybe you call it shopping, which easily turns into materialism; or looking good, which easily becomes vanity; or moving up, which easily crosses the line between "need," and "status," or pride, or having a good time or relaxing, which can easily be a drug or alcohol addiction. Whatever you call it, if it's the thing that drives your choices and decisions instead of God, then you are following an idol.

God should be the first priority in your life. Here's one way to check whether He's first or not. Let's look at the last line in that verse, "They did not ask, 'Where is the Lord?'" This is a way of expressing a desire to seek the Lord. I want to ask you a question. Did you wake up this morning and seek the Lord? When you had to make that decision today, did you seek the Lord for advice? When you go to sleep, will you ask, "Where is the Lord?" Are you seeking Him throughout the day, or are you so tangled up in the world that you don't ask that question?

God must be so upset that His people are not seeking Him and upset that they have given up the only valuable and lasting thing they had, which is their identity in Him. In Jeremiah 2:11–13, God says, "...

But my people have exchanged their Glory for worthless idols." They have traded this priceless relationship with God for worthless things that will rot, rust, and fall apart – some for big houses, fancy cars, and designer labels. Has that designer laid down his life for you? It would be like trading bars of gold for dirt. Sounds stupid when we word it that way, doesn't it? And yet, we still do it.

God goes on to warn us, in Jeremiah 2:19, that "'Your wickedness will punish you; your backslidings will rebuke you. Consider then and realize how evil and bitter it is for you when you forsake the Lord your God and have no awe of me,' declares the Lord, the Lord Almighty." You've probably said or received the same message at some point: Stop and think about what you're doing, about how bad it is for you and how awful the consequences of your choices are. Stop and consider. Have you connected the dots between your choices and your circumstances? What were you thinking? I can remember people asking me things like that "back in the day." And no, I didn't stop and consider, but I do now. How about you?

I will tell you this: If you're a Christian, you know when you are screwing up. It's not like you can go la-di-da down the road, thinking you're not doing anything wrong. You know you've drifted from God; you know your walk isn't what you want it to be. You know you are not following God's perfect plan for your life. We ignore God and His instructions for our lives and put other things first. As I'm writing this, football season has just begun, and I know many Christians with box seats or season tickets, believers who will choose to put football ahead of God and go to the game or stay home and prepare to watch the game on TV, rather than worshipping God on Sunday mornings. Football games are great, but not when they become a higher priority than God.

If you had a standing appointment with a loved one, and he or she shrugged it off for chips, dip, and touchdowns, you would feel as if you'd been let down, that the value of your relationship had just been discounted to the clearance rack. From God's view, that looks a lot like forsaking Him, like losing our awe and fear of Him.

God calls His people to account when they do that, and He reveals their hypocrisy at the same time. "They have turned their backs to me and not their faces; yet when they are in trouble, they say, 'Come and save us!'" (Jeremiah 2:27). You and I both know there are many people walking around, looking at God, being at church, and then going out the door and not living a Christian life. Their faces are on God for an hour on Sunday morning, but for the rest of the week, their backs are turned – until somebody gets sick or they have a marriage problem, a money crisis, or whatever, and suddenly, they're calling out to God, asking Him to save them. We'd never do that. Or would we?

God says that is hypocritical. We say the same thing when someone does it to us, ignores us, and then suddenly acts like our best friend when they need something only we can give. And we've done it to others. In Jeremiah 2:28, God responds to hypocritical people, "Where then are the gods you made for yourselves? Let them come and save you when you are in trouble!" Well, let's get this right. You spend all your time focusing on the things of the world, like what you are going to get, how you are going to get it, and who's going to notice, but now there's trouble, and you go and pray to God for help. And you're surprised when you don't get the answer you want?

In today's language, God is in essence saying in Jeremiah verse 2:28, "Hey! You love cocaine and now you're in trouble? Call your drug dealer; I'm sure he'll be sympathetic. You love your alcohol, and now you got problems? Call the liquor company. Love your money, your golf clubs, your house? Call your banker, your golf pro, and your realtor; see if they'll rescue you. And all those names you love to drop so you sound important? Call one of them to bail you out. Let's see them save you. Oh, they can't. And now, you need me?" So, let me ask you another question. How much of your prayer time is about asking God to fix your problems? How much time do you spend simply thanking God for what you have and praising Him for who He is?

God proceeds to give perhaps the scariest analogy I have ever seen in my life by comparing such behavior to a marriage. In Jeremiah 3:1, God gives Jeremiah these words to say to the Israelites: "If a man divorces his wife and she leaves him and marries another man, should he return to her again? Would not the land be completely defiled?" Let's get this picture that God is presenting. Husband divorces wife, wife marries someone else, should he take her back after that? Wouldn't that defile him? Or vice versa? Yes, it would defile him. The verse continues with God speaking, "But you have lived as a prostitute with many lovers – would you now return to me?" You've been running around on Him (cheating on God), so to speak, by putting many things of this world ahead of Him. You've cast Him aside and ignored Him. You've given your time and affection and love to other people and other things, and yet now, when you have a need, you're coming to Him, expecting help. Do you see your hypocrisy toward God as easily as you see it in other people?

In our human relationships, the normal response to someone doing this to us is to blow them off. Is this the final word? Does God blow us off when we're the ones behaving this way? Does God leave you there crying while He turns His back? No, absolutely not. In His great love for His people, He invites them to return. Consider Jeremiah 3:12–13, "'Return, faithless Israel,' declares the Lord, 'I will frown on you no longer, for I am merciful,' declares the Lord, 'I will not be angry forever. Only acknowledge your guilt – you have rebelled against the Lord your God ... and have not obeyed me ....'" Sounds like an amnesty period. Just come on back, tell Me you screwed it up, and I'll give you another chance. Return to Me; I won't be mad at you forever.

Why would He say that? "... for I am your husband ...." Complete, perfect, amazing, incredible love. "'Return, faithless people ... for I am your husband ...'" and in 3:22, "Return, faithless people; I will cure you of backsliding."

From God's perspective, this isn't some passing, casual relationship He has with us. When we say yes to God, we are committed to Him in the same way we are committed to someone when we say "I do." We aren't capable of fixing the problems we cause in our relationship with Him unless we turn back to Him, admit what we did wrong, and choose to go forward together. When we do that, He says He will heal our backslidings. This invitation to return is always available to His children, but returning to God means repenting by turning away from what drew us away from Him in the first place.

Sounds pretty clear. Fess up, repent, return, and get back in step with God. So, why isn't everybody doing it? Why isn't everyone leaping at the chance for amnesty? We do it for library fines or tax issues, but we don't see ourselves needing it spiritually because hey, we're saved. Yet, God says that we act like silly children when we do that. Think about your own family. You'll never disown your kids, but when they act as if they have no responsibility to live up to certain expectations, you discipline them, and you probably aren't inclined to shower them with gifts.

God is looking at our unwillingness to return to Him and says, "My people ... are senseless children; they have no understanding" (Jeremiah 4:22). I'm sure all you parents can relate. You only want the best thing for your kids. You are only telling them what to do because you love them, but they just don't do it. Silly children, they just don't get it. And neither do we, because God says (in the context of not returning to Him) that we have no understanding. We don't get the implications of continuing down our own path.

I can tell you from experience how true that is. Did I know – did I have the information, did I hear all the messages and warnings – that the lifestyle I was living before I knew Christ was harmful and even dangerous? Of course, I did. I had all the info, all the disclaimers, warnings, and lectures, but I had no understanding, and I always thought I could keep it together. And you say, "Well, you weren't in church, and that's why this doesn't apply to me. I have understanding because I'm in church, and I read the Bible." Maybe so. Maybe not. Some of you have read the Bible all your life, but that doesn't mean you have understanding! If you did, you would do what it said. That's what God is saying to the Israelites and to us. Do you understand what's in store for you if you don't repent and return to God? At the time Jeremiah was writing, it was a final warning about their being conquered and carried off into captivity because of their disobedience to God's commands. I'm not saying this is about occasional disobedience or something you do out of ignorance of what God's Word says. What God is pointing at here is a persistent lifestyle of disobedience and hypocrisy, and He will only tolerate it for so long and will only give you so many chances before He will force you to face up and confess.

I can't speak for you, but I can tell you I personally would prefer to face up and confess on my own, rather than digging my heels in, thinking I'm gonna pull one over on God. Why? I'll let Jeremiah answer that. In 5:24–25, God goes on to say that, "They do not say to themselves *in their hearts, [emphasis mine]* 'let us now fear the Lord our God.'" I have a question for you. What are you saying in your heart right now? Are you just nodding along, yeah, yeah, whatever, this doesn't apply to me so I'll skip this part? Do you have any fear in your heart for God right now? That is the problem that Israel had back then. It wasn't in their hearts. Get this right: God says I have this perfect plan for your life, and I know exactly what I want to accomplish for you. I know exactly why

I created you. Before the foundation of the world, I created you. Before you were in your mother's womb, I knew who you were and every hair on your head is numbered. I have the perfect plan for your life, but your disobedience and your actions have interrupted that for now. You interrupted it, and you stopped God's blessings from coming to you.

So, how can you change that?

"Stand at the crossroads and look; ask for the ancient paths, ask where the good way is, and walk in it, and you will find rest for your souls" (Jeremiah 6:16). God tells the Israelites to go back to the tried and true ways of their ancestors and to walk in those ways. Then, you'll have rest, peace, and joy in your souls. Doesn't that sound good? Peace, joy, rest for your souls. Sounds simple enough, but what do those silly, senseless children do? At the end of verse 16, the Israelites respond, "We will not walk in it." Rather than choosing the path to peace and joy, they're choosing to stay on the path of the world that's already caused them so many problems.

How about you? God gives you the choice too. Stay on your pot-holed path that keeps making you frustrated and troubled? Or turn back to God's path and blessings? It's not what you *say* that reflects your answer; it's what you *do* that proves it. Do you nod along with the pastor as he preaches, and then go back out Monday morning just like you were in the world? Before you answer, let me tell you that God has more; He tells you what happens if you don't come back to Him.

Jeremiah 6:21, "Therefore this is what the Lord says: 'I will put obstacles before this people. Fathers and sons alike will stumble over them...'" That sounds like fun (NOT!). Want some more potholes and obstacles to happiness? Think it's hard getting your local highway department to come out and fix that hole in your road? You ain't seen nothing yet, friends. If God puts a pothole in your life's road, you'd better pay attention because it won't just make you stumble; it's going to affect your family and others too.

Yet in spite of obstacles and stumbling, the people persist in doing things their way, in continuing to backslide, "... They cling to deceit; they refuse to return. I have listened attentively, but they do not say what is right. No one repents of his wickedness, saying, 'What have I done?' Each pursues his own course..." (Jeremiah 8:4–6). Do you refuse to return to God? He is listening to you ... but what is He hearing? Are you saying the right thing? Is He hearing you say, "What have

I done? Lord, I am coming back. I repent. I'm sorry?" Or is He hearing you say, "God wait, I'll get to you later. I'm handling this."? Are you pursuing your own course or God's?

God knows the difference. He sees it all, even if your words sound right to the people in the pew next door, and he sees what's in your heart. In Jeremiah 16:17, He declares, "My eyes are on all their ways; they are not hidden from me, nor is their sin hidden from my eyes." God sees everything. He sees all your actions. He even knows your thoughts before you think them (Psalm 139:2). Well, of course, He does. He created you in the womb (Psalm 139:13). He created you before the beginning of creation. He knows the plans He has for you (Jeremiah 29:11).

So, why in the world would you want to do things your own way when the One, the One who made everything that ever was, is, or will be, has a plan for you? Do you have the ability, the power, the strength to do something better than God? Then how come you're not on top of the world?

Somewhere at home I know I have some photos of myself as a young, high-flying guy, and I can tell you I looked bad. And it's not just goofy-hair bad or dumb-clothing-styles bad, but I mean I literally and physically looked bad. I can see the toll that my lousy life plan was already taking. I call those my "befores." I keep them, so I can remind myself when I need it, when I'm being tempted by an old sin, that that's not the way I want to look. That might be the way some have fixated on me, but not God, and if God sees me differently, then there's real hope. I'm God's kid now, and I have a new life photo. It's all airbrushed and perfected the way God sees me.

Do you have "before" and "after" pictures? Or are you still fixated on your "before"? If you're relying on your own ability, power, and strength and not putting God first, you will continually drift back to the "before" look, and you'll miss out on many blessings in this life and the next. God is always ready for us to show up for the "after" photo, but we have to decide to show up. The first step is to "Turn now, each of you, from your evil ways and your evil practices, and you can stay in the land the Lord gave to you and your fathers for ever and ever" (Jeremiah 25:5).

In the New Testament, the message is the same. "If we confess our sins, he is faithful and just and will forgive us our sins and purify us from all unrighteousness" (1 John 1:9).

Are you searching for God with your whole heart? Let me repeat: God makes an amazing promise to us! He says, in Jeremiah 29:11–13, "'For I know the plans I have for you,' declares the Lord, 'plans to prosper you and not to harm you, plans to give you hope and a future. Then you will call upon me and come and pray to me, and I will listen to you. You will seek me and find me when you seek me with all your heart.'" You will find him when you search for him with all your heart, not when you're focused on the world, not when you've got a buzz going, not when you're hitting on someone at a party, not when you're doing the wrong thing. *You will find me when you search for me with all your heart.*

When I finally turned to God, I had to seek Him, and I still have to seek Him with all my heart to keep from backsliding into my old ways. We all do. He knows that. And that's why He promises to be there for us if ... *if* we seek Him. He gives us the choice.

So what now?

How do you seek Him with all your heart?

One way we seek after God is through His Word, the Bible. We get to know His character and the things He promises for us and expects of us, and we learn that the boundaries He has for us are there for our protection. We also seek after Him by worshipping Him at a Bible-believing church and by spending time with Him in prayer. These are all things we learn to do over time, and it is a lifelong process. Scripture encourages us to persevere and pay attention so that we don't drift away from God. "We must pay more careful attention, therefore, to what we have heard, so that we do not drift away" (Hebrews 2:1).

In Colossians 2:6–7, it says "So then, just as you received Christ Jesus as Lord, continue to live in him, rooted and built up in him, strengthened in the faith as you were taught, and overflowing with thankfulness." If you're "rooted and built up," it means you're anchoring yourself to Christ and growing from His "root." Are you being taught how to do that by going to a Bible-believing church? Are you reading scripture for yourself and asking how the verses you read apply to you? Are you walking in Jesus Christ, meaning are you living according to how He would have lived? Are you abounding in thanksgiving? Start thanking God for everything, *every thing* you have – for each item of food in your house, for clean water, for indoor plumbing and air conditioning. That'll help you overflow with thanksgiving!

Then, learn how to get your mind onto heavenly things. Give thanks for the things you have, but don't focus on them, don't be caught up in possessions or in wanting more things of this earthly life. Colossians 3:1–2 says, "Since, then, you have been raised with Christ, set your hearts on things above, where Christ is seated at the right hand of God. Set your minds on things above, not on earthly things."

Focusing our minds on earthly things can lead us right back into our "before" photo, into old addictions and habits, and into being ruled by someone or something other than God. And it's not just physical stuff, either. It's also those natural human responses we need to overcome by focusing on Christ and not on ourselves. A few verses later in Colossians 3, Paul spells it out for us: "Put to death, therefore, whatever belongs to your earthly nature: sexual immorality, impurity, lust, evil desires and greed, which is idolatry ... rid yourselves of all such things as these: anger, rage, malice, slander, and filthy language ... do not lie to each other ...."

That's a long list of things to learn to recognize in ourselves and then learn how to put them to death! And what do we put in their place? Compassion, kindness, humility, gentleness, and patience, and we are to bear with one another, forgive one another, and love one another (Colossians 3:12–14). Show the qualities of Christ. Let the peace of God rule in your heart. Let the word of Christ dwell in you richly. Live your "after" life now – live it abundantly with the peace and love of Christ.

And if we don't? All I have to do is look at my "befores" or get a call from Tom, and I remember what it was like. I remember what it was like to wander in that wilderness, crippling myself and putting myself into a position where I would be in captivity to something or someone that did not have my long-term best interest at heart – someone or something that would not be there when I called out for help and needed to be rescued. I've been there. And I don't want to go back.

Are you there now? Is there a "Tom" calling to you from your past, reminding you of what you were? Are you being tempted to return to something other than God?

Or is there a Jeremiah in your life right now, calling you to turn to God? Like the Israelites and like me, you have a choice to make. God is calling. Will you answer? Can't sleep? Is your stomach hurting? Are you aching from something God has shown you during this blunt look at real life? Then, take heart. God is speaking to you. Meditate on these specific verses from Psalm 51 and cry out to him.

Psalm 51

1 Have mercy on me, O God,
  according to your unfailing love;
  according to your great compassion
  blot out my transgressions.
2 Wash away all my iniquity
  and cleanse me from my sin.
3 For I know my transgressions,
  and my sin is always before me.
5 Surely I was sinful at birth,
  sinful from the time my mother conceived me.
6 Surely you desire truth in the inner parts;
  you teach me wisdom in the inmost place ...
9 Hide your face from my sins
  and blot out all my iniquity.
10 Create in me a pure heart, O God,
  and renew a steadfast spirit within me.
11 Do not cast me from your presence
  or take your Holy Spirit from me.
12 Restore to me the joy of your salvation
  and grant me a willing spirit, to sustain me.
16 You do not delight in sacrifice, or I would bring it;
  you do not take pleasure in burnt offerings.
17 The sacrifices of God are a broken spirit;
  a broken and contrite heart,
  O God, you will not despise.

Dan the Man

Four men, different legacies. Two were good friends of mine, and one I simply knew from church. The other one is Daniel, of Old Testament fame. I've learned a few things from looking at their lives and the choices they made or didn't make.

The first two men left this Earth a few years ago. They were very good friends of mine. One of them, Rob McNamara, a great guy from my high school days, had a brain aneurysm, was on life support for a day or two, and then his wife had to make the hard decision to pull the plug. She did, and he died. Along with his wife, he left two wonderful children. He was my age, late forties, sweetest guy you'd ever want to meet. I'd known him since we were 12 years old. Rob was the "do-anything-for-you" kind of wonderful guy – the type you would think deserved to go to heaven.

Shortly after that happened, I got more bad news that my good friend, Eddie Eade, passed away. He had a heart attack on the 18th hole while golfing with his 16-year-old son. Eddie was 43, an amazing guy, just amazing. I'd known him for 10 years. He had a very interesting story. He was a drug addict, crack cocaine specifically, rough stuff. His wife was divorcing him. He had three young kids at the time and couldn't get his life together. He came down to Florida. We talked, and he decided that he wanted a different chance at life. He accepted Jesus Christ as Lord and Savior, kicked his drug habit and reconciled with his wife. For the last 10 years of his life, he was the most on-fire Christian man you would ever want to see. He witnessed in prisons and at meetings for Alcoholics Anonymous and Narcotics Anonymous. Everywhere he went, whether it was work, the golf course, prisons, or the flea market on Saturday, this guy was a walking testimony for Jesus Christ.

So, I've been thinking about how incredible this was. Here were two great guys, close friends of mine, men I admired and loved and respected very much, but they went to two different places. Then, I thought how sad that was too.

You could look at Rob's actions, the way he lived his life, the things he did, the people who loved him, all those things, and you would think that if anybody *deserved* to go to heaven, he'd be the one. Unfortunately, to the best of my knowledge, he did not make the decision to accept Jesus Christ as his Lord and Savior, and so I do not believe that he is in heaven.

Then, we had Eddie, who made that decision, and without a doubt, we can say for sure where he went the moment he was done with this tent called his body. God was smiling at him, saying, "Well done, good and faithful servant! Come and share your Master's happiness."

Doesn't seem fair, does it? That's what I thought. Not fair at all, because Rob really was a terrific guy. Then, I realized that what I think is fair doesn't matter. I'm kind of unreliable that way, probably like most people. For example, if you ask me if it's fair that I get a speeding ticket doing 50 in a 30 mile-per-hour zone, I would say absolutely not. That speed limit on that stretch of road should be 50, and you would agree if you drove that same road. It's just not fair. But you know what? It's the way it is; that's reality. The requirement on that road was 30, and I didn't fulfill the requirement, and I got penalized for it.

I also think it's fair that I be the next 10 million dollar lottery winner, but just because I think something is fair or not doesn't change anything. So, whether I think Rob not going to heaven is fair or not isn't the point. See, I'm looking at what he did and how he lived – his actions and his works – and God says it's not about actions, and it's not about works. It's about believing God with all your heart and saying yes to Jesus Christ as Lord and Savior.

The point that came home to me so clearly is that once your life is over, you don't have a choice. So you'd better say yes up front because it will not matter what you *did* in this life. It will only matter what you *professed*, what you said you believed about Christ, and whether you accepted Jesus Christ or not. I hope and pray that anyone reading this book, this very paragraph, anyone who hasn't said yes to Christ will not close this book or finish this page without making that choice, that decision. Don't assume that you are immortal and that your time is far off, because believe me, Rob and Eddie did not wake up on their last mornings expecting to die. And I believe only one of them, Eddie, is in heaven today.

And Eddie changed history. It's really not unusual for a Christian man to change history because it's God working through believers who makes it happen. But how, exactly, did Eddie Eade change history?

Let me back up a little. I told you that 10 years ago, he came down to Florida. What I didn't tell you is that he was the brother-in-law of my business partner, who had come to me one day and said, "Jack, my brother-in-law has a big drug problem, do you think you can help?"

Me? Yes, me. I've had some experience in this area, as you know, so I was a likely source, whereas my partner had no clue about how to talk to Eddie about such things. So, I said, "Yeah, and here's what we do. Let's fly Eddie down from Buffalo and tell him we might have a job for him and that will give me the chance to talk to him."

So, we do this; we fly Eddie down. I take him out one night, and my partner conveniently goes away. The two of us are sitting there at a table and I tell him, "Eddie, I can see it. If you don't change your life, I'm seeing your funeral. It's a cold Buffalo morning, cold and gray, and dark. Your mother's there, and your father's there, and they are weeping. And you're just gone, and it is so sad. Eddie, I believe that God has given me a vision of what your funeral is going to be like and what your life is going to be like if you don't change it." Then, I asked him that night if he wanted help, and he said yes. He soon gave his life to Christ, turned his life around, and from that point on, he became, like I said, the most on-fire Christian you would ever want to meet. He stayed like that for the next 10 years, right up until he died. And for those 10 years, he changed history – first by accepting Jesus Christ, and then by being obedient to Jesus Christ.

History is something you see after it's happened, after it's all over, right? Well, I got my history lesson at Ed Eade's funeral. It started at his wake, where there was a waiting line for two hours. This line went out the funeral hall as they had never seen before. Hundreds of people, maybe a thousand, were coming in that night to pay their respects to Eddie because he had impacted so many people. I sat there talking to his sister, and I told her this was going to be amazing. Could you imagine all the people going to heaven someday and God asking them, "How did you get here?" and they all say, "Ed told me. Ed Eade showed me the way." This guy's legacy is phenomenal.

Then, at the funeral service at Calvary Chapel, down in Fort Lauderdale, the place was packed. The pastor talked about Eddie's life, and at the end of this sermon, he gave an invitation, and people were getting saved – at the funeral! Eddie influenced others, not only during his life, but also after his death.

The most incredible of these stories happened with Eddie's daughter, Rachel. At a reception after the service, she said, "When the pastor asked if anybody needs God, I raised my hand and then I put it down real quick." And here, I am quoting her directly: "And then I felt my hand being lifted up, and I looked around, and there was nobody there, and I saw Eddie's blue thumb, Eddie had a crushed thumb, remember?" (It happened in a factory accident.) Rachel knew it was the Spirit of God using Eddie's life and even his death to make sure that she didn't miss out, to make sure that she made the decision that day and would find her place in heaven for all eternity. So, people got saved at that funeral sermon, and Eddie Eade changed history for a whole bunch of people ... and so can you and I.

How? Simply by saying yes to God and yes to God's gift of salvation, and yes to obedience, as we walk and live the abundant Christian life, no matter what is in our past. Just look at Eddie.

I will never forget what he told me a long time ago. The "before Christ" Eddie was not a good guy. He'd spent time in jail, and when he got saved, he said that somebody had come into jail and preached to the prisoners, and he would never forget that guy because that guy was the first person to plant the seed of God in his life. It had such an impact on him, and when I was witnessing to him, when he flew down from Buffalo, he specifically mentioned that to me. I said, "Eddie, let me ask you a question, did you ever tell the guy about the impact he had on you?"

"No," he said. "I never saw the guy again in my life. He came to the jail that one day and preached, and he was gone."

I thought, wow, here is this guy, this minister or lay person, who went into a jail to witness to inmates, who was being obedient to God by giving a message, and he walked out of there and will never know until he gets to heaven what impact he had on Eddie's life directly and on countless others indirectly. Preaching in that prison on that date might have been a small thing to him, but not to God. And it's the same for you and me. We may not necessarily know the impact we have on other people's lives, directly or indirectly, but we can make and change history for the better if we are simply obedient to God in our daily living.

So, we looked at my friend Rob and my friend Eddie, and there are two lessons in their lives for us. First, if you want to spend eternity in heaven, you have to make the decision to accept Jesus now, before it's too late. Don't assume life is going to keep on ticking your way. Second, our obedience to God can change countless other lives, even if we don't know it this side of heaven. When I get to heaven, I'd rather hear God tell me how many people were there because of me, rather than having to answer to Him for all the people I never told about Jesus.

Now, let me tell you about the third fellow and the life lesson we can learn from him. Not long after Eddie's death, I got a call from a man named Carl Rogers. I knew him several years ago because he went to my church for a little while. Very nice guy, young and smart, too, but he had a tough past, including alcohol abuse. You could see he wasn't living the life he wanted, but he was coming to church and struggling with his past and his issues. I believe he accepted the Lord, and he was trying to do the right thing, and I really admired that. So, one day, I got a call from him and his wife. I hadn't seen or heard from him in five years.

"Jack," he says, "I've got a problem."

"What's up? How can I help?"

He said, "Here's the deal. I went to become a commodities broker, the guy I worked for ripped me off, I lost everything, and in a few days, I'm gonna be homeless. I'm gonna be out on the street. I'm living in a sleazy hotel in Delray Beach with my wife and three kids in this one room; we have nowhere to go; and we have no money. I'm working in a bagel place now and I have no car."

Turns out Carl smacked up his car in a drinking fit a few weeks earlier, so I assumed he'd gone back to his alcohol as a result of the pressure he believed he was under.

I said, "Carl, I love you, you are a great guy, and I want to help you, but here's the problem. Let's say that we get you some temporary housing or get you out of this crazy mess you are in at the moment. What is going to change a month or two from now or even three months?"

Carl didn't say anything, but at least he hadn't hung up the phone.

"Here is what I believe is happening, Carl. First, I believe God wants you in this spot right now because He loves you and wants your attention. I believe you are the luckiest man in the world today."

"Lucky? How you figuring that?"

I said, "Yeah, buddy, lucky, because this only cost you your money. Nobody is sick, nobody is dead, and you have your kids. God has your attention the easy way. We are just talking about money for now, but Carl, I'm telling you, you are standing at the crossroads and how you respond will determine what happens the rest of your life. God loves us too much to let us waste our lives. You're a child of God, and He wants you to have this abundant life." Still no dial tone on the other end, so I kept going. "You know what, Carl? You need to turn and walk with God. Do like it says in Matthew 6:33 – seek first the kingdom of God and His righteousness and all these other things will come. That means you need to come back to God now, so you can live your life happily the right way. Or you can continue to run from God like you have been, and you know what you can expect? More of the same. Except I don't believe in the future you'll get off as luckily, with God just taking your money."

We all have to make the same choice every day, don't we? We have to choose to turn to God and do life His way or keep on running from God and stumbling through life our way.

It's like this story about being pulled over for speeding. You're driving along, and a police officer pulls you over with his flashing red light. You roll down your window, and he's walking over and very nicely asks, "Can I have your license and registration?"

You say, "Well, what did I do wrong, Officer?"

He says, "License and registration, please."

And you say again, "Officer, tell me what I did wrong."

"Sir," he says, "I would like your license and registration."

"Well, I'm not going to give it to you."

"Really? Guess I'm going to have to exert some force. Get out of the car. Now."

And on it goes. You keep resisting, up until the point that he's going to club you with a nightstick, slap on the handcuffs, and drag you off to jail because he is going to get what he wants. Why? Because he is in a position of authority. Does he really want to club you or harm you? No. All he wants you to do is be obedient and cooperate.

It's a good picture of what I was trying to communicate with Carl. I know, because God has had to communicate like that with me. Here we have God, who loves us and who is our father and only wants the best for us, and he's saying, "Jack?"

"Yes, God?"

"Be obedient, so I can bless you in all your life."

"Yes, God."

"Carl Rogers?"

"Yes, God?"

"Be obedient so I can bless you in all your life."

And how does Carl respond? "Well, God, why should I be obedient?"

"So I can bless you in all your life."

"What if I don't want to be obedient?"

And on it goes. Carl (or you or I) keep at it, and the more we resist God, whether we do it silently or at full scream, the more force God will have to exert in our life because ... why? Because He is mad at us? Because He hates us? No! Because He loves us so much that He cannot bear the thought of His children wasting their lives. He loves us too much, so absolutely, as our Father, He is going to do whatever He needs to do to get us into a position where we will be submissive and obedient and where He can bless us. That is God's motive.

It's been a few years now, and I haven't heard from Carl, but I still learned something from him, and that was the importance of recognizing those crossroad moments in my life. And when I do, I make sure

I hand over the "license and registration to my life" to God, so God doesn't have to slap the handcuffs on me to get my attention.

So now, let me tell you what I learned from this old guy named Daniel. He's the last guy on my list that I wanted to tell you about. I hadn't planned on spending much time with him, but I was preparing for a sermon not long ago, and God basically told me to head to the Old Testament and read the book of Daniel.

"Okay, God," I say, "I'll read the book of Daniel." In my mind, I still had a different message I wanted to talk about, but God said, "No, Jack, we are going to read the book of Daniel, and you're going to preach from that."

"That's nice, God, but are you going to tell me what the message is?"

So, I obediently began reading the book of Daniel, looking for the message, and sure enough, God showed me what He had in mind. We can look at Dan the Man and see what he did that caused God to bless him so abundantly in his life. Hopefully, we can each hold up a mirror to our own lives and ask, "Am I succeeding in the same areas as Daniel, or am I falling short?" If you realize you're falling short, I hope you'll amend your behavior quickly.

Just as a quick foundation, the book of Daniel tells the story of a young Israelite named Daniel who is taken away from his home and family by the Babylonians when they invade and conquer Israel. He spends the rest of his life in a foreign land, and the book recounts his faithfulness to God amidst an extremely pagan culture. Daniel and a few of his friends, considered by the invaders to be handsome, intelligent, strapping youth, are singled out for royal treatment. The Babylonians figure, hey, why kill these guys if they can be of some use? Let's train them up in our ways, and we'll be able to use them. As part of the process of indoctrinating them into the Babylonian culture, they wanted to feed Daniel and his friends wine and food that they thought would make them strong and well. "But Daniel resolved not to defile himself with royal food and wine" (Daniel 1:8).

Daniel *resolved* not to defile himself with the royal food and wine, not to compromise with the culture around him. So from the earliest point of his "privileged" status, Daniel stayed true to God. His mind was already made up. He didn't have to think, "Am I going to defile myself?" Instead, he knew he had a relationship with the Lord, and he had faith in the Lord, and he knew exactly what he was going to do. Do you? Do I? It should be second nature to us to think that way, so that when (not if) we're offered something from the world, we already know how to answer. For example, if a prostitute walked up to me, I would say no, thank you. I wouldn't have to think, "Gee, she looks nice, should I or shouldn't I?" It would be ridiculous for a mature Christian believer to have such a thought! And for Daniel, the thought of defiling himself with the royal food and wine was equally ridiculous. God was his first priority.

After Daniel had been in Babylon for a while, King Nebuchadnezzar had a crazy dream and was desperate to find someone to interpret it for him. When none of his wise men could, he threatened them all with death. This included Daniel, who asked for time to interpret the dream, and then prayed to God for help. That night, God gave Daniel the interpretation, and Daniel expressed his gratitude to God in chapter 2, verses 20–23: "Praise be to the name of God for ever and ever; wisdom and power are his. He changes times and seasons; he sets up kings and deposes them. He gives wisdom to the wise and knowledge to the discerning. He reveals deep and hidden things, he knows what lies in darkness, and light dwells with him. I thank and praise you, O God of my fathers: You have given me wisdom and power ...."

Daniel thanked and praised God for the wisdom and knowledge, and power he had received as an answer to his prayer. Do you and I do that? Do we ask for those things? And are we grateful to God for the wisdom, knowledge, and power we receive? Or do we just kind of say "Thanks, God!" as we hurry through the day, thinking "Thanks for saving me, and yeah, I'll get to heaven whenever but right now, I have to live my life." Shouldn't we be grateful on a daily basis for the wisdom and knowledge, and power that we have received *so that* we can live our lives?

Daniel had full confidence that God was God. He didn't doubt it. He didn't dispute it. As part of the dream that he was interpreting, he described the empire that would conquer Babylon and the empires that would follow, and he was able to explain from the dream that "In the time of those kings, the God of heaven will set up a kingdom that will never be destroyed ...." (Daniel 2:44). This was going to be an eternal kingdom, so God is telling Daniel that there is going to be a heaven. Daniel believed that if God said there was a place called heaven that could never be destroyed, not by any kingdom, no matter how powerful, then absolutely there was a place called heaven. Are you that certain?

More time passes in Babylon, and Daniel's friends are told they must worship a golden idol that King Nebuchadnezzar created. You've probably heard this before; it's about Shadrach, Meshach, and Abednego. And even though Daniel isn't in this story, he has spent a great deal of time with his friends. His relationship with God has affected them, so much so that here is how they reply to the king when told they are to worship the golden idol: "O Nebuchadnezzar, we do not need to defend ourselves before you in this matter" (Daniel 3:16). Can you imagine? They tell the king in no uncertain terms, no, we are not going to bow down and worship your golden idol, and we are not even going to tell you why. We don't have to go to court; we are not going to defend ourselves in this matter. In verses 17 and 18, they say, "If we are thrown into the blazing furnace, the God we serve is able to save us from it, and he will rescue us from your hand, O king. But even if he does not ... we will not serve your gods or worship the image of gold you have set up."

Wow! The God they served is the same one you and I serve, and He is able to rescue not just them, but also you and me from the burning furnace. But does He *have* to?

Apparently not, because I've seen some Christians burn in a furnace, figuratively speaking. They weren't *rescued*. So, how do I explain that? The same way I explain many things. Look at Jesus Christ on the cross. The night before it all happened, He said, "... My Father, if it is possible, may this cup be taken from me. Yet not as I will, but as you will" (Matthew 26:39). *Father, take this cup from me, can't we come up with another plan? I know this is Your will, but maybe there is an alternate plan, a plan B that doesn't have me nailed on the cross.* Yes, Jesus asked if there was another way, but ultimately, He said, "Yet not as I will, but as you will." Here is the desire of My heart: that Your will be done, not Mine.

Can we truly say those same words when we are about to enter the furnace of bankruptcy, the chemo schedule, the lawyer's office, or the unemployment line? Not every Christian who cries out to be rescued from the furnace is actually rescued from the burning furnace. Not every sick Christian praying to God not to die doesn't die. But guess what? They are rescued by God, spiritually. Shadrach, Meshach, and Abednego didn't know whether God would let them burn in the fire or not, but they knew for certain that if they did burn in the fire, they would be with God. That, to them, was the rescue. They knew that they couldn't lose, and as harsh as that sounds, we have to look at our "furnaces" the same way. If God chooses to rescue me from the fire, great, if not, then I'm with Him in heaven. Like Paul said, "To live is Christ, to die is gain." What he meant is it's great to be here on Earth doing the Lord's will but I long to be in heaven because then, I get to be with Jesus face-to-face.

Now, here's the end of the furnace story for Shadrach, Meshach and Abednego. It's in Daniel 3:25. Guess what? King Neb (the new shortened nickname I just gave him because his name is so long) says, "... Look! I see four men walking around in the fire, unbound and unharmed, and the fourth looks like a son of the gods." They were delivered, delivered on the spot. God delivered them from the fire, and when they came out, they didn't even smell like smoke!

God delivered them from the fire. God is always with us. God is with you and me every step of the way, and God will always deliver us from the fire, but our definition of deliverance (and its timing) and God's definition might be two different things. God has supernatural powers. And the same power that saved the three of them from the furnace, the same power that raised Jesus Christ from the dead, is the same power that is alive in you and me today. "I pray also that the eyes of your heart may be enlightened in order that you may know the hope to which he has called you, the riches of his glorious inheritance in the saints, and his incomparably great power for us who believe. That power is like the working of his mighty strength, which he exerted in Christ when he raised him from the dead and seated him at his right hand in the heavenly realms..." (Ephesians 1:18–20). The mistake we make is that we don't access that power; instead, we try to do things in our own limited human power.

Speaking of getting a grip on the limitations of our human power, let's keep going in Daniel. In a flashback sequence in chapter 4, more time has passed since the whole furnace incident, and in spite of all the great things he had to say about God after the three got out without being smoked, King Neb would not humble himself or acknowledge God. In fact, Neb got so outrageously conceited that he took the credit for making all the splendor of his kingdom. Bad move. God fulfilled a prophecy about this and took away Neb's mind. He became like an animal living in the wild and grazing in pastures. His nails grew like spikes, and his hair grew like bird feathers (Daniel 4:31–32). See, God had already warned Neb this would happen unless he acknowledged "... that the Most High is sovereign over the kingdoms of men ...." It took a few years, but finally, Neb looked up and acknowledged who God was, and he got his sanity back, just as God had promised in Daniel in 4:26–27. King Neb had lost his mind and, for a season – years, actually – he had lost his power to run the kingdom.

So, I ask you, do you have a grip on the limits of your human power? Are you taking credit for something that should belong to God? Or has something been taken away from you? Are you at a crossroads in your life like my friend Carl Rogers in that hotel room? God will gladly restore to Carl, you and me, our life and stuff and joy if we would simply turn to God and put Him first by taking to heart and acting on the words of Matthew 6:33, "Seek first the kingdom of God and his righteousness and all these other things will be added unto you." I know I've told you this verse a ton of times in this book, but it's that important, that critical. It is literally the key to everything, the necessary first and crucial step to living the abundant Christian life!

Will you, like King Neb, finally come to your senses and acknowledge that heaven rules, acknowledge it not just with your mouth as a passing thought, but also with your life and with your actions?

Daniel had tried to warn the king beforehand to "renounce your sins by doing what is right, and your wickedness by being kind to the oppressed. It may be that then your prosperity will continue." This warning for Neb is as true for us as it was for him. Renounce our sins. Do what is right and then our prosperity can continue, not before. That prosperity is not necessarily financial prosperity. It's about spiritual joy, the peace that transcends all understanding so that you are happy and peaceful and joyful. God's peace is like nothing we can ever get from the world.

Finally, King Neb gets it, and in Daniel 4:34, it says, "At the end of that time, I, Nebuchadnezzar, raised my eyes toward heaven, and my sanity was restored. Then I praised the Most High; I honored and glorified him who lives forever." The king turned his eyes back to God, and his sanity was restored. Sound familiar? Reminds me of the prodigal son who lost everything, turned back to God, and everything he lost was restored to him by his father..

Is there something in your life that you need God to restore? Does it feel as if God has forgotten you, left you to fend for yourself? Perhaps God is allowing a furnace in your life to heat up and you want to hide or run away; or perhaps it's pride creeping in and taking over, blinding you as it did King Neb. Regardless, as believers, as sons and daughters of God, heirs to the throne of Jesus Christ and ambassadors of God, our only hope is to turn back to Him. He always welcomes us back, always loves us, and picks up from where we last left Him. The key to life is that you have to turn back. You have to lift your eyes to heaven and acknowledge God, and your understanding will return to you.

God doesn't forget his child, but maybe you, his child, forgot him. Don't be like King Neb and suffer for seven years before turning back to God. When King Neb finally turned and acknowledged him, God blessed the king, giving him back his reason and honor and splendor. Lost any of that and want it back? You know what to do.

King Neb goes on, in verse 37, to "praise and exalt and glorify the King of heaven because everything he does is right and all his ways are just. And those who walk in pride he is able to humble." Neb is praising God, and he is realizing that all God does is right. You and I need to make that realization too. We don't have the ability or the right to question God. I can't say, gee, God, I think six of these things you said are right but the other four, well, two I'm really not sure of, and two I just think you are wrong, so I'm going to toss those out. It doesn't work that way. It's like the requirement for salvation: it's not our game, we didn't create ourselves. Just the opposite. We are the *created*, not the creator, so we don't get to make the rules.

Neb says those who walk in pride, God is able to humble. If you are walking in pride, God will humble you and bring you to your knees. So, how and where are you walking today? Are you walking in pride, or are you walking with God? Here's how you can tell the difference: The pride walk is anything that is not the God walk. It doesn't matter what you call what you are doing. If you are not walking with God, you are walking in pride. That's it.

What does it mean to walk with God? It means you have a relationship with Jesus Christ that is so evident that everybody who sees you knows you are walking with God. I'm not saying at Dunkin' Donuts that you take a Bible and slam it on the person's head in line in front of you. That is not what I am talking about. What I'm talking about is that wherever God has put you, whatever your profession is, wherever your home is, whoever you are, however God made you, your life glorifies and reflects Jesus Christ out of love, and not obligation.

The difference between doing something out of love versus out of obligation is in our attitude. I can have a tantrum and start grumbling, "Lord, I can't believe I have to go and reflect Jesus Christ everywhere I go. That really stinks. It's almost as bad as going to school." Or, I can focus on how much God has done for me and given me, and instead of grumbling, I could say, "Wow, Father, I can't believe all the stuff you've done for me. I love you so much and not only did You bless me with a life and give me your Holy Spirit to teach me all things, but every day, I can communicate directly with you and I know you love me. Then, when it's all over on Earth, I get this amazing place in heaven as a reward, and I never die and I am with you for all eternity. This is the greatest deal ever!"

Which attitude do people see in your life? Joy and happiness? Or something else?

Back in Babylon, others became jealous of Daniel and his relationship with the king, so they passed a rule, knowing that Daniel wouldn't obey it. The rule was that you had to pray only to King Neb, and if you prayed to any other god, they were going to put you in the lion's den and have you torn apart. We already said that Daniel made his mind up, and he belonged to God. His second nature kicked in automatically, so it didn't matter what anybody said or did, he would continue to worship God alone. The Bible tells us King Neb was tricked into signing this new law by the people who didn't like Daniel, and he realized too late that Daniel, whom he really liked and loved, was going to suffer under this law. In fact, King Neb was totally bummed out, but as king, he couldn't change the law because in that day, once the king gave his word, that was it.

"So the king gave the order, and they brought Daniel and threw him into the lion's den. The king said to Daniel, 'May your God, whom you serve continually, rescue you!'" Even King Neb believed that Daniel's God could save him. Why? Because he'd seen for himself how Daniel served his God faithfully and how God had been at work in Daniel's life and in the lives of Shadrach, Meshach, and Abednego. He saw Daniel's love and faith and he believed it, and that is what made him believe that God would rescue him.

Others believed in Daniel's God because of his demonstrated faith. Neb believed in Daniel's God because of Daniel's faith. And others will believe in our God because of our faith too. They will see God working in our lives. They will see God living in us and they will want it. No wonder God blessed Daniel. I think Eddie Eade and Daniel might be good friends in heaven right now because they shared this same quality on Earth. They impacted others by believing and trusting God and allowing others to see God acting in their lives.

What else did Daniel do that brought him such blessings? He wasn't afraid to confess. He confessed his own sins, as well as the sins of others, and accepted responsibility for the consequences of Israel's sin, even though he, personally, had not participated:

> O Lord, the great and awesome God, who keeps his covenant of love with all who love him and obey his commands, we have sinned and done wrong. We have been wicked and have rebelled; we have turned away from your commands and laws... We and our kings, our princes and our fathers, are covered with shame because we have sinned against you... Just as it is written in the Law of Moses all this disaster has come upon us, yet we have not sought the favor of the Lord our God by turning from our sins and giving attention to your truth. (Daniel 9:13)

Daniel knew that the nation of Israel had been taken captive by Babylon because they had rebelled against God's Word. This disaster came upon his people because they had not sought the favor of the Lord by turning from their sins and giving attention to the truth. Whether Daniel personally did those things or not isn't the issue; he is living the consequences of others' actions.

Do you have disaster in your life? Carl Rogers had disaster. He has not sought the favor of the Lord by turning from his sins and giving attention to God's truth. If things are not going the way you want, and you are not living a joyful, peaceful Christian life, then turn from your sins and give attention to God's truth.

You have a choice to make. My Pastor, Truman, preaches a sermon called "Are You Bitter or Better?" I love that sermon because he talks about how bad things are going to happen to everybody. What are you going to do with the circumstances? Are they going to make you bitter or better? If you don't turn to Jesus Christ, then you are going to be bitter, and if you do turn to Him, then you will be better for it.

Carl might still be trying to handle his drug problem without God, but I can tell you that without divine intervention, I was as captive and enslaved to drugs as Israel was to King Neb, and so is Carl. Maybe your issue isn't drugs, but most of us have been held captive by certain choices that we have wrestled with for a long time. I can assure you, as a former drug abuser, that God sending His people into captivity reminds me a lot of something called "intervention," which is when people who love you tell you that if you do not change the way you live, then you are heading for a crash, and you will probably die. That's why they do an intervention. It usually is for someone who has a major drug, alcohol, or gambling problem. Whatever the issue is, if there isn't any intervention, people almost always lose their spouse, kids, job, and home, and that's just for starters. The people that love this person, are they doing an intervention because they don't like him, or they want to harm him? No. They do it because they love him so much that they want to save his life and God does an intervention in our lives because He loves us too much to let us die or mess up our lives, or miss the blessings He has for us.

I know intervention can work. Remember Eddie Eade? His teenage son Evan was breaking his heart, going down the same path that Eddie had gone down when he was a kid. It was ugly. Evan was into drugs and being disobedient, and Eddie didn't know what to do. I remember praying with Eddie on many nights for his son, praying that he would turn around, that he wouldn't die or wind up in jail. Eddie was frustrated, and he couldn't get anywhere with him. Finally, after many tears and prayers, he decided to put him in a lock-up home called

Teen Challenge. It's a Christian center. Evan was there for about a year or a little longer, and he came back a changed man. Some time later, I saw Eddie with Evan at a birthday party for my partner's daughter. I asked Evan how it was going. He was happier than I'd ever seen him because he was working with his father in business. He said the best part of his day was at 5:30, when he would sit in his father's office for the next 30 minutes and watch Ed in action, working the phone, closing sales, and doing business. Evan thought it was so cool and not long after that, Eddie died, and I thought how cool it was that before God took this man home, He let Eddie see that, indeed, his son had been delivered back to him.

The point is that Ed loved his son so much that, no matter how painful it was to send Evan away kicking and screaming, Evan went. Not by choice, but shouting how his father must hate him to send him to a place like that. Ed didn't hate him; he loved him. Rest assured that God will treat you and me the exact same way because He loves us. If God would send his chosen nation into captivity in order to get them to deal with their disobedience, why should we think He's not going to make us deal with ours? If God needs to do an intervention in a specific issue in our lives, He will. He'd prefer that we obey and get His full blessing, but if it's tough love we need, it is tough love we are going to get.

In Daniel 9:18, Daniel is approaching God in prayer; listen to what he says about God's character: "We do not make requests of you because we are righteous but because of your great mercy." If Dan the Man couldn't stand before God and make requests based on anything he had done, then neither can we. As Daniel, we make our requests simply based on the blood of Jesus Christ at the cross. Are we grateful for God's mercy? And if we are, do our lives reflect it, or do we take it for granted?

Later, Daniel is physically overwhelmed during another vision where an angel of God is speaking to him. He says, in 10:17–19, "'How can I, your servant, talk with you, lord? My strength is gone and I can hardly breathe.' Again, the one who looked like a man touched me and gave me strength. 'Do not be afraid, O man highly esteemed,' he said. 'Peace! Be strong now; be strong.' When he spoke to me, I was strengthened and said, 'Speak, my lord, since you have given me strength.'" In another translation it says, "Do not be afraid, oh beloved one." Hey, you and I are the highly esteemed and beloved of God! We are God's kids; how awesome is that? And yet, sometimes, I complain to God about how all these burdens have gotten me down. I can't breathe. I have no strength left, and God says, "Oh beloved one! Don't be afraid. Peace I give you, my peace that transcends all understanding, I give you. Be strong now; be strong." Daniel couldn't be strong on his own, and neither can we. The only way we can be strong is with the strength of Jesus Christ in us.

And you say, "Right, Jack. And exactly how do I do that? How do I have Christ be strong in me?"

It's simple. You let Him be in charge. You let Him rule in your life, and you will have strength in your life. If you are God's kid, why would you mope around miserably?

As the book of Daniel is coming to a close, it assures us that "many will be purified, made spotless and refined, but the wicked will continue to be wicked. None of the wicked will understand, but those who are wise will understand" (12:10). Are you wicked or wise? God's Word is clear. Are you going to choose to understand it or not? It's black and white; it's yes or no; there is no in-between.

Here is the last thing that I've learned out of Daniel, in chapter 12, verse 3. God is speaking to Daniel and really to all His children: "As for you, go your way to the end. You will rest and then at the end of the days you will receive your allotted inheritance." At the end of the days, you and I will receive our allotted inheritance too. What a great promise.

God says go and do until the end. Do what? Do what is right in the eyes of the Lord. Wait on the Lord, trust in the Lord, and you will receive your reward.

Daniel went faithfully to the end, doing what was right in the eyes of the Lord. How about you? Will you go like him?

Or will you go like the other two men I described? Will you go like Rob McNamara, living a good life and doing good things for people and being an all-around nice guy? Unfortunately, according to God, that won't get you to heaven.

Will you go like Carl Rogers, a Christian in name only? You accepted Christ as your Lord and Savior at some point but gave up. Maybe you're sitting on the edge of disaster, still trying to do things your way. Wasn't it your way that got you into that spot in the first place? You can keep running from God, or you can choose right now to run back to Him and be obedient, so He can give you the blessings He's been holding for you. Time's passing.

Or will you go like Eddie Eade? He was on fire for God, and he used his time to change history by being obedient to Christ. He produced fruit for God. God has a message for every believer today. That message is that life is short, and you do not know when God will call you home. Don't be like that withered fig tree that Jesus came upon on His way back to the city (Matthew 21:18–20). When he saw that it had no fruit but only useless leaves, He spoke and ordered that it would never bear fruit again, and the tree withered quickly. Why keep a fig tree that isn't producing any fruit? Jesus was upset that the tree was not bearing fruit, not doing what it was created to do.

In Luke 13:6–9, Jesus tells this parable: "A man had a fig tree, planted in his vineyard, and he went to look for fruit on it, but did not find any. So, he said to the man who took care of the vineyard, 'For three years now I've been coming to look for fruit on this fig tree and haven't found any. Cut it down! Why should it use up the soil?' 'Sir,' the man replied, 'leave it alone for one more year, and I'll dig around it and fertilize it. If it bears fruit next year, fine! If not, then cut it down.'"

Go live like Daniel and Eddie, bear fruit in your life, and do it now! Be not like the fig tree. Why? One fig tree that was not bearing fruit was withered, and its life ended by God immediately. Another was given a little more time to get its act together and do what it was created to do. God is waiting and watching for your response to His call on your life. However, He won't wait forever. At some point, the choice won't be yours any longer. So, don't blow it with God!

George Foreman: Hanging out with the heavyweight champion of the world. George had a new short lived comedy series we were discussing, and of course he is an ordained minister and a true champion for God.

George Steinbrenner: At spring training with George some years ago, I'm not sure if George was considering offering me the Yankee GM spot but at that point I was only interested in ministry opportunities. Seems like the Yankees have fared OK without me.

Derek Jeter: With Derek Jeter when he was a rookie... I told him to work hard, have faith in God and things would turn out just fine... looks like I got that one right!

Don Mattingly: I told Don to make sure they spelled his name right on his baseball card, so we decided to take matters into our hands and not leave anything to chance.

Gary Carter: A great Christian man who has inspired many, and ran the MLB baseball chapel for many big leaguers. He's laughing because I told him he could take the afternoon off and I'd catch in the Joe DiMaggio legends game. He didn't think it was funny, but I meant it!

Dan Marino: Super guy and one of the greatest quarterbacks ever. Here we are on the golf course in Lake Tahoe; if I remember correctly, we were talking about what steakhouse in South Florida was the best. My vote was New York Prime in Boca Raton.

Joe Namath: Great quarterback and a NY legend. Joe and I shared some of the same battles off the field as we struggled with addictions, but you won't find a nicer guy. My prayer for Joe is that he has found the peace of God and is enjoying every minute of his life.

Keith Jackson: An NFL superstar, we are discussing his future broadcasting career at a television conference in Las Vegas.

Kim Alexis: I had the opportunity to consider many of television and Hollywood's top actresses, starlets and models for use in TV shows and commercials so it seemed people were extra nice to me, obviously because they thought I could pay them. For the record Kim was genuinely nice!

Dan Quayle: As Vice President of The United States... I remember telling him we should "do lunch" if he becomes President... as you can see he just laughed! Never made lunch.

Pat Sajak and Vanna White: I ask the hard questions, so when I asked Vanna if the wheel was "fixed" she just grinned... I think Pat was starting to panic, especially with the photographers around. A good time was had by all!

David Hasselhoff and Henry Winkler: These guys were discussing a new project they wanted to do together... of course I told them they could always count on me... anyway they never called.

Eric Estrada: When Eric is your friend, he's your friend for life. A great guy and someone I really wanted to use in an infomercial, but it seems his face was already in most infomercials I was watching at the time. Anyway we had a lot of laughs and as you can see, hugs also!

Regis Philbin and Kathy Lee Crosby: My idea was they come to Florida and shoot the show live down there... that wasn't going over so well... so I suggested a whole week of shows on Jesus Christ... I'm still waiting!

Buzz Aldrin: Joining astronaut Buzz Aldrin, I asked, "Buzz, which do you prefer moonwalking or a morning jog? By the way was Bill Lee really a spaceman? Buzz took my joking like the true American hero he is.

Burt Reynolds: Burt is a Florida State football alumni and a great proponent of the arts and theatre in South Florida. Of course, his TV and movie career speaks for itself. I told him I thought we should do a movie about FSU football and he should play Coach Bowden. But we didn't know Bowden had no plans of retiring... he's still going.. and so is Burt!

Geraldo Rivera: I was a kid when Geraldo broke the Willoughbrook story and became famous. All I wanted to know now was how do I get a moustache to grow on the side of my face.

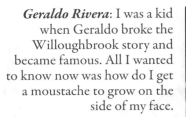

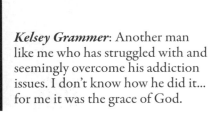

Kelsey Grammer: Another man like me who has struggled with and seemingly overcome his addiction issues. I don't know how he did it... for me it was the grace of God.

Dan Ackroyd: From *Saturday Light Live* to *Ghostbusters* to looking like he was considering an executive career. I told him to stick to comedy!

Jenny Jones: Pulling a switch on Jenny Jones asking her the questions in a segment she was doing for ETV. Never made it on air. That was the beginning and end of my interviewing career.

Martin Lawrence: One funny dude... I asked him why he was wearing dark sunglasses at 10 in the morning and he said "its all about image, baby." Like I said, a funny man!

John Tesh: I asked John if he could play any Springsteen songs on his piano? It's obvious one of us is a serious journalist... can you tell which one!

Jenny McCarthy: She had just became known back then and I was talking with her Dad who wanted to talk about TV projects for her. Most of her fame up to then had come from posing in magazines. Based on her "exposure" I didn't think it was a good fit so we never worked together.

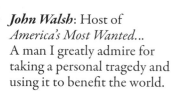

John Walsh: Host of *America's Most Wanted...* A man I greatly admire for taking a personal tragedy and using it to benefit the world.

Sargeant Slaughter: Showing me, literally, how easy it would be to snap my neck like a twig. At that point, I made the executive decision to keep quiet about any doubts I had that wrestling might not be real!

Jimmy Smits: At the Superbowl with Jimmy Smits in Miami. Game was a blowout but we had a blast behind the scenes.

Joan Rivers: Very sweet lady and genuine. I always thought she was a shrewd businesswoman... who knew she'd be such a great "apprentice?"

Ed McMahon: Best advice I ever got in business came from Ed. He said even when he was doing all those Budweiser commercials and other TV shows with Dick Clark, he never strayed too far from the well, that being *The Johnny Carson Show*. His success on Johnny's show is what allowed him to do all these other things. I applied that lesson "never stray to far from the well" to business with great success. Never go to far away from what is working. These days I'm still using Ed's principals but now for God and His business of life.

Bruce Springsteen: Backstage with 'The Boss' in Ft. Lauderdale, FL, just in time to celebrate his 60th birthday. I quote one of his song lines when I preach to reach the hearts of lost people that gets them thinking, "it's a sad man my friend/who's living in his own skin/and can't stand the company." Bruce's music has been a constant in my life since I was a teenager... and if you've seen one of his live shows you know there is nothing more exciting.

Chris Hammond: A true Christian brother... walks the walk all the way. 100% sold out for God and an inspiration to me as a Christian. Here's Chris and me (with Roy White) at Yankee Fantasy Camp. I got to pitch a few innings in most of the games that week and Tommy John even said I was good, of course it was all in my distracting windup. (I remember watching Juan Marichal as a kid) and my full menu of pitches "slow, slower and slowest." Chris is a champion for Christ and I especially enjoy our conversations when we share our testimonies, thoughts and hearts for God. Chris is a true light in a world of darkness and I'm proud to be his brother in Christ.

Relief In Mississippi: Cleaning up after hurricane Katrina. The devastation was indescribable, with shattered homes, shattered lives and mostly shock on people's faces. I will never forget the humbling experience of those that lost everything continuing to thank us (the Hearts and Hands relief team I had organized from our church) for coming to help them. A reminder to me, as God's Word tell us, our possessions are meaningless and our relationship with God is everything.

Jack-Harness Driver at Play: My hobby! In my driver colors, I drove harness horses as an amateur in over 40 races. I haven't done it seriously for the last 5 years since my daughter, Talia, was born. But don't count me out; I just might make a comeback!

Camera, Lights, Action – Jack on the Set: Here I am watching over the TV crews. I loved television production... it's a job that I never got tired of and it was never boring. No two days were ever the same. Just happened I loved God and ministry even more.

Jack Serving God: **T**here is nothing I enjoy more in my life now than preparing for a message and then having the privilege of delivering it in a church. God has blessed me in truly allowing me to do that so often and in so many different churches. I do not take it for granted nor do I take lightly the responsibility of being prepared to deliver God's message. Of course, it's God and His Spirit that speaks to people through sermons and messages, but it is my true joy to be used by God to serve.

Peter Walks on Water

I was a full-time pastor once, back in 2003. Well, sort of. Unofficial and full-time for six weeks.

I thought I'd test my thinking; see if this is maybe something God had for me as the next phase of my career. You're probably thinking hey, not a bad idea, being a pastor – no answering to Wall Street about shareholder value, no boss breathing down your neck, and lots of flexibility, plus you get to figure out what you're going to preach on each week.

For six weeks, I'm at this little church in Hallandale Beach, Florida, 100 on their membership roll and maybe 60 showing up on Sunday mornings. I literally shadowed and worked full time with the pastor, Bob Dyshuk, a true man of God who became a close friend and a mentor to me. Whatever he did, I did; if it was visitation or witnessing, counseling, or just running to get janitorial supplies, everywhere he went, I went ... 40 hours a week plus Wednesday night, Saturday, and Sundays for most of the day, getting things set up and ready for the worship service, following up with people after it's over.

And I see the impact on Pastor Bob and his family every day. I'm having breakfast with them, lunch with them, dinner with them; I am with them every single step of the way. I really developed this tremendous burden, and I believe that after six weeks there, God cleared it up for me. I was not called to be a pastor, not in 2003, anyway. I just wanted to preach. But at the end of the six weeks, I did ask God why I went through all this. Now, looking back with some perspective, I know it was to see if I would be obedient to God, and I was. I did what the Spirit told me to do, and because of that, I'd say this was one of the times in my life when I've felt closest to God. I also believe the reason I was down there was so that going forward for the rest of my life, I would rise up alongside pastors and help my pastor and other pastors in the future. Now, I understand what they go through.

So, I came out of these six unbelievable weeks, and man, I was fired up. It was a tough six weeks, but there were incredible blessings of seeing God at work in so many ways in lots of different lives, things I couldn't have seen if I'd stayed home.

I remember saying to God, wow, thanks for that opportunity, thanks for the great training, thanks for what I believe is preparation for the next mission You have for me, thanks because, as a result of this, I am really walking closer to You. This was like a mountaintop experience. Ever have one? They're awesome. And as I already said... temporary!

The next thing I knew, Satan started tempting me just as he did Jesus, and it was unbelievable. It went on for over a month, starting at the moment I thought I was the highest spiritually. Satan just came in and started supercharging my flesh, stirring up my desire for material things at a time when the business that I had sold and a couple of other interests I had couldn't pay me because money was tight. Business was horrible, so all of a sudden, the cash flow that was supposed to be coming in was not there. All this worry started filling my head, and suddenly, I'm focused on dollars and what-ifing the future, rather than being filled with the Spirit.

Then, one morning, I went to the racetrack to drive and jog some horses to relax. This is when the movie *The Passion of the Christ* had just come out, and one of the guys there starts talking to me, asking me a question about Jesus. And I wasn't *there*. I was stuck in all that worry about cash flow and what-ifs, so wrapped up in my own stuff that I was ineffective in my response and then this guy brings over one of the veterinarians and says, "Hey, doc, come on over here. What do you think about Jesus?"

Now, here I am with these guys who usually never talked about God, and I've got this wide open door to tell them about Jesus and about salvation, and what happens? I mumbled something, but I knew I was ineffective, and I got really uncomfortable, which is not me at all. I talk about my faith all the time with anyone. If that wasn't bad enough, a third guy joins us and jumps into the conversation about Jesus, and they are all ganging up on me about why I believe. I'm like this baseball player up at bat and striking out. I'm thinking this is horrible. I am supposed to be a witness for Christ, and instead, I had nothing – no inspiration. They're lobbing these easy pitches at me, and I am striking out. I got slaughtered.

God revealed to me that this was definitely an attack from Satan and that I should expect nothing less. Because the closer I get to God, the more Satan would like to interrupt my life and distract me, and I needed to chase this off with prayer. But I have to share with you that I am tired of fighting. It's a fight, and I'm tired of it. I'm tired of not feeling spiritual. I'm tired of getting the snot knocked out of me by Satan because this is a constant, tough battle we are in. Do you have a battle going on right now that just won't quit? One that's wearing you down until you feel like walking away or rolling over and giving up because you can't figure out what's next. Is this a time when you just can't find your way out of a situation?

Through this struggle, God spoke to me and gave me a very simple and famous verse, John 14:6, "I am the way, the truth and the life." He reminded me there is no other way, there is no other truth, and there is no other life. I can't count on my stuff, my cash flow, or my what-ifs. Go anywhere else for direction, for "truth," for what we humans call "life," which usually refers to living the good life materially. Go anywhere else for those things, and you won't find them. God isn't going to change His standards when I feel as if I got the snot kicked out of me because I let my spiritual life rest on the mountaintop while I went back to the flatlands.

That's a lesson I needed to use with my son, Ricky. He was about 15 at the time. We were trying to get him to do better in school, and I tried punishing him and taking stuff away, thinking, surely that has to work, right? Wouldn't he want to get back his computer and television? It didn't work, and actually his grades got worse. It was in fact, as if it had no effect on him.

Some of you parents who have more experience than I do know what's next. We get desperate, and we think, hey, bribery sounds good, why not? So, I offered Ricky a deal (and we knew he was capable, otherwise we would never have made this offer): Okay, son, if you get all B's and A's on the next report card, Mom and I are going to get you a new car this summer. You have to work and pay for gas and insurance, but we are going to get you a new car.

Maybe you've tried this same thing at your house. You can figure out what happened. Nothing. He doesn't do it. He doesn't get the grades, and I have to tell you this is mind-boggling to me. What is up with that, anyway? If someone had offered me a car at age 16 for doing something I was perfectly capable of doing, I would have done it in a heartbeat! There would have been no stopping me. And, of course, the report card comes out, and we have to have "the conversation." I'm driving him to one of his baseball practices, and he's asking about the car. I said, "Ricky, I am not going to lower the bar for you every time you fail. You didn't get the job done; the deal's off."

I thought about God and how He must look at us the same way. How often is God saying, "Hey, Christians, I want you to have all this stuff, all these blessings, and here is what I would like you to do. Obey." Then, we don't do it.

I wonder sometimes if He's scratching his head, going, what is up with that? I can't believe Jack wouldn't do something he's completely capable of doing. Did I not speak clearly enough? Didn't he want the blessings of God? That Jack guy says he wants My blessings, but...

Does God look at me with the same sadness and disappointment that I have felt for Ricky? To be clear, it's not a lack of love because, obviously, I love Ricky the same whether he gets the job done or not, but I'm stuck in disbelief that he couldn't motivate himself to do something that was so clearly in his best interest, that would so clearly benefit him and help him. I had to tell him more than once that I would not lower the bar for him. "Ricky, now you don't get the car. Instead, you can get a job and buy a car, and you have some money saved up and maybe we will let you spend that money to buy a car, but you don't get that gift. You missed that blessing from us."

God used this experience with Ricky to have me take a look at myself and to show me that, if I am not obedient to God, and I don't do what He tells me to do, I will be learning that same lesson – that God will not lower the bar. God knows we are capable of obeying Him because, as believers, we have His Holy Spirit in us to enable us. He will not give blessings to you or me when we choose to disobey His Word. We're the ones who lose out, just like my son, because God wants to do great things through us if we will obey Him.

Erwin McManus is a preacher who speaks at Promise Keepers, where he once said that "God wants to make history through you. God wants to accomplish great things through you." The kicker is that it can't happen if we stay in a state of disobedience. Sometimes, though, I believe our disobedience is a result of doubt, which is part of the human experience. I read a lot of history and biographies, and not just Christian ones. A common observation about man is that doubt plays a part in just about everyone's life at some point. Even the people who accomplished great things in this world had moments where they doubted themselves, where they felt inadequate or overwhelmed by the challenge they were facing. I've passed through such phases before, and I'm sure that before God calls me home, I'll pass through the Doubt-Detour again. What's next? I don't have certainty about the future. Then again, neither did one of our founding fathers, George Washington, who was a man of faith. He had an early victory in Boston, but afterward, his army was worn down, causing him to retreat to New Jersey. What should he do? Quit?

You know the story. He makes a decision to cross the Delaware, wins that battle, goes on to win a few others, and America is free. Had he not taken the chance, had he not believed in God, had he not had the faith that God would deliver him, I doubt America would be what it is today.

Washington knew, as you and I should, that one person alive with the power of God is an unbeatable force. The Apostle Paul understood this too.

In Acts 9:3–6, Paul was on his way to Damascus when he was dramatically stopped by a blinding light. He fell to the ground and responded to someone calling his name by saying, "'Who are you, Lord?' 'I am Jesus, whom you are persecuting,' Jesus replied. 'Now get up and go into the city, and you will be told what you must do.'"

What I find so interesting is that Paul didn't first respond with

"Lord, what do you want me to believe?" It wasn't about belief, it was about action. Paul said, "Lord what do you want me to DO?" Paul was told to go into the city and with the help of his traveling companions, and he did just that. His conversion was not a change of creed, but a dynamic change in the entire direction of life, a change in the way he would live his life, a change in his life's work and conduct. The instant Paul knew Jesus was God, he responded by asking Jesus what Jesus wanted him to do.

Was that my first question when I realized that Jesus is who He said He is? No. Is that my first question as I come upon problems or challenges? Not often enough. Is it yours? I was thinking about that and also about Erwin McManus saying that God wants to make history through us, and a couple of very popular scriptures came to mind.

The first was the story of blind Bartimaeus in Mark 10:46–52. Jesus is passing by, and Bartimaeus calls out a couple of times for the Son of David to have mercy on him. Jesus stops and asks him, "What do you want me to do for you?"

Can you imagine the Son of God standing in front of you, asking you that question? What do I want God to do for me? Are you and I going to stand there and shuffle our feet and shrug, and say, gee, I don't know Jesus. Come on! What *specific* thing would you like God to do?

Bartimaeus gets it right. "Rabbi, I want to see." Pretty specific, huh? And Jesus says "your faith has healed you," and He gives him his sight. Jesus grants him his request with his faith. Bartimaeus also did something after his request was granted. The Bible tells us that he immediately followed Jesus. Immediately. He didn't think about it, didn't go home and talk about it, didn't lay out plans, or do a spreadsheet analyzing if this was in his best interest or not, didn't ask what was in it for him or what did he have to lose. He simply, immediately followed Jesus.

Now, I'm putting myself in the scene and changing the name. "Son of David, have mercy on me."

Jesus stops and says, "Jack, what do you want me to do for you?"

"I want to see." I want to see spiritually and know You, and see my life through Your eyes. And Jesus gives me spiritual sight and continues down the road on the way to the work He still needs to do, and what do I do?

Am I following along behind Him? No. I'm asking myself if following Him is what I want to do. Why?

Why haven't I followed Jesus down the road, even though my faith has been rewarded? My focus is on me, not Him. Would it be in *my* best interest or not? What are the ramifications for *my* life? What would *I* have to give up, and what do *I* have to lose? God has proven His loyalty, love, and faith to me, and I have proven my resistance, stubbornness, and lack of faith to Him. All these things, I believe, have stopped me from receiving the full blessings of God.

By the way, when I say "following Jesus," I don't mean coming to church. I am talking about really following Jesus with your life, giving your life up to Him and obeying Him.

Jesus has the same question for every believer: "What do you want Me to do?"

How would you answer that if He were in front of you right now?

When you finish reading this chapter, get alone someplace, and answer that question. I hope that answer isn't about getting material possessions because that's not what scripture promises.

Do you want to experience the full blessings of being close to God and following Him? I sure do. I've been there, and I've lost it by trying to coast through the spiritual warfare in my life on the power of my mountaintop experience. I understand now that experiencing the full blessings of being close to God means learning how to keep our eyes on Jesus. If we don't, then we get caught like I did at the track, caught unprepared to defend my faith and just waiting to be slaughtered and feel ourselves sinking under the weight of the enemies' attack.

That reminds me of Peter walking on the water. You know the famous story, beginning in Matthew 14:22. Jesus sends the disciples across the lake in a boat, and in the wee hours of the morning, He walks across the water to join them. The disciples see Him and are terrified, they think it's a ghost. And Peter, just like the rest of us, doesn't believe it's Jesus, so he tests God by saying, "Lord, if it's you ... tell me to come to you on the water." "Come," He said." Then Peter got out of the boat, walked on the water, and came toward Jesus. But when he saw the wind, he was afraid and, beginning to sink, cried out, "Lord, save me!" Immediately, Jesus reached out His hand and caught him. "You of little faith," He said, "why did you doubt?"

We do the same thing as Peter – we doubt. We test God. "Prove it, God; just prove that it's you." And we test Him a little more. "Lord, if it's You, tell me to come out of my routine ... tell me to take this job ... tell me to witness to my neighbor ... tell me to do" – do what? What do you doubt that God is saying to you? If you are doubting it's Him, then check the scripture. He will only tell you what's consistent with His Word.

Peter gets out of the boat, and at that one moment, he believes, without a doubt, in the supernatural ability of Jesus Christ to enable him to walk on water. There is no doubt in his mind that Jesus is cap-able of doing what He promised He would do. Jesus says the same to you and me. Come, you know it's I. What are you afraid of? Peter walks a little way on the water, and then the Bible is very specific: Peter hears the wind and gets scared, and begins to sink. He hears the wind. He got distracted; he took his focus off of Jesus. How often in our lives do we hear Satan's wind or the wind of the world – the distractions of everyday life? For me, the winds howled full of cash flow questions and what-ifs, howled loud enough to distract me from Jesus and to cause me to sink under the weight of the attack that morning. I missed the blessing of having God's Spirit enabling me to speak truth to those three men because I was all about *me*, instead of all about *Jesus*.

I'm talking from experience. I'm focused on God, on the moun-taintop experience, on how close I'm walking with the Lord, so close I feel as if I can walk on water – until – until my job, my obligations, my sin, my whatever. Those things make some noise and distract me, so I have to pay attention to them because what will happen if I don't? Peter took his focus off the Lord, and he sank. He would've drowned if Jesus hadn't saved him. The same exact thing happens to us when we take our eyes off the Lord. That wind is always out there, trying to knock us off course.

Seconds later, Jesus says to Peter (and to you and me), "you of little faith, why did you doubt Me?" Jack, where's your faith, why do you doubt? Come, I have the ability and the power to work through you. I want to do great things through you. Are you willing?

And Then, we say "Prove it, God; just prove that it's You." And we test Him a little more.

Did God take His hand off Peter? No. Does God take His hand off us? No, we take our eyes off God. We doubted what we were sure of. There is no reason I should be wrestling with these issues, except one, which is that I have Adam's blood going through my veins. I'm a sinful human, and that is why Jesus died on the cross for my weaknesses and me. Yet, I can't use that as an excuse. Look at Paul. I am so impressed by what he did, but you know what? I could be as good as Paul and so could you, so could every believer because Paul was just a man, just a human who did truly live by faith. He did whatever was necessary to obey God. He ran the race. He made his body his slave. Each and every day, he did what he had to do. He didn't sit there like I do, thinking great thoughts, yet accomplishing nothing. I waste much time thinking of all these grandiose plans, rather than acting on them, rather than doing the right thing each day, and letting God work through me. I have the ability to do great things like Paul, but do I have the will? Am I willing? Or do I just want to talk about my good intentions? Sometimes, it comes down to just one simple thing – shut up and get going.

All of us wrestle with the deception of good intentions. If we think about doing enough good things, we seem to convince ourselves we've actually done them. Then, often, the opportunity to really *do* one of those things is lost forever, and we're left feeling empty.

It makes me think about the prodigal son in Luke 15. I'm wondering what he must have felt like at the moment he realized he had blown it all. What was it like that very second, when it hit him that it was all gone – all the money and the stuff – all just partied away? The only thing I can equate it to, and hopefully, you guys cannot, is drugs.

When I had my drug problem, I remember what it was like when the drugs ended. The problem wasn't getting high; the problem was coming down. There's a sinking feeling in the pit of your stomach that one moment when you say, "Oh no, I'm out of stuff, and I'm going to come crashing down soon." It was the worst feeling you could ever imagine. I have to believe that the prodigal son had that same sinking feeling in the pit of his stomach, too – that "I am going to crash" sensation. How devastatingly stupid and defeated he must have felt.

Sometimes, even now, I feel like that, not because I squandered wealth, but rather because I squandered time by trying to do this Christian life on my own. Imagine how Peter felt when he was looking at Jesus on the cross, knowing he'd denied him three times. I wonder, while Jesus was slowly dying, did He ever look Peter right in the eyes? Peter must have felt so disgusted and dejected, and depressed, knowing he had failed his God. That's how I feel when I know I've screwed up or disobeyed.

The good news is I don't have to stay in that state. Like the reunion between the prodigal son and his father, the parable is for us: we can repent and turn back to God, and God, who has been watching and waiting for our return, loves us no matter what. After that morning at the track, I did a lot of confessing, and I felt that love from God, just as I'm sure you do when you think you have failed God for whatever the reason is, and you get right with him. But remember, this life we live is an ongoing spiritual battle, and Satan is a strong adversary. He loses in the end, but in the here and now, the way we can win and be victorious is to stick close to God.

By now, you know that my background is in advertising and television. I just love tag lines and slogans, so as I thought about being tired from the spiritual fighting, I thought, hey, what I need here is a slogan, a motto to help me stay fired up. How's this? "Jack Levine, stirred but not shaken." Catchy, huh? (I got that idea from 2 Corinthians 4:8–18). You can stir me, but you can't shake me; you can knock me around, but you can't shake me. No, it's not catchy; it's sad that I would think I could rally myself with some advertising slogan. Get real. It might play on Madison Avenue, but it certainly doesn't have any power. Only God's all-surpassing power can give me the ability to stand straight and tall – not me, not some advertising slogan or rallying cry. Paul goes on to say in that passage that "We are hard pressed on every side, but not crushed; perplexed, but not in despair; persecuted, but not abandoned; struck down, but not destroyed." Paul knew that all he needed was God's power, not his own (2 Corinthians 4:7–9).

Paul was more qualified than most to write about relying on God's power. In 2 Corinthians 1, he talks about the hardship he and Timothy faced, saying "We were under great pressure, far beyond our ability to endure, so that we despaired even in life. Indeed, in our hearts we felt the sentence of death. But this happened that we might not rely on ourselves but on God, who raises the dead." Get this right – I believe all the things that have happened to me – drug addiction, divorce, unemployment, to name a few of the bigger ones – all these have happened that I might learn to stop relying on myself, which seems painfully obvious when I look at the list of failures in my life and that the only person I am to rely on is God. God, God, God, who raises the dead.

What is dead in your spiritual life? A marriage, a career, passion, joy, peace, hope? Only God can raise things from the dead. If Bartimaeus could ask for something specific, so can you. Jesus is waiting for your answer to His question, "What do you want Me to do for you?"

I know there will still be times when I'll be more like Peter than Jesus, when, like Peter, I will fail God. I'll deny Him. I'll fall asleep on my watch. I'll sink while walking on water so that I can no longer rely on myself.

I believe good things will happen because of God, not me. With me in the way, I can accomplish nothing. With me out of the way, God can accomplish and make history through me. And it's the same for you. I believe all of my problems are the result of my taking my focus off Jesus and placing it on the world. As soon as I do that, it means I've dropped my guard. I've dropped the armor that God gave me to defend against Satan's attacks, and I become vulnerable.

Shadowing a pastor for six weeks showed me how important it is to keep my eyes on Jesus, not on the wind and the waves of what's happening around me. A pastor's life is often surrounded by such turmoil because he is, by the nature of his job, brought into the winds and waves that are crashing into the lives of his congregation. If he takes his focus off Christ, he will surely drown. Pastor Bob taught me to let the noise of the world flow around me, rather than letting it distract me. When I practice doing that, I can tell that God is lifting me higher, and I won't have to ask Him to lower the bar because I got worn out from fighting and worn down from temptation and quit.

So, my friend, what do you want Jesus to do? And when he answers you, will you immediately obey?

The Only Thing That Matters

Sometimes, we make things so much more complicated than they should be or than Christ ever intended them to be. Are you tired of the merry-go-round of the world and its stuff – anxiety, fear, competition, finances? Want to get off the ride, but you're afraid that if the thing suddenly stopped, you'd be hurled into space?

The good news is that right now, if you are resting in the perfect love of Jesus Christ as a believer in Him, then for you, there is no fear or worry about the future, no fear or worry about a loved one dying, about you getting sick, about unemployment, or financial ruin. This perfect place of rest comes only from a love relationship with Christ. Perfect rest. Sounds like hype for an island resort, but it's not.

God offers every believer in Christ the opportunity to come into this place of perfect rest with Him. It's a rest for your soul – an insurance policy that your soul will be peace-filled. This exact same perfect rest was first offered to the people of Israel and now is available to everyone. It is available through the life of Jesus Christ, and we get it by putting our faith and trust in Him. God is offering every believer today the privilege and opportunity to come into perfect rest with Him.

The problem for so many of us Christians is that we're still riding the not-so-merry-go-round of life, and as a result, we know nothing of this perfect rest. We get on the carousel and pick an animal to sit on – the "worried-about-health" pony or the "credit-card-debt" frog – and we go around and around, and at the same time, we go up and down, constantly in motion.

Sometimes, we might even switch to a different animal. We get some big bad news all of a sudden, and hey, it's two steps to the left, and we climb up on the big gray elephant named "unemployment" or "divorce." Been there. Ridden lots of those suckers. It's a bouncy ride. Anybody getting motion sick yet?

We get caught up with fear, with dread, with worry. We beg God to spare a loved one's life, our jobs, or whatever the ride du jour might be. So where is the perfect rest of God? Where is that peace?

In Matthew 11:28–30, Jesus says, "Come to me, all you who are weary and burdened, and I will give you rest. Take my yoke upon you and learn from me, for I am gentle and humble in heart, and you will find rest for your souls. For my yoke is easy and my burden is light." So, why don't we see more people leading the joyful life that God gives us? What's the failure? The failure is lack of faith. Remember the disciples in the boat? Jesus is sleeping, they're crossing the Sea of Galilee, and a storm comes crashing in. The disciples panic and wake Jesus up, shouting about how they're all going to drown. Jesus quiets the storm and asks them, "Where is your faith?" (Luke 8:24–25).

When you reside in this state of perfect rest with the Lord, you do not fall prey to fear. It does not exempt you from suffering and feeling pain. God said that we would have trials, tribulations, and suffering while here on Earth. These happen to everyone, but your soul, mind, body, and spirit will be at rest throughout all these.

Why? Because you know that God is in control of everything concerning you. Everything.

I learned this lesson myself in an interesting experience some years ago while flying back from the West Coast with a friend of mine named Bob. Those are good flights for sleeping, so I was catching some z's somewhere over Kansas probably, when I was jerked awake by some severe turbulence. I grabbed Bob's arm and screamed, "The plane is crashing."

"No, Jack, it's turbulence."

I tightened my grip on Bob's arm and continued screaming.

"No, it's crashing; it's crashing." I mean, I really believed we were going down, and this was it.

He pried my fingers off his arm, grabbed my shoulder, and shook me. "Jack," he said, "it is just turbulence."

"Okay." I finally exhaled, but I am telling you I didn't like the rest of the flight, and I sure didn't sleep anymore. Shortly after that, I was supposed to go on a business trip to Atlanta, and I said to my business partner, "I'm not going. Forget this trip. You go if you want, but I'm not going."

He said, "We're going, but I understand you are a little shook up from your West Coast flight, so we'll just delay the trip a couple of weeks."

I said, "Okay. That works." A couple of weeks went by.

He said, "Time to go, Jack."

"I'm not going."

"Yes, you are."

"Listen, you don't get it. I thought my last flight really was my last flight. I am not getting on any more airplanes. I need more time."

He stared at me for a minute, and then finally said, "Jack, do you believe in God?"

What kind of stupid question was that? "Of course, I do."

"So, if it's your time, and God wants you up in heaven, you're going, right?"

Not such a stupid question after all. "Right."

"And Jack, does it matter if you are on a plane or not?"

"No."

"And if it's not your time, you can go on all the planes you want?"

I got the point. "Okay. Book the flight." A sense of peace that I hadn't expected filled me when I finally acknowledged that, absolutely, God is in control of my life. When He says, "time's up," it doesn't matter where I am or what I am doing, I cannot *do* anything to affect God's timing (like avoid airplanes), though I do have to be ready for Him. And the first step to being ready is to have a relationship with Jesus Christ, so I can know I will be in heaven.

Then, that same understanding just spread into the rest of the way I was living. Being ready for God was about more than just my salvation; it was about how I was living day to day. Was I living for Him or for me? Was I living a life of turbulence because I'd forgotten to look to God first and find His rest? I was so focused on living "my" life that I lost sight of what Paul said in Galatians 2:20, "I have been crucified with Christ and I no longer live, but Christ lives in me. The life I live in the body, I live by faith in the Son of God, who loved me and gave himself for me." If we're saved, then we live for Christ. I knew I was saved, but did I really know what it meant to live for Christ?

I spent some time meditating on that, and God laid a verse on my heart – Galatians 5:6, "For in Christ Jesus neither circumcision nor uncircumcision has any value. The only thing that counts is faith expressing itself through love." For the people of that day, circumcision was an external sign of faith that represented a commitment to live by God's law – outward actions. But we all know in our own lives and can certainly study it in the Old Testament that outward conformance to rules does not mean that our hearts are involved. Just think about the last time you watched a kid having to apologize! The words "I'm sorry" can be made to sound so sweet, even while the faces are frowning, the hands are still in fists, and the words are so fake! So, Paul is reminding the Galatians (and us) that the outward *symbols* of faith do not have any value. In our day, it's not what we say or do or what church we attend. It doesn't matter whether we eat meat or don't eat meat or whether we wear our Sunday best to church or go casual. What has value in God's sight is faith expressing itself through love.

Sounds pretty simplistic, especially when you think about all the ways we can complicate our faith. Let's really walk through the verse and make sure we understand everything behind those words.

What counts ... what matters to God ... if we want to know what matters to *Him,* to be able to understand "faith expressing itself through love," we first have to have a relationship with Him. That's where we start. I can't do what matters to you if I don't know you; I can't express love to you if I don't know how you would define "love." Just think about the cultural differences in expressing love – Would you feel loved if I gave you a herd of goats? If you're a typical suburban American, you'd think I was insane, but in a different part of the world, you'd probably be thrilled with that expression of love.

When we're in a relationship with someone, we want to please them. It's the same with God. Hebrews 11:6 says, "And without faith it is impossible to please God ..." so if I want my expressions of love to please God, then those expressions of love have to come out of my faith.

What is faith? Faith moves beyond salvation, beyond simply accepting Jesus into your life. The classic definition of faith is found in Hebrews 11:1, "Now faith is being sure of what we hope for and certain of what we do not see." It's more than just believing that God exists – more than just believing that Jesus is the Son of God and that he died on the cross for my sins. "Faith" is *trusting* what that person – God – says. "Faith" is *acting* on the belief that what God says is true, and it will come to be, even when all your feelings and circumstances say otherwise, even when you wake up suddenly, and you are convinced that the plane you're in – your job, your marriage, your health crisis – is going to crash. This means that even though we can't see the heaven God is talking about, we believe it exists and that we'll be there with Him one day. That even though we can't see the reason for the trials and troubles and sorrows we face, we know that God is with us through them all, using them to teach us and mature us so that our joy will be complete, and we will lack nothing. We believe without doubt that God is still in charge, like it says in Romans 8:28, "And we know that in all things God works for the good of those who love Him ..."

Faith enables our spiritual sense to function; it's the gas for the engine of happiness. Where faith is defective, the result will be inward numbness toward spiritual things. If your faith isn't on target, you will be numb to the Holy Spirit's teaching, and you will miss out on all the blessings God wants to give you.

Faith is not a once-done act, like salvation. Faith is a continuous gaze at Jesus Christ. Faith is constantly fixing our eyes on Jesus (Hebrews 12:2). Some have said that faith "is the eye that sees everything in front of it but never sees itself." When we are looking at God, we stop looking at ourselves and our weaknesses and faults.

That's what faith is, but what do we do with it? The simple answer to that is that we make it our priority. To make it a priority, we choose to do those things that will build it up, educate it, strengthen it, rather than tearing it down or acting like we did before we got faith, and we certainly don't do stuff that will weaken it. The only way to know how to do all that is to really stay in God's Word and get close to Him.

When we do that, we give the Spirit access to our hearts and minds, so he really can teach us all things, and that takes time – a whole lifetime.

We can't possibly learn everything at once that the God of the entire universe wants us to know. We have human, three-dimensional minds with limited capacity, and God knows that. He allows each of us to learn at our own pace, but He absolutely does expect us to learn.

I have to do what the Bible calls "draw near to him." Hebrews 10:22–23 says, "... let us draw near to God with a sincere heart in full assurance of faith ... Let us hold unswervingly to the hope we profess, for he who promised is faithful." To develop my faith, I draw near to God, fully believing Him, and I don't swerve from that belief. That "hold unswervingly" bit leaves no wiggle room. Don't swerve. Don't let the world get us caught up, so we swerve away from our faith, take our eyes away from God, and go back to the world we know. That's what we *don't* do.

We also don't retreat when things get tough. God specifically says in Hebrews 10:38, "But my righteous one shall live by faith. And if he shrinks back, I will not be pleased with him." That warning against shrinking back or retreating is a lot like "don't swerve." It's like we're turning away from our faith, and remember, without faith, it is impossible to please God. If you swerve or shrink back from your faith, God will not be pleased. You'll still get into heaven, but you won't have the victorious, abundant, joy-filled life on Earth or the other rewards that God wants to give you.

Rewards? Yes! Here is the full version of Hebrews 11:6: "And without faith it is impossible to please God, *because anyone who comes to him must believe that he exists and that he rewards those who earnestly seek him* [emphasis mine]." If you have faith in God, then you can be certain He will reward you for seeking Him. If you are certain of that, why wouldn't you spend all your time seeking Him? Why would you spend your time doing anything else? It's like being offered a huge bonus plan at work, a plan that says you can get the big bucks if you stay focused on your objectives. At my old television production company, we had a simple formula in one of our divisions. We instructed our employees only to call companies that spent $1 million in advertising, whose product had wide appeal to people all across the country, and who advertised in national magazines. Whomever they called had to meet those criteria, otherwise, don't call them. Why? Because we knew from experience that if our employees followed our plan (our road map), then they would be successful beyond their wildest dreams, and likewise, if they did not follow our plan, they would fail miserably. Simple, right?

If I told you to go out into the street and find a guy with a blue suit, blonde hair, and red tie, and that every one of those guys you find is going to give you $1,000, would you go and talk to anybody else? No. You would be looking for guys who fit the description all day long. Well, God says you must believe that He rewards those who seek Him. If you believe that, then shouldn't you be seeking Him with all your heart? Why would you spend your time doing anything else?

Sometimes, the rewards are for here and now, and other times, they are waiting for us in heaven. Consider what is called the *Hall of Fame of Faith* in Hebrews 11. This chapter recalls many of the ancients who acted in great faith despite outrageous circumstances and pressures from others to turn away from their faith. I won't go over all the names, but let's look at a few just to get the idea.

There's Noah, whom was warned by God about things not seen, and in holy fear of God, he built an ark. He was the laughing stock in his day, the God freak, but he persevered for years to build the ark because he believed God and never doubted. Noah got his reward – he and his family were spared from the flood and got to start all over. His faith gave him a do-over. You ever want one of those?

By faith, Abraham obeyed God's instructions to go to a place he would later receive as his inheritance. He obeyed, even though he didn't know where he was going. Can you imagine uprooting your entire life without knowing where you were actually going? If God were to call you on your cell phone and tell you He has this great plan for you, but you have to leave now, and He'll tell you whether to go north or south, east or west, would you do it? Well, God, no, I've got this family, this job, the kids would be unhappy if I did that. But God simply says, go and trust Me, obey and I will reward you, I have a plan for your life, I know where you are going, your job is just to obey and have faith. Yet Abraham went, and he received rewards he could never have imagined. In his old age, he received a son, along with the promise that all the nations of the world would be blessed through him – a reward in his lifetime, named Isaac, and an eternal reward he could only see once he was with God.

What about Moses and his birth parents? By faith, they hid him for three months after he was born because they knew he was no ordinary child. They weren't afraid of the king. They acted on faith and trusted God to intervene on behalf of their son. By faith, Moses, who grew up in Pharaoh's household, refused to be known as the son of the pharaoh's daughter. Instead, he chose to be mistreated along with the people of God. Why suffer through all that when he could have taken the easy way out and enjoyed palace life with the Egyptian royalty? He had faith in God, he trusted God, and he believed God for the future, both on Earth and in heaven. His reward? Being one of, if not the greatest, leader of the nation of Israel and probably having the most intimate relationship with God of any person who has ever lived. And that was just while he was alive. Can you even imagine his reward in heaven?

The list goes on, and it ends with some names of people who were martyred for their faith, people who didn't receive the rewards on Earth, not as we think of rewards, anyway. Our generation seems to be hard-wired to think of rewards as a windfall in the market or perhaps bonus points we can use for free airline tickets. Aren't we always wondering how quickly we can get enough points to cash in for a prize?

The people in the *Hall of Fame of Faith* are amazing, because in Hebrews 11:13, it tells us that many of these people were still living by faith when they died. They didn't see the things that God promised while they were alive – the Messiah, the Christ – they only saw from a distance. They didn't know the impact they were going to have on people, on history, and on life, so why were they faithful? Because they were certain there would be rewards later. Talk about delayed gratification! The most important thing that those people could do with their lives was to express their faith in God through their obedience. They responded to God and focused on pleasing Him, instead of trying to please themselves or others, because they were certain of who God was.

I ask you today, are you responding to God's voice? Do you realize you can be in that same kind of one-on-one relationship with God?

Just think, it's you and God, like Abraham and God, Moses and God, Noah and God. Now, it's you and God, the creator of the universe, your Lord and Savior, telling you about His promises and what He wants you to do. If you don't have that relationship with God, or you don't have the Holy Spirit working in your life, then I encourage you to examine your belief system. God wants to talk to you. He wants you to open up your heart and let Him in. God's greatest desire is for us to be in close fellowship with Him, and that we love Him, and enjoy the full benefit of all He has to offer.

The writer of Hebrews encourages us to be like those people in the *Hall of Fame of Faith* – to express our faith by the way we live. "Therefore, since we are surrounded by such a great cloud of witnesses, let us throw off everything that hinders and the sin that so easily entangles, and let us run with perseverance the race marked out for us. Let us fix our eyes on Jesus, the author and perfecter of our faith, who for the joy set before him endured the cross, scorning its shame, and sat down at the right hand of the throne of God" (Hebrews 12:1–2).

Since we are surrounded by such an incredible crowd of witnesses, a few of which I just named, such as Noah and Abraham, we're supposed to get rid of everything that hinders and entangles us so that we, too, can persevere in our faith like those Bible heroes did. It's as if we are being given a spiritual pep rally, and we're being told that if Noah or Abraham could do it, so can we. We can obey and get the great rewards, and "all" we have to do is throw off everything keeping us from obeying God completely. "All" we have to do is get rid of the sin that so quickly entangles us and keeps us from having a relationship with God. If that's "all" it takes, why aren't we doing it?

That's the usual approach to understanding the *Hall of Fame of Faith*, but in my opinion, there's a problem with that. We need to take it one step farther. I had the same problem at my company with my employees not following the instructions on what type of accounts to call. We gave our people everything they needed to identify and call the right kind of accounts. It was a basic sales formula, so why didn't they do it? The same reason we don't follow God's simple formula that we know works – because we are human.

Because we are human, we have a problem – a heart problem. The problem is that greatness comes from a sincere desire to achieve your goal. Whatever the goal, you've got to really want it and be willing to go to any lengths to get it. So let's say, just like the Bible's *Hall of Fame of Faith*, I show you the sports stars of my day, such as Michael Jordan, John Elway, Ken Griffey, Wayne Gretzky, and I say look at everything these guys have done. I could encourage you and admonish you to study them and be like them. But what happens? Most people will look at Michael Jordan, for example, as one of the greatest basketball players ever, shake their heads, and say, "I can't do that. I'm not going to invest the time that he invested. I don't have his natural talent."

You know what? Here on this Earth, that may be true, but God, in His wonderful ways, gives us a much better plan. He says look, all you have to do is believe and have faith in Me, and you are guaranteed to succeed at this faith thing. (He doesn't promise that we'll all be as good an athlete as Michael Jordan is, though.) This is about our faith. There are no ifs, ands, or buts. If we have faith and believe God, we can succeed at the faith thing. So, when we look at our *Hall of Fame of Faith*, the issue is not whether we have the *ability* to be like them, as it would be in sports, but whether we have the *desire* to do what they did, as in, do we have that same heart's desire? Without that desire to live by faith and please God, we will not be willing to go to the lengths necessary to reach that level. I think you will find that having that desire is the key between happiness and pain, between the life of joy and suffering, between a life of peace with God or separation from God.

Can you throw off the things that hinder your faith? Can you throw off the hectic pace of the world, the status your job brings, or other people's opinions of you? You *can*, because you have the Holy Spirit in you, but *will* you choose to exercise that ability? What about specific sins like pornography, drugs, rage, hatred, and jealousy? Will you throw away the sin of loving money? Will you run with perseverance the race that God has marked out for you? You can *have* faith, but it doesn't do any good unless you *express* it by taking action that shows your love for God and His Word, just like you can *have* a car in your garage, but you won't *go* anywhere unless you use it.

No matter what the obstacles, Christ has marked out ways for each and every one of us. How do we know that? Because God told us. He predestined us to be adopted into His family (Ephesians 1:5), He has a perfect plan for our lives (Jeremiah 29:11), and He has good works He wants us to do (Ephesians 2:10). So, if we are obedient and follow

Him, we will see that plan come to fruition just like the people in the *Hall of Fame of Faith*. But keep in mind, we have a choice to make. We're all on the merry-go-round of life, but as believers, we can choose either motion sickness on Earth by focusing on self and circumstances, or we can choose God's rest, joy, comfort, and the peace of God that transcends all understanding by fixing our eyes on Christ as we live out each day's circumstances.

The choice we make will be reflected in our priorities, and our priorities will demonstrate our faith. To say it another way, as I wrote in a college poem, "We see the signature of our souls reflected in the actions of our lives." Our priorities will be an expression of our faith, and as we know, the only thing that counts is faith expressing itself through love.

When we are expressing something, we are active and our actions are visible to others. As others see what we are doing, they will draw some conclusions. This is why we have to look at how we are living our lives, so we can really see what we are expressing to others as our priorities. Paul understood this perfectly. In Galatians 2:20–21, he stated how he lived, "The life I live in the body, I live by faith in the Son of God, who loved me and gave himself for me." While Paul was on Earth, he was working, relating, resting, and living, doing all his daily stuff *as if* it were Christ actually doing those things. Paul could say that, and his life proved it. If I say that, does *my* life prove it? Does yours?

We need to train ourselves up and be ready to do the same thing as Paul. How do we do that? By deciding what's important. We have to believe that we really do need to be ready, because if you don't believe you need to be ready, then you don't have to decide.

If somebody is sitting next to you with pains in his chest, you scream "heart attack" and get him to the hospital because you believe that's what's happening. Spiritually, then, we need to do the same thing. We need to decide. Do we believe that it's important to stay focused on God or not? No matter what we *say* for an answer, what we really believe about that question is going to show up in our priorities. That point came home to me in a conversation with my son, Ricky, when he was 16. I asked him to rank his priorities for me.

"Playing my saxophone first, baseball is second, spending time with my friends and family is third, and fourth is schoolwork."

I said, "Schoolwork doesn't count because there are some things in life, some obligations that we have to do, regardless." But I was curious about something. "Ricky, let's look at the saxophone thing. You stated that your number one priority is the saxophone, but you take a half-hour lesson once a week, and we have to make you practice half an hour three days a week. That doesn't reflect to me that it's a priority in your life."

I'm just using that example to say that we shouldn't kid ourselves about what our priorities are. Do not say your priority is God and Jesus Christ and living a life of faith when you are not demonstrating, or expressing, it in your life. It doesn't fly. Your life should reflect the worth you place on your priorities. What's it worth to you to have a relationship with God? What does God say it's worth?

His Word says, "The only thing that counts is faith expressing itself through love." If your priority is God and Jesus Christ, then people should be able to see it in your life. If they *can't* see it, something is wrong. If they *won't* see it, then that's their problem, but if they are watching you and can't see it, then you have a problem. Are you in a right relationship with God through His Son Jesus? If you are already a believer, then spend some time drawing near to God, reading His Word, and asking Him to show you where you need to refocus your priorities so that people will see Him at work in your life.

When our focus is out of whack, it's easy to slip into the mode of just talking about our faith being a priority, instead of actually living that way. To fix that, we need to "... fix our eyes on Jesus, the author and perfecter of our faith ..." (Hebrews 12:2). Keep our eyes fixed on Jesus. It's like being in the marching band. If you want to stay in tune and in step, you keep your eyes on your drum major, the one calling out the instructions, and you do not look around at the other marchers, the fans, the players, the refs, or anyone else. Otherwise, you will stumble, lose your way, and cause problems for others in the process. That's what happens to us when we shift our focus off God and allow it to become "God and the radio," "God and the self-help books," or "God and what my friends say."

When I stop fixing my eyes on Jesus and start noticing the turbulence of life, my changing circumstances, or my fleshly desires, the motion sickness will kick in and cause me to lose the rest that He promises. And it will also cause me to stop expressing my faith through love.

Rest? Or motion sickness? It's a choice. While God says how long my life will be and when it will end, I have the freedom to choose to focus on Him and enjoy the ride or focus on everything but Him and suffer the consequences.

I choose to fix my eyes on God, because when I do, I will find that promised rest from the turbulence surrounding me. When I do that, I am free to express my faith through love to God and to others. It's so simple. The only thing that counts is faith expressing itself through love ... Is my faith and your faith in God being seen by others in the way that we live?

Is Church Good?

In 2004, I preached at a church in Coral Springs, Florida, and had a great experience. I got to meet the youth pastor there, a terrific guy. We'll call him "Bill."

Bill called me about a week later. "Listen, Jack, I have a buddy, a guy named Charlie. I've been witnessing to him for a long time. Says he was saved, now he's kind of down and out on his luck, and he has a major, major drug problem he's trying to deal with. Says he's trying to get his life back together but doesn't seem to quite get it."

"How so?"

"He was kind of focused on God for a while but now it seems like his focus is in a lot of other places. He asked if you would talk to him."

"Absolutely." I'm always willing to talk, if the opportunity arises, where my life experiences could benefit somebody else.

So, I met with Bill and Charlie, and we talked for about four-and-a-half hours. Finally, Charlie says to me, "Jack, how did you turn your life around? How'd you do it? I just can't seem to turn my life around."

After four-and-a-half hours, I thought I'd already explained it, but I went ahead and told him again. It was easy for me because I really wasn't satisfied with my life the way it was. I'd reached the point where

I truly believed there had to be more to life than the life I was leading – more purpose, more reason than just existing. And you know, God made this promise that if I would seek Him, I would find Him, so I worked at seeking God, and sure enough, God wasn't a liar. I found Him. He revealed Himself to me in 1991, and since then, I can tell you that life has just gotten better each and every day.

So, Charlie says, "Yes, yes, yes, I understand that that's wonderful, but I still need to know more, you know? Tell me more; tell me how you really got there."

I scratched my head and wondered what I'd left out that might satisfy his need for "more," but I couldn't come up with anything. "Well, Charlie, there isn't more. It's really simple. All I did was turn to God by reading the Bible. I started praying, I started attending church, and God spoke to me in many ways. He spoke to me through my quiet prayer time with Him, through other believers, and pastors' messages."

"That's it?"

"Yeah. God just made it clear to me who He was and what He had done for me, and I was so grateful for what He'd done."

Charlie exhaled loudly. "Well, I don't go to church. I mean, yeah, I *went* to church, but I can't go there anymore."

Can't go to church? A sudden picture of some of the characters who might be lingering in the shadows of his life flashed through my mind. "Uh, why is that?"

He shrugged. "The people. They're all hypocrites. They say one thing and do another."

I know I'm supposed to be ministering to this guy, but I can tell you that lots of un-minister-like thoughts ran through my mind. "Okay, well, that's interesting. But you say you're saved, so tell me, what do you do to bring yourself closer to God?"

"I do a little of this; you know, I talk to God here and there."

After nearly five hours with this guy, I'm realizing I've got this person in front of me who claims to be saved but doesn't want to spend time in church because he thinks he can "do church" on his own with God, yet he has no real plan for getting to *know* God. And he hasn't made the connection himself (that he keeps asking me for) of how he can turn his life around.

I'm not surprised at his viewpoint, really. It's our natural inclination to think we can do things without God, even when we can't change the basic physical things in our lives that are making us miserable.

In a sort of technical, picky way, Charlie is correct about one thing, and that is that having a relationship with Jesus Christ, a true, saving relationship, does not require you to ever set foot in a church. The only requirement to have a relationship with Jesus Christ is that you accept him as your Lord and Savior. So, technically, splitting hairs, Charlie was correct ... and that was even more reason I was kind of annoyed at him.

I silently sent up a few prayers of repentance for my own attitude, and then sat there lovingly and patiently explaining to him why I go to church. I do it because I want to. I come to church because I want to worship God, because I love God. It's an overflow of my gratitude for what God has done for me. It has never been an obligation for me to come to church; it has always been a privilege.

So, there we sit. I talk to Charlie a little bit more and just focus on him, explaining that he needs to have his own relationship with God, encouraging him to seek God on his own. I tell him that God will speak to his heart clearly. When we finally part company, I give him a few tapes of past sermons, and I think, okay, this is it, God; hopefully, You worked on his heart.

I get a call a few days later from Charlie, and he says, "Okay, so like, I listened to the tapes. Now what?"

"What do you mean, now what?"

"No, no, no, you don't understand. I want to do what you did. You gotta tell me what you did. How did you do it? How did you stop the drugs and turn your life around? How did you do it?"

I felt as if I were hitting rewind on the tapes that I'd given him about giving my life to God, reading His Word...

"No, Jack, no," he says. "No more scripture. I just want to hear what your secret was."

"You don't get it, do you, Charlie? There is no secret." It was obvious the answer was right there, but he didn't want it. It was as if he had a deadly disease (and in reality, he did; it was his drug habit), and I told him straight out I had the cure and held it out to him, and he refused to take it. What do I say to him now? What would you say to the Charlies in your life?

So, that whole Charlie thing got me thinking... why are you at church, and others aren't? Why am I there on Sunday, but Charlie isn't?

Charlie didn't think church was good. He didn't think church was necessary. He didn't think he needed to be there. He thought he could do it on his own, even though he kept begging for help to do something he hadn't been able to do on his own. Makes him sound kind of stupid, doesn't it, until God reminds me that, without His grace, I was doing the same thing.

It got me thinking that many Christians are like Charlie. They say they're trying to find God but refuse to look where He is. Think about it. If you want to find me, a good place to come is my house. I'm usually there a lot. So, if you want to find God, a good place to look for Him is in His house. So, why don't people look there?

I started to think about the excuses that people, whether they're believers or not, have given for not coming to church. I made this list... and wondered how often you and I have used these when we let our sinful, rebellious nature get the upper hand. You see, we can be *in* church physically and still not *be* there spiritually.

Excuse #1: I don't have to go to church to spend time with God. I can do that on my own in my own way.

Honestly, I believe that is a perverted view of God's truth. You see, that's about doing it *your* way. Most of us can look at lots of things in our lives that we did our way that haven't turned out so great. We have to ask whether what Charlie wants, and the people that think like him want, is the same as what God wants. So, what does God want? He wants us to spend time with Him. He calls us His children. We are heirs to the throne of heaven. We are brothers and sisters with Jesus Christ. We are sons and daughters of God. So, we're *family*. How about spending some time with family? With your Father? The Bible says in Hebrews 10:25, "Let us not give up meeting together, as some are in the habit of doing, but let us encourage one another – and all the more as you see the Day approaching."

I told Charlie that when it comes to church, I come to worship God. I don't come for the music. I don't come for the pastor. I do benefit from these things, and God speaks to me through them, but I'm not there as if I were part of the paying audience at a Springsteen show. I'm not there to say, "Hey, Pastor, you know what? You did great last week, but this week you're a little off." I'm at church for God. I want to worship and obey *God* – that is why I come.

Because of that, I'm personally not very judgmental of what music is played, what message is preached, or what color the carpet is, because that's not my call. A lot of people are concerned about it, though, which is a shame. I truly feel that until we get to the point where we can commit to the fellowship of our church and stick with that commitment, even when the preaching or the music, or the carpet isn't exactly what we want, we'll still have a generation of disconnected people floating from church to church.

I remember John F. Kennedy's inauguration speech when I was a kid, when he said, "Ask not what your country can do for you. Ask what you can do for your country." My advice to you would be very similar: ask not what your church can do for you; ask what you can do for your church. It's too easy to walk away. "I don't like this, that guy or that thing is not right, this one is more traditional, that one's not." God put each of us somewhere for a reason, so if we are part of God's team, we should be lifting up our leaders and our pastors. Have you ever really sat down and prayed for your pastor or the leaders of the church? If we're looking to see what we can give, rather than what we can get, we'll suddenly find ourselves beginning to fit into the fellowship and being used by God! And there aren't many things that feel better than that.

I could almost have some respect for that "I don't need church; I can do it on my own" routine if it were followed up with successful results. If you can pass the test without doing the work, you're a lot smarter than I am. What if you were in school and decided not to go to class because you can learn all that stuff on your own better than you can in school? Really?

Okay, so how'd you do on the test? If you ace the final exam, maybe you can make that argument for not needing church because you can "do it" on your own. But if you're failing the class, well, you're not doing so hot on your own, are you?

When you "do church" on your own, in your own way, how are you doing with those tests that life throws at you? Getting A's? Or less than what you'd hoped? If Charlie is still seeking out other people for the answers that God has so clearly placed in front of him, then surely he is missing something.

Are you pulling a Charlie by continually ignoring (or avoiding) what God has to say on a subject and, instead, continually seeking out others' secrets for how to do things? What are you still trying to handle on your own? Finances? Addiction? Parenting? Purity? Anger? How's that working out for you?

If you're still "trying to handle it," then maybe it's time to turn to the Teacher and His book for instruction. One quick way to know if you're handling it on your own is to listen to yourself explaining your solution ... if it begins with "I think" or "I feel," then you are probably missing the same things Charlie missed. Another quick test is if you're still looking for answers after exhausting your own (and others') solutions, then that's a clue, my friend. So what do you do now?

Here's a starting point. Pick an issue you continually worry about or struggle to find the right way to handle. Either on your own, or with the help of a more mature Christian, search the Bible for input that applies specifically to that issue. Use a concordance to find applicable verses, and then use a commentary to study what those verses mean.

Excuse #2: People in church are hypocritical.

Well, no surprise there. I am a hypocrite, and Charlie is right. People in church are hypocritical. How dare I say that? I didn't. God did. Look at Romans 3:10, where He said, "... There is no one righteous, not even one." Only Jesus was righteous, only Jesus lived His life perfectly. If we could have been righteous and lived perfectly, and never been hypocritical, then Jesus would not have had to die on the cross as a sacrifice for you and me. He wouldn't have had to pay our sin debt so that we could be free, abundantly free here on Earth now, and eternally free with God in heaven.

If we're looking for perfect people, then we can look straight at Jesus. When we do that, we realize that everyone else we look at, including that reflection in the mirror, is not and never will be perfect. So I ask you, is there someone you've criticized or dismissed because they didn't live up to your standard of perfection? Confess it to God, and if need be, seek that person's forgiveness as well.

If you're still hung up on labeling "churchy people" as hypocrites, stop for a minute and think about how things look when you apply that same standard to yourself. Are you willing for God to show you the answer to that? Ask Him to show you those times that you've been hypocritical. Maybe you worship on Sunday, then curse about your employer during the week. Or do you get on a tirade about rude drivers, and then cut someone off in traffic? Do you keep the extra change when the clerk makes a mistake, rather than making sure the transaction was handled correctly? How about that income tax filing or that item you claimed as a business expense?

Excuse #3: I'm not going to church because all they want is my money.

Right again, sort of, but actually churches want more than that. We want *you* because God wants you – your heart, soul, spirit, and strength. And by the way, if you study scripture, you'll see that it's not your money in the first place; it's God's. He's just letting you use it for a while.

So, churches want money. Why wouldn't they? All they want to do is build God's kingdom, which is a hospital for souls. Hospitals need to be open. They need to pay electric bills and doctors; and spiritual hospitals, the churches, need to pay for utilities, supplies, staff, and pastors.

Do you know to whom you are giving money? Think about it. You "give" it away all the time to others, based on what you value. For example, how much have you "given" to a guy named Calvin Klein or Louis Vuitton? Or to Bass Pro Shop or the Sharper Image? Or Starbucks? Or late fees on your bills? Interest charges on credit card debt? Do you even know where your money is really going, and how much is for needs versus wants?

Do you say you care about the wellbeing of others? Prove it. Did you value someone's need for spiritual care this month? Do you complain about teenagers' attitudes, rather than supporting the youth group and pastor that gives them alternatives to the street?

Excuse #4: I'm not going to church because the messages hurt my feelings and make me feel bad.

If you only want to hear what makes you feel good, you are never going to grow up. This mentality is exceedingly childish and self-centered and prevents you from learning how to handle the business of life. Relationships and plans and dreams will fail a lot of times. You will screw up things you thought would be a piece of cake.

Maybe you are attending church but you're using this "feelings" excuse to keep from committing to it. You haven't joined, and therefore, you are not taking on your part of the responsibility for your Christian family. The real heart of this excuse is that you don't want to hear God's truth; instead, you want your version of it.

So, how's your version working out for you? Life full of roses and big successes? Peace in the home and peace in the heart? Perfect health and bank account?

If you want a feel-good version of the truth, how about I just change all the truth for you? No planes crashed into the World Trade Center Towers in New York City on September 11, 2001. Nobody died in the world this week. There is no war in Iraq. People are not starving in America, Christians aren't being persecuted across the globe, and smoking a lot of pot over time won't kill your brain cells. Oh, yeah, and by the way, you are the most gorgeous and intelligent person that ever was. Feel better?

I can't help but think about my dad. As a young man, I used to ask him for advice. Now, as an older man, I still ask him for advice. The difference is how I respond to what he tells me. The young me got mad at him for telling me what I didn't want to hear. One day, he just looked at me and asked why I bothered seeking his advice if I didn't want to hear what he had to say. He told me flat out, "Hey, you don't want the truth? Then don't ask me, because if you ask, you're going to get the truth whether you like it or not."

Do you sometimes think that you have a better truth than God does? For what subject? Have you thoroughly searched the scriptures and dedicated yourself to studying that subject? How does your version line up with his? Do you ever get mad at God when He doesn't give you the answer you want? Why? What part of your life needs some advice right now? What scriptures have you chosen to ignore because you don't like what they say?

Excuse #5: I don't go to church because Christians don't do what they say others should do.

This one's kin to hypocrisy with a little twist. Sure, I can talk the talk, but do I walk the walk? I try to, as best I know how.

I'm like a baseball player who goes out every day and practices and trains and studies. I do everything I can to go out there and live the life that God told me to live as well as I possibly can. Sometimes I fail, and the "baseball fan" (perhaps you) looks at me and says, see, Jack stinks. That's why I don't go to church, because Jack can't bat a thousand at the game of Christianity that he is always talking about.

Now, who's the hypocrite? That same baseball fan would think that a player batting 300, which means he misses 70 percent of the time, is amazing. And what about football? If you complete your passes seven out of ten times, you're the greatest – but wait a minute, you still missed three out of ten! How come that quarterback doesn't stink? Why doesn't the fan say, see, that's why I don't go to football games – because they only succeed at seven out of ten passes.

Am I a terrible Christian if I can't walk the walk perfectly? No, and neither are you. There is no such thing as perfection on planet Earth.

There is perfection when we get to heaven, where we'll be made perfect. There is not perfection down here. We are supposed to train our bodies. We are supposed to master our flesh, and God's Spirit is supposed to be in control so we can go out there and fight the war and do the best that we possibly can. But it's not about being perfect.

So, if church can't make me perfect, why go? Well, hey, why does the baseball player keep playing? Because he wants to get better and believes that, with the help of his coach, he can improve. The coach says the same thing all the time – keep your eye on the ball. Jesus says, "Keep your eye on me." So, I do. I'm keeping my eye on the ball, but I still miss, so I take more practice time, more training. I get better and better. I work harder and improve, little by little, season by season. It works for ballplayers. And it works for Christians ... but you have to show up for practice.

Are you showing up for practice? I mean not just showing up at church, but being there with all your heart, soul, mind, and strength. Are you studying the game plan – the Bible? If you had to create your own "baseball card of faith" with your faith statistics and performance on it, what would it say? What would it say if those closest to you wrote it? What would it say if someone you didn't know, a "fan" who was observing you, wrote it? Where do you need to spend more time practicing a principle your Coach is trying to teach you? What would "improvement" look like this season, then the next and the next?

Excuse #6: I don't go to church because it's not entertaining.

Yeah? Neither is breathing, but it's awfully important. Church is not a Broadway show. God doesn't invite us to church so we can critique a performance or to see if the pastor inspires us today. He didn't invite us here so we could gossip about the musicians or the singers or to kill time before something more fun starts on Sunday afternoon.

There is no place in scripture where God assigns us the role of secret church inspector to grade the congregation on how they look or how friendly they are. What's really underneath that excuse is the notion that somewhere, you'll find a church that does things the way *you* like. That's not in the Bible, either.

Instead, how about we look for a church where they do things God's way? It's supposed to be His house, where His family comes together to worship a living Savior out of gratitude and thanksgiving for the blessings we've been given – given, mind you, not earned. How about we come to church to listen to God, so we can learn? That means we have to shut up for a while. I'm a pretty average guy, and I can only learn when I'm listening ... I have never taught myself anything new when my mouth was moving.

Are you attending a church now because God is there, or would your reason start with something about what you prefer or what's convenient for you?

If you left a church, then why? Was God not being honored, or were you not being entertained or pampered?

Does your reason for choosing a church revolve around what it does to serve *you* (entertains you, pays attention to you, calls you, fixes your car, and so on) or does it revolve around how you can serve God and others?

Excuse #7: I go to church, but only out of obligation.

Who is holding a gun to your head? It's not God. Often, this reasoning goes along the lines that not attending will make God mad at you.

God will not be mad at you if you don't come to church. As a matter of fact God doesn't want you here if you don't want to be here. It's like being on a date with somebody who doesn't want to date you. Most of us have probably experienced that once, and that's enough.

Knowing that someone is with you because they feel an obligation rather than a desire is no fun.

God knows our hearts. Instead of getting mad that we don't want to worship Him, I believe He gets sad. Imagine ... He's adopted you into his family, has guaranteed you an inheritance that can never be taken away, even by the IRS. He's given you brothers and sisters, but you would rather be sleeping late or doing a crossword puzzle than spending time with Him. Excuse me, but if that's how you treat someone who loves you so much, He was willing to die for you, then how are your other relationships going?

God wants people to worship Him in spirit and in truth, not those who are there in body only. If you're going to church out of obligation, you have to ask yourself if you're really a Christian. You aren't a Christian just because you live in a certain place, because your grandpa was a preacher, or because you go to church. Each person is accountable to God for his or her own life. Have you ever admitted to God that you are a sinner – that without Him, you are hopeless and helpless? Have you ever told God that you believe Jesus is who He said He is – that He took the punishment you deserved from God so that you could have a relationship with God? Anyone can even believe that much, but still not be a Christian. You become a believer – get saved, become a Christian – only when you ask Jesus to come into your life and be the LORD over your life. Have you done that? If you haven't, will you do it now? Ask Him to be the Lord of your life, and ask Him to give you a desire to worship Him and to teach you how to do it.

Ask yourself, when you're in church, are you really *there*? Worship is acknowledging who God is and what He has done for us. When we get that right, we develop a grateful, humble attitude. How's your attitude? Grateful? Your ability to breathe, move, see, smell, touch, taste, hear, drive, work, laugh, cry, earn an income, read a book – all these are from His hand. We worship the ATM machine when it lets us make a withdrawal, yet we forget who enabled us to do and have the job that put the money there in the first place. When was the last time you went outside and thanked God for everything you have and everything you see – for creating everything, and I do mean *everything*? Have you ever done that? Now is a good time to start.

Let me give you an example. Imagine it's hotter than blazes outside right now, 104 degrees in the shade and humid beyond belief. What if I told you that we were going to work out in the field, and we were going to work ourselves very, very hard, shoveling dirt all day? Oh, and guess what? Water is sparse today, and you are going to be pretty thirsty, but you may only get a little sip or two. And there will be no food – sorry about that. The shovels and the rocks you are going to be lifting are heavy as heck, though, and I can promise you one thing: at the end of the day, you are going to be sore, hurt, sunburned, thirsty, and hungry. You might say, "Well, I don't know. That's not a particularly good feeling for me. Can you get somebody else?"

But what if I told you that tonight, after that long, hard day, after we complete all the work, we are having the party of all time? We are having an *unbelievable* party. There will be filet mignon, baked Virginia ham, and pizza (all my favorite foods), and everyone gets as much of their favorite foods as they can eat. And to make it even better, there will be whatever kind of entertainment you love by the best entertainers, who will be there performing for you. When I go, Bruce Springsteen is going to be playing for me. Maybe for you, it's somebody else. And because I know you are sore, the world's best massage therapists will be there. They'll have ice packs and heating pads that will not only heal you of the day's work, but will also make you feel better than you ever have in your life, better than new. People are going to feed you grapes. It is going to be unbelievable.

So, I want you to do some hard work today. And by the way, the work you'll be doing is helping to build a few buildings here in the church. We are going to build God's kingdom. Okay. Now we're all in. It's well worth it. I am going to suffer a little bit today, but as I'm suffering, I help build God's kingdom, and tonight, we are having this unbelievable celebration party, and I'm the guest of honor.

That's a picture of our lives here on Earth. Obviously, this is just an analogy. The pleasures of God in heaven are far, far beyond some good food and a Bruce Springsteen concert. When I go to a Springsteen show it's over after three hours. But in heaven, the treasures never end;

they never rust or fade. The reward of heaven is God himself, and God is eternal and infinite. No matter how long we're in heaven, no matter how many billions of years we are there, we will never run out of new things to enjoy about God. Being with Him will be far, far better than any concert we've ever been to, any vacation we've ever taken, any high or thrill we've ever had, and we'll just enjoy Him more and more, as eternity goes on! What a gift that is! And the irony is, we build up that treasure by not settling for all sorts of lesser rewards here on Earth.

In Matthew 6:19–21, Jesus instructed his disciples not to build up treasures on Earth, but rather treasures in heaven. Let's look at what He says right after that. Jesus has a way of cutting right to what's important. He tells them not to spend their time pursuing earthly riches, because He knows if they do that, that's where their hearts are going to be. He also knows they'll be wondering about some natural concerns. They're going to think, "Well, that sounds good, but I have to eat, don't I? How am I going to feed my family?" Look what Jesus says:

> Therefore I tell you, do not worry about your life, what you will eat or drink; or about your body, what you will wear. Is not life more important than food, and the body more important than clothes? Look at the birds of the air; they do not sow or reap or store away in barns, and yet your heavenly Father feeds them. Are you not much more valuable than they? Who of you by worrying can add a single hour to his life? And why do you worry about clothes? See how the lilies of the field grow. They do not labor or spin. Yet I tell you that not even Solomon in all his splendor was dressed like one of these. (Matthew 6:25–29)

Jesus is saying, "Hey, God has this under control. He's doing things on a level of detail that you don't even understand. He's providing clothing for even the little flowers over there – nice clothing, too! Do you think he's going to leave you naked and hungry?"

God says in Jeremiah 17:10, "I the Lord search the heart. I test the mind even to give every man according to his ways, according to the fruit of his doing." You reap what you sow. This is not about your salvation. Once you accept Jesus as your Lord and Savior, you are going to heaven, no matter what. This is about your *reward* in heaven. God clearly says we are saved, based on faith in Jesus Christ alone. That's crystal clear, but He has also told us clearly that, on Judgment Day, we are going to be *rewarded*, based on what we *do*.

Jeremiah, an Old Testament prophet (which means that God literally spoke through him to the people), said: "This is what the LORD says: 'Let not the wise man boast of his wisdom or the strong man boast of his strength or the rich man boast of his riches, but let him who boasts boast about this: that he understands and knows me, that I am the LORD, who exercises kindness, justice and righteousness on earth, for in these I delight,' declares the LORD" (Jeremiah 9:23–24)

That is what you should glory in – that you understand and know the Lord. He says, "I am the Lord, and I delight in exercising kindness, justice, and righteousness on Earth. And I delight in the fact that you understand and know Me." Understanding and knowing Him better is ultimately the work that's rewarded! That's number one on the list. And it only makes sense, because being able to know Him better and more perfectly is ultimately the reward itself.

We come to know Him through the things we've talked about in this book. We know Him through dying to ourselves, through relying on His help to give the devil the boot, through suffering, through embracing the incredible love of the Father, through having a relationship with God through prayer, reading the Bible, and being part of the church body. All of these things bring us greater understanding and appreciation for the God who has drawn us close through the sacrifice of his Son.

Ultimately, the awesome Christian life is about one thing: *knowing God*. The better we know Him, the more we love Him. The more He blesses us, the more He expands our ability to enjoy Him. And that goes on into eternity!

That's the God we serve. That's the God who bought us with His Son's blood. That's the God who allows rebels and sinners to see and enjoy, and bask in His glory for eternity. The God who said "Let light shine out of darkness" made His light shine in our hearts to give us the light of the knowledge of the glory of God in the face of Christ (2 Corinthians 4:4b–6).

That's the secret that I was offering Charlie – the secret to turning his life around, so he could live the life he imagined. And that's the secret that he never accepted.

That's the reason we go to church, in spite of all its imperfections. We stop making excuses, so we can get to know God better and better.

And the more we know Him, the more we love Him, and the more we can see past this working life to the party that awaits us in heaven.

That's the life you always imagined – the awesome Christian life. We have it forever, and we can start living it *now*. It's ours for the taking. This gift, this present, this life – this is it, baby. It is time to get in the game and swing the bat.

How to Enjoy Life

If you get ice cream and let it sit there, it melts. It drips onto your hand, your pants, and down on the floor, and you can't eat it anymore, and you can't enjoy it because all it's done is make a mess. Enjoy it while you've got it.

Same with life. It comes in lots of sizes and flavors, but it only lasts a little while, so either you can enjoy it, or you can let it melt away and make a mess in the process. What's the point of having it if you're not going to enjoy it?

You know that "Footprints" poem and the part about how God physically carries you through the hard places in your life? During a recent quiet time when I was reading my Bible, I was searching for God's answers to some questions in my life. After spending time in the Word, I felt as if I were a three-dimensional, living example of that "Footprints" message. More than any time in my life, I sensed God lifting me up, cradling me in his arms, and encouraging me along. Needless to say, I was as grateful as you could imagine to God for the crystal clear answers He'd given for my questions. Afterwards, I went to take a shower before going to work, and that's when I started to cry. I was overwhelmed with joy on the one hand and gratitude on the other — gratitude not just for the revelation He had given me that morning, not just for showing up in the biggest way ever, but also for the fact that He had made my heart obedient to His will.

But what if I hadn't shown up to meet with God? What if I hadn't opened my Bible that morning? I would have missed some of the greatest blessings I ever got in my life. It was just amazing how God laid on my heart that there is always a payoff for being there with Him. It might not always be immediate, but there is always a payoff.

My pastor, Truman Herring, constantly encourages us to be at church because we'll never know the blessing we could miss if we don't show up. Honestly, I can't tell you that I walk out of church every Sunday morning shouting about how my life changed because of what I'd just heard, but I can tell you that I am always inspired. I always get a blessing from God by coming to church. Some of those blessings are more apparent than others are, but I know if I weren't there, I would miss out on them (and sometimes, by just being there, I wind up being used by God as a blessing to someone else). And the thing is that you don't know which day will be the "amazing blessing day." Just as Jesus said, you don't know the hour or the time that He is coming. This isn't the NFL where they tell you the date of the Super Bowl, and everybody in the nation tunes in and enjoys that once a year event. This is God. And He shows up every Sunday, and every other day, you come to meet Him.

Fortunately, we don't have to wait for one big event per year to enjoy our lives, although some folks do live that way, letting parts of their lives just melt away, waiting for something better to happen, searching for the big "IT" that will finally make them happy. Unfortunately, they're never going to find IT, because the source of our true happiness is not an IT but a WHO, specifically, God. What we often fail to realize is that IT is often a tactic used by our enemy, Satan, to keep us from being blessed. The more we pursue IT, the less likely we are to see how much of our ice cream has melted, how much has been wasted.

On the other hand, God, who created us and wants to bless us, has given us great advice and guidance on how to enjoy life, advice that might surprise you.

So, the first question I want to ask you is what place does IT have in your life? What do you look to for enjoyment that excludes God? And in particular, if IT is something you don't want others to know about, then IT is a problem between you and God and will keep you from enjoying the life He wants you to have.

IT was a problem for me, for a time, until I had to face something I'd never expected to as a Christian – Satan had a place in my life, and I'd venture a guess that he does in your life too. I'm being totally honest here because I hated to admit that revelation. Instead, I wanted to stand up and shout to anyone listening that Satan had no place in my life.

Unfortunately, at the time in 1998, that wasn't completely true. I didn't realize it until my buddy Roger Spencer preached on sharpening our axes and fighting Satan, and he reminded us that God tells us to take off the things that hinder and so easily entangle and to not let Satan get a foothold in our lives. Roger talked briefly about television in his personal life and the impact that pornography had on him as he was flipping the channels. Unfortunately, it's rather easy to access that kind of stuff on cable, network, and satellite TV, now that there are over 500 channels.

I went home after that, and I thought about it and then got busy with life, but it came back to me a few days later. I realized something unpleasant, but that I believe I have to say. I'll bet most of you, and I'm talking mostly to the men, have a place in your house where Satan lives. Maybe it's not in your house. Maybe it's in your office or your car or your safe deposit box. It's a different thing for each one of us. It could be a pornographic magazine, evidence of a gambling trip, a drug stash, or something as seemingly innocent as pictures of a girl you once loved. I don't know what it is, but you do, and you haven't thrown it out of your life. You keep it tucked away somewhere, and you only visit it in secret when nobody is looking.

Are you squirming in your seat? Good. Because until you deal with it, you will not be able to enjoy life God's way.

How often do you pull out that porn magazine or look at the picture of that old girlfriend? How often do you have money that you shouldn't have earned a particular way? Certainly, you're not proud of that thing, because I bet if I walked into your house, I wouldn't see it on your kitchen table.

I'm not asking you about something I haven't already had to deal with in my life. I had something in my house for a long, long time that

I was never willing or able to get rid of. As I continued to think about Roger's message, though, I realized that was where Satan lived and any time I secretly went and opened that compartment and took that thing out, I let Satan out.

Now, thanks be to God, I finally obeyed His prompting to get that thing out of my house and out of my life. It doesn't belong in either place, anymore.

What's silly, though, is that my first thought was to simply move it. I could put it somewhere else, maybe the safe deposit box because I don't really want to look at it or have it at home, but I also don't want to completely get rid of it just yet. The thought didn't last long. God made sure of that.

"Jack," I sensed God speaking to me, "if all you're going to do is move it, then you might as well put it in your living room and make it an idol, and say 'Hey everyone, this is where Satan lives.'"

When God put it that way, I knew what I had to do. I had to throw it out of my life completely.

Do you have just that one, last little supposedly "harmless" thing stashed away in secret, whether it's in a safe in your home, tucked into a drawer, or in a filing cabinet in your den? Whatever hiding place you're using, that's where Satan lives. Again, I promise you that until you deal with that, you will not be able to enjoy the life that God wants you to have.

What you must realize is that Satan is in your house *with your permission*, and if you think you can keep him contained in that little box, you're wrong. If you think he is not smart and if you think he won't use that thing you're hiding to get a foothold farther into your life, you're wrong. Maybe nothing's happened yet, maybe your secret's safe for now, but Satan will wait for it. He'll wait for just the right opportunity, even if it takes six months or a year or more, he'll wait. He'll wait until you can't stand it anymore, and you have to go to that thing, and when you do, you open the door to his first attack.

As I dealt with my particular thing and threw it out of my life, I actually said out loud "Satan, you can't live in my house anymore. I've let myself off the hook to this point because I never thought about how it represented you, Satan, but now I understand, and it has to go." All of us need to look into our houses and what we are hiding and get rid of whatever it is, because really if you have to hide it, it's not good. If you're hiding it, something's wrong.

Now, the irony for me is that sometimes there are things we aren't hiding, and we don't realize we ought to get rid of! Not long after that epiphany about needing to get rid of those secret things, I had the privilege of leading a discussion session after Roy Isbell, an 80-year-old retired pastor and true man of God, preached a great message on sorrow, sin, and death. The morning of that event, I left my house in a little bit of a rush, but I got there in time to hear Roy's preaching. When he finished, I got up and led the discussion.

Afterward, a member of our church, Bruce Frcek a new believer and all-around great guy, came up to me and pointed at my chest. "What's with that shirt?"

"What do you mean?"

"Why are you wearing that shirt?" Bruce asked.

I looked down at what I was wearing and shrugged. "It's just a harness racing shirt with the name of a horse, 'Red Bow Tie.' That horse got the world record for running the fastest mile for trotters his age."

"Yeah," he said, "but it's got a Budweiser emblem on the sleeve."

A Budweiser emblem. Big deal. I was sleepy, I grabbed a shirt out of my drawer, saw which one it was, thought about it for one split second, and figured this is no problem. Usually, I wear a Jesus shirt to a men's ministry meeting at church, but I figured, hey, it's a Saturday morning, no big deal. I'm not going to be hypocritical just wearing certain stuff outside and certain stuff in church. No problem. I yanked on the shirt and hurried out the door ... and now, I wondered why Bruce was making it an issue.

Then, two more people came up to me, and to top it off , one of them was my pastor's wife, Connie.

"Jack," she asked, "why are you wearing that shirt?"

It slowly dawned on me that the shirt wasn't okay, not because of what it said, but because it was me wearing it, and my church family held me to a higher standard of accountability than the rest of the world because of my relationship with Jesus Christ. And I believe God also holds Christians to that higher standard because of our relationship with Him. People are watching me, watching us as Christians, and making assumptions about what we represent. Wearing that shirt was not the end of the world, but this small emblem on it bothered my friends and my church family. Other people, both inside and outside the church, notice things about us that we don't. And what they notice affects them, so if we're not careful, it can affect our credibility as a Christian. How could I enjoy my life in Christ if that happened?

So, did that shirt take away my credibility? No, because these guys love me, they know me, and I thanked them for pointing it out. It was a good lesson for me. I would hate to be out there in the world wearing that shirt, trying to witness to somebody, and they say, yeah, this guy with a Budweiser shirt on is gonna tell me about Jesus? Even though I thought it was just a harness racing shirt, I'd overlooked the Budweiser thing on it.

Some of you might be shaking your heads, thinking how can he be making such a big deal out of a shirt? If you enjoy it, wear it. I can understand that thought process, but as I've grown in my faith, I've come to the realization that my enjoyment of life isn't tied up in a shirt or a car or a *thing*; it's directly tied into my God and pleasing Him. Does God care about a T-shirt with a Budweiser emblem? Who knows? Does God care about how that *shirt* or that *thing in my life* I hang on to affects other people or how it affects the image of Him I am supposed to be reflecting, representing, and portraying to the rest of the world? Absolutely!

People are watching. It's way too easy to blow the one opportunity you might have today to witness to someone. My pastor gave an example of the preacher who was on a bus, and the bus driver, knowing the passenger was a preacher, gave him ten cents extra change to see if the preacher would give it back. The preacher passed the test by returning the money that wasn't his, but later said he cried, thinking if he hadn't been faithful with such a little thing, he could have lost his witness over a lousy dime. It's not worth a dime, and it's not worth a shirt.

Those are just a couple of examples of the little things that so easily entangle us and cause us to lose our way as Christians and prevent us from enjoying life God's way. Paul warned us in Hebrews 12:1, "... let us throw off everything that hinders and the sin that so easily entangles ..." Surprisingly, another lesson I've learned is that some of the things that so easily entangle aren't hidden in our homes or our offices, but they are hidden in our hearts, such as attitudes or sometimes misunderstandings about the scriptures that can affect our credibility as witnesses to a watching world and our ability to enjoy life God's way.

Take Galatians 5:13, for example. This is a verse I stood on for a long time. "You, my brothers, were called to be free. But do not use your freedom to indulge the sinful nature; rather, serve one another in love." According to this verse, I'm free. I might still wear that shirt. I'm a Christian, I'm saved, and God would love me no matter what I wear, right? Right. But God also says in 1 Corinthians 10:23–24, "'Everything is permissible' – but not everything is beneficial. 'Everything is permissible' – but not everything is constructive. Nobody should seek his own good, but the good of others." If I am seeking the good of others, then I am not out there advertising beer on my shirt. Why does it matter?

It matters because we are charged with a responsibility in 1 Corinthians 10:31–32, "So whether you eat or drink or whatever you do, do it all for the glory of God. Do not cause anyone to stumble..." If one person didn't believe my witness or thought I was sending a hypocritical message because of that shirt and therefore turned away from Christ, I would have caused him to stumble. So, that shirt went into the garbage.

After that, I kind of scrutinized the rest of my stuff – the clothes, the books, everything – and while none of it was being hidden from anyone, and I wouldn't worry about anyone from my church seeing them, I knew that some of those things added nothing to my life in Christ, so out they went too.

God's timing is so good. After throwing away that shirt, I found myself in my quiet time in the book of Proverbs, seeking wisdom for a matter. God directed my heart to Ecclesiastes instead and had me linger there.

I said, "God, that's pretty weird." But that's where I went and that's where I stayed, and that's where God gave me the answer I'd been seeking. What was my question? "God, how do You want me to enjoy life?"

I wasn't being sarcastic, as if criticizing Him for taking away all the "fun stuff" since I'd been saved. I was being sincere. God created me and knows me through and through, and He sees the big picture that I can't. Maybe there is something He wants me to learn – something new that I'd never considered but would thoroughly enjoy.

Ecclesiastes is not a book that we tend to spend a lot of time in, so I'll give you a little bit of background on King Solomon. In his day, he was the wisest, richest man in the world. God bestowed on King Solomon more wisdom than anybody ever had, and it wasn't just scientific wisdom like Einstein had, but rather, emotional wisdom, life wisdom to know everything. In addition to bestowing all this wisdom on him, God made him the richest man in the world. So believe me, when I say that Solomon had everything a man could ever want or dream of, and at one point in his life, he set out literally to find the answer to happiness.

After searching, experimenting, learning, and consuming, he made a very wise observation, "What profit has a man from all his labor for which he toils under the sun? One generation passes away, and another generation comes. Man cannot express it; the eye is not satisfied with seeing or the ear filled with hearing. That which is then is what will be, and that which is gone is what will be gone. There is nothing new under the sun; there is no remembering of former things, nor will there be any remembrance of things to come by those who come after".

What profit does a man get from all his labor?

We labor, every one of us, but what's the profit in it? Is it that we get paid at the end of the week, and we get to put food on the table? That we work really hard and get to go on vacation once a year? We get to drive a nice car? Is that it?

He went on to say that "One generation passes away and so will the next, and who will be here to run the earth after us? There is nothing new under the sun."

You say, "Wait a minute, Solomon. There's the Internet; you didn't have that. And that horse and buggy routine got replaced by automobiles. Radio got replaced by television." And you're right, but Solomon is speaking of human nature. Technology will continue to change, but as far as the make-up of man and his mind and heart, there is nothing new. It's always the same. Even back to the time of Plato and Socrates, philosophers were asking the same questions about the meaning of life that people ask today. Why am I alive? What am I doing? What's the purpose? They had the same deep thoughts and sought the contrasts in life, and tried to solve problems the same way that Solomon and many other Old Testament people did.

ments, try to please people, try to please ourselves, and then we pile on *stuff* that we think will make life meaningful and watch what happens. Now we've got *two* houses that need maintenance and alarm systems. We've got a cabinet full of money, which means we worry someone will steal it. We have nice dishes and fancy silver utensils, and we wonder if the maid is going to take any, and we buy insurance to protect the stuff. Where, exactly, does enjoyment enter in? How can you enjoy those things when they come with such burdens?

Are we so busy acquiring, paying for, maintaining, and protecting our things that we never actually enjoy them?

The wisest man in the world, King Solomon, tells us that the guy who *doesn't* have this stuff is better off because he's like a child who doesn't have these worries.

"Okay, Jack," you say, "I hear you. So what is the answer to the question about how to enjoy life?"

Don't ask me; ask Solomon! Here is his answer in Ecclesiastes 2:24–25: "A man can do nothing better than to eat and drink and find satisfaction in his work. This too, I see, is from the hand of God, for without him, who can eat or find enjoyment?"

Solomon says nothing is better for man than he should eat and drink, and find satisfaction in his work, but we can only do that with God. So, the first step to enjoying your life is to make sure you are connected to God, and we do that only through a relationship with His Son, Jesus Christ, not through the acquisition of THINGS.

Understand this – God is not out to make life miserable and boring by saying you can't have some ITs in your life, things that you enjoy such as a nice car or a great vacation. However, He does want you to know that they will not bring lasting happiness – only a relationship with Him will do that. If your joy and happiness are based on that relationship with Him, then those ITs can come and go and not cause you any heartbreak.

Once we are rightly related to God, we are in a position to be able to do what Solomon says, and that is to eat, drink, and find satisfaction in our work. Are you eating? Drinking (and I don't mean alcohol)? Working? Most of us do those things every day. Well, then, are you finding satisfaction in those things and enjoying them? Yes, no, maybe, some days, never? Or maybe you're thinking there is some specific thing or person, or destination out there with your specific brand of happiness attached to it.

Think again, Solomon says, think again, because I did all the market research for you. I spent my money, time, and effort trying to "find" happiness, only to "find" that happiness comes from enjoying God. Then, the work that you do, the family that you have, the life that you lead, all will be enjoyable and of great blessing to you. It all starts with enjoying a relationship with God. Enjoy the day Solomon teaches. It is the only day you have. It's called "today," and it's called the PRESENT, and it is truly a gift to you from God.

Solomon advises us to enjoy those things while you have them, before they melt away, and if you don't, you are blowing it in a big way. He observed that rich or poor, God has given us all the same basic ice cream in life – people, food, drink, and work. And in those things, we can find enjoyment and satisfaction *because* we know there is more, there is eternity with God, and that takes what otherwise would be meaningless and gives it great hope and purpose, thanks to the privilege of knowing and loving God.

Solomon is not saying you have to have a job you love. There are some circumstances beyond our control. Solomon encourages us that, with God's help, we can still find satisfaction in that job and do it well, and in that, we can find enjoyment.

He went on to say, "He who loves silver will not be satisfied with silver; Nor he who loves abundance, with increase ... So what profit have the owners except to see them with their eyes" (Ecclesiastes 5:10–11, NKJV). You want more money? Fine, but how many steaks do you eat at a meal? One. Maybe the big guys can have two. How many cars can you drive at a time, and how many houses can you actually live in? One. No matter how many houses or cars you have, you can only really live in one or use one at a time, and the others just drain the bank with upkeep, insurance, loans, security systems, and more. Does that sound like something to be enjoyed?

Solomon saw all that and told us that accumulating stuff is foolishness because it doesn't bring satisfaction. None of us should be surprised by that because we've all learned it over and over again. As kids, we just knew the latest walkie-talkie, bike, or sound system would make life perfect ... and IT didn't. As adults, we just know that a different job, a bigger house, a new car will make life perfect ... and IT doesn't.

And still, we pursue those things that claim to make us happy but don't. I know. My early career on Madison Avenue as an advertising executive was spent trying to fool you, the consumer, into thinking that STUFF would make you feel happy, special, loved, envied, and satisfied. I lied. Consuming STUFF will not get those results. And neither will so many other things we try in an effort to enjoy life and pursue happiness, many of which make us look like fools, destroy relationships and families and careers, or ruin our health and life itself. I know. I spent a lot of years doing drugs which nearly killed me, while destroying other parts of my life until I went to God.

And even if it's not drugs, we'll find that, without God at the core of our lives, we will work, worry, and compare ourselves to others and · get stomachaches and headaches and backaches (yes, most are caused by stress), wondering what will happen. Without God, wisdom is meaningless, as are pleasures, folly, work, advancement, and riches. The quest to find pleasure and enjoyment in life is a tactic of the enemy to keep us distracted from the true source of enjoyment, and that is God. At the end of Ecclesiastes, as Solomon summarizes the results of his market research, I can tell you that Madison Avenue would have fired him because he concluded it's not about them; it's about God. Solomon brings us right back to God:

"Now all has been heard; here is the conclusion of the matter: Fear God and keep his commandments, for this is the whole duty of man" (12:13). Fear God; meaning be rightly connected to Him. Keep His commandments; meaning simply, obey His Word. When we do that, we can stop worrying and start enjoying life!

In Chapter 11, verses 8 and 10, Solomon concludes: "However many years a man may live, let him enjoy them all. So then, banish anxiety from your heart and cast off the troubles of your body ..." He didn't say we wouldn't have anxiety and troubles, he said we are to banish them and cast them off ... in other words, get rid of them. I do that exactly as God instructed in 1 Peter 5:7, "Cast all your anxiety on him because he cares for you." I lay them all at God's feet.

I'm standing in awe of God. I'm showing up to spend time with Him every day, and it's worth it. Why? Because He's showing me how to enjoy the life He wants me to have before it melts away.

Humbleness

One day, I was thinking about how much I love my older son, Ricky (a teenager at the time). I hope that doesn't embarrass him. If I had my way as a father (and I'm sure that any parent can appreciate this), Ricky would know every single thing that I know. He would absorb every bit of wisdom, every fact, everything I could teach him. My desire is that he would learn all that stuff today and have it and use it, so that he would have the best possible life going forward. Wouldn't it be great if he didn't have to make the same mistakes I did?

But I realized something. I realized through practical experience as a father, and as a human, that it doesn't work that way. There are some things that Ricky learns from me right away. There are other things that he will learn later as he goes on in life, and there are some things that he will never learn from me at all, no matter how much I want him to.

And God must look at us the same way. It is God's desire that we would learn his instruction manual, the Bible, inside out – that we would have the benefit of all His wisdom and knowledge, so we wouldn't have to suffer and struggle, and we would have it all down. But God knows that some people learn right away and some will learn as they go along, and some won't learn until they see God face-to-face in heaven because they won't learn it while they're down here on Earth.

I know for sure that my love for Ricky is not based on how much he learns from me. As a matter of fact that has nothing to do with it. Yes, it is a desire of my heart that he learn these things, so he can have a better life, although I love him just the same, whether he does or doesn't. God loves us just the same, regardless of how quickly we learn the things He would have us learn. If it were any different, it would mean that God's love was conditional, or based on something we could do – dependent on our works, rather than His grace, rather than it being simply His gift that we should enjoy in this short earthly life we each have.

Who wouldn't want the people they love to learn important lessons without having to experience all the pain? The way I figure it, if I can get the point God is making without having to *feel* the point poking me in the chest or biting me in the butt, the better off I'll be and the better off those around me will be too. And that includes you. God has been working on me, and I am offering you the benefit of my lesson while sparing you from the pain of it.

Look at Luke 14:7–11, where Jesus is eating dinner at the house of a prominent Pharisee. Not only are the Pharisees testing Him, but they are also watching Him, trying to find anything they can use against Him. However, Jesus is watching them and has something to say about their behavior:

> When he noticed how the guests picked the places of honor at the table, he told them this parable: "When someone invites you to a wedding feast, do not take the place of honor, for a person more distinguished than you may have been invited. If so, the host who invited both of you will come and say to you, 'Give this man your seat.' Then, humiliated, you will have to take the least important place. But when you are invited, take the lowest place, so when your host comes, he will say to you, 'Friend, move up to a better place.' Then you will be honored in the presence of all your fellow guests. For everyone who exalts himself will be humbled, and he who humbles himself will be exalted."

Jesus makes multiple references in the Bible to humbleness and humility, and He is constantly telling us to humble ourselves. It is interesting to me because He doesn't say that He will humble us, although He will do that if we don't respond accordingly, and I'll cover that later, but rather, He is telling us that we need to humble ourselves.

All right, then, if I need to humble myself, how do I do that? And what does "humble" really mean? Good questions. My dictionary gave me a couple of helpful definitions of humbleness. One is that "you're reflecting, expressing, or offering in a spirit of deference or submission." The other is "that you are not proud, you are not arrogant, and you are not assertive."

Let's look at that spirit of deference or submission. Deference means submission or courteous yielding to the opinion, wishes, or judgment of another. I might have an opinion, but out of deference to my pastor, I will yield to his decision, demonstrating that in my mind and heart, he is more important than me. And is it just for our pastor that we should have a spirit of deference and submission? No! First and foremost, we are to have that spirit toward God, because every single thing we do in our lives, every action we take, every thought we think, every word we say should be in a spirit of deference to God. We should be going to God first and asking for guidance. That's what a humble person should do. Why? Simple. Because God alone has the perfect plan for your life. If you believe God, and you believe He has the perfect plan for your life, then obviously you want to defer to Him for the way to get there. You want instruction to come from Him.

Does that mean I only "take orders" from God? Not exactly. We also are instructed to submit to authority, as long as it doesn't cause us to contradict God's Word. "Everyone must submit himself to the governing authorities, for there is no authority except that which God has established. The authorities that exist have been established by God" (Romans 13:1). God's design includes governing agencies that are to govern for our good, and so we are to submit or defer to them as well.

How about that other definition? Why are pride, arrogance, and assertiveness bad? I wondered about this because there are some things I feel I've earned the right to be proud of. There are some things I'm very good at. Those traits are certainly admired in sports and in business. The problem with pride and arrogance and assertiveness is that, in God's economy, those characteristics suggest that we are in control, not God. That's the big mistake.

For you sports fans, contrast God's instruction to humble ourselves with the celebratory dances and actions of certain pro athletes. Their actions are designed to draw attention to how great they are, but in God's sight, it's foolishness because they are just doing their jobs. Why does any employee, whether it's a pro sports player or a local businessman, think it necessary to adore themselves and say, "Look at me, I'm the greatest!" when they are simply fulfilling their job description? Just imagine if your waiter or waitress did that! "Hey, aren't I great? I didn't spill your drink!" Suppose the mail carrier did that after putting the envelopes into each mailbox. "Look at the way I put that letter in your mailbox. I'm the greatest mailman of all time." You would think he was crazy. Come on, that's his job. Proverbs 27:2 tells us, "Let another praise you, and not your own mouth ..." Did you get that? If praises are to be said about you, let someone else give them, not you. Other people and God should be the ones telling you how great you are, which is certainly in contrast to the athletes, politicians, and many famous people of this world. Why are we to be different and not praise ourselves? Because the praises of man are not to be sought as our reward (Matthew 6:2, 5, 6). We do not need applause and praise from other people to pump ourselves up. Our desire should be to hear God say, when we get up to heaven, "Well done, good and faithful servant" (Matthew 25:21, 23).

Another definition of humble is to not be assertive. In our culture, being assertive has to do with *self*. It has to do with confidently expressing yourself to get what you want, and it often is associated with improving self-esteem. Did you catch the focus on self? If we are focused on confidently expressing *our* wants, desires, and goals, then we cannot be humble, and we cannot focus on what God wants.

Humble has a sister word with a similar meaning, and that word is humility. I was doing some research and learned that humility is "the quality, or state, of being humble." If you have humility, then you are being humble, and a humble person lacks all signs of pride, arrogance, and assertiveness. Having even a small amount of any of those qualities would be sin to God.

Synonyms for humble include lowly, modest, unassuming, and

meek. That last one, meek, really bothered me. I don't want to be perceived as meek, but the problem is that I'm thinking meek equals weak, and it doesn't. For those of you who are familiar with karate and other martial arts, you know that these people are some of the strongest people you will ever see, but they never use their power unless they are attacked. They are humble, and they speak softly – you've heard the phrase "Speak softly, and carry a big stick?" That's them. They don't think it is necessary to tell you how strong they are or how great they are. They know their strength and they have it if they need it. I wouldn't consider them weak. Quite the opposite.

Would you consider Jesus weak? I wouldn't. When Jesus got aggravated in the temple, He knew what to do. He turned over the table of the moneychangers and cleared the place! We are not to be weak, but there is a difference between having physical strength and knowing that you have the power of God in your life. God said all things are possible with the power of God. Knowing we have that power and walking around with it doesn't mean we are to use it out of arrogance and pride.

The opposite of humble is conceited. Do you know conceited people who believe their talent and abilities have gotten them where they are, that their success had nothing to do with God? Some Christians believe God is lucky to be working through them, as if they could accomplish anything apart from Him. Apparently, they've overlooked John 15:5, "I am the vine; you are the branches ... apart from me you can do nothing."

Bruce Wilkerson, who wrote "The Prayer of Jabez," told this story once. As he was about to preach, he remembered he had sinned. He didn't say what the specific sin was, but he asked God for forgiveness before he went up on stage to preach, and the Spirit of God spoke to him and said, "Do you realize where you would be if I took my hand off you?" And He said he got down on his knees and cried. He realized that everything he did and everything he accomplished was simply and only through God because God's hand was on him. We need to have that same realization in our lives.

In 1 Peter 5:5–6, God says, "All of you, clothe yourselves with humility towards one another, because, 'God opposes the proud but gives grace to the humble.'" Did you catch that? We are supposed to show humility toward one another, not just toward God. That's a little tougher; don't you think? That means no pride, no arrogance, and no assertiveness toward each other. Why? Because God opposes the proud and gives grace to the humble. Would you like to be God's enemy? Does it sound like fun to have God opposing you all day long?

I don't think so!

"I want some grace, God."

"Really, Jack? Then humble yourself."

As the verse concludes, in verse 6, it says, "Humble yourselves, therefore, under God's mighty hand, that he may lift you up in due time." That is a promise from God, a promise that if you humble yourself, He will lift you up when the time is right. That is God's time, by the way, and He will not be hurried.

So, let's get back to that parable Jesus told about taking a seat at the table of honor. He is very specific – don't do it. Don't grab that seat of honor, that title, that whatever it is you try to do to make yourself seem more important than you really are, because anyone who exalts himself will be humbled. We can see that so easily when it happens to others, and yet, we are often blind to our own self-exaltation.

Let's look at that in terms of our lives and in our relationship with God. Do not believe for one minute that you are worthy of the place of honor here on Earth. You are not. I am not. We are worthy of death and eternity in hell, and if not for our Lord and Savior's sacrifice on the cross, that's where we – all humanity – would be. We are invited to God's feast in heaven because of what Jesus did for us on the cross, and not because of anything we did on our own. Our works, the things we *do*, get us nowhere, and we all fall short of the glory of God (Romans 3:23), and as such, we should be grateful to God, instead of boasting about ourselves.

Let me put it like this. Say you're a fan of sports or rock-n-roll or science, and I invited you to see Bruce Springsteen (if he were your favorite), or Dan Marino (for those of us old enough to remember), or a great scientist like Albert Einstein, or a great inventor like Ben Franklin. Say, I brought you to meet these people. I find it hard to believe that you would say to Springsteen, "Yeah, you are pretty good, but I write better songs than you," or that you would look at Marino and say, "I'm a better quarterback than you," or that you would say to Albert Einstein "I'm impressed but I think I have a better formula."

I think you would be sitting there, humbled, in awe of the knowledge and ability of the person you're with. I doubt that you would be shooting your mouth off. I'd like to think you would be very respectful and very humble because you didn't get to sit with them and meet them based on anything you did. You don't know Springsteen. You don't know Marino or Einstein or Franklin. The only reason you're even there is because I got you in. I got you the meeting. I set it up. You are in on my ticket, and as such, I would think you would be on your best behavior.

That's how it is with us and God and heaven. We are saved, and we have a place in heaven because God gave it to us, not because of the things we did. Salvation is a gift from God. It is not based on works. Nobody earned it. Nobody deserved it. It's a gift (Ephesians 2:8–9). I would think that, out of respect and gratitude for the gift, absolutely we would be humbled. God says, "By the way, Jack, where is your gratitude? I paid the price of your ticket into heaven with the life of my Son, with His blood on the cross. Remember that? You couldn't pay that price, Jack, but I paid it for you."

Where is my gratitude, and where is yours? Is it buried beneath an attitude of pride and arrogance?

Have we humbled ourselves in front of God, or have we exalted ourselves? We mentioned that a little earlier. What happens if I don't obey God and don't humble myself? I am God's child, and He is my Father. If you are a parent, what would you do with a disobedient child? You'd discipline him or her, right? Same with God and His kids (us); we are His children, and God would have to do that for us. How? Sometimes, it's by removing some stuff. My kids usually get something taken away – a privilege or a freedom or a physical or material possession. When God disciplines us, He might do that, or He might choose tools like our finances or our relationships. There is usually some loss of something we consider important. Why? Because God loves us too much not to do it. Because He wants us to have His full blessing. He wants to lift us up and exalt us, but first, if we don't deal with our attitude, He will have to help us along, so to speak.

Parents, if you had a disobedient child, who was ruining his life, running away, was into crime, and you had to put him into military school to keep him from winding up dead, would you do it? Of course, you would, even if your kid didn't want to go and hated you for it. As a matter of fact that kid would probably think you were the worst parent in the world at that point. So why do it? Because you love him. You do it to save that child's life.

On a less intense scale, if your child was being disobedient, you would take away their privileges so that she could learn, be blessed, and have all the benefits of life. You discipline your child, not so that he or she would lose their life, but so that they would find it.

Maybe you're not a parent, but you have a sibling or a spouse, or a best friend who is ruining his life with a drug problem. Would you put him into rehab whether he liked it or not? Yes. Why? Because you love him. You'd do an intervention because you want what is ultimately, long term, in that person's best interest.

In the examples I've given, the troubled person is not humbling himself; he is continuing on his path, his way, unwilling to defer or submit to others, and in the end, it will destroy him. "There is a way that seems right to a man, but in the end it leads to death" (Proverbs 14:12).

It is God's preference that we humble ourselves. This is a spiritual do-it-yourself project that we can take on with God's blessing. God promises that, "He who humbles himself will be exalted." In Psalm 51:17, it says, "The sacrifices of God are a broken spirit; a broken and contrite heart, O God, you will not despise." God wants your spirit broken. Is a broken spirit aggressive or prideful? Of course not. Did you see the newspaper picture of Saddam Hussein (the former Iraqi dictator) when he was captured and came out of the hole in 2003? That was a broken spirit, but guess what? They cleaned him up, fed him, and he got cocky again.

Unfortunately, we're like that with God. He bails us out of an emergency – someone is dying, or there is some financial crisis or health crisis or some other crisis – and we pray, and God bails us out, and then what? For two or three days, or even a couple of weeks, we are the most humble people in the world ... and then we forget. We are right back to ourselves, back into doing what we want. God wants us humble and broken. What's the downside for us if we choose not to humble ourselves? Go back to Psalm 51:17, and you'll see that if we don't have a broken spirit and a broken and contrite heart, then God will despise us. That's right. "God opposes the proud, but gives grace to the humble" (Proverbs 3:34, James 4:6).

In Proverbs 18:12, God says, "Before his downfall a man's heart is proud, but humility comes before honor." If your heart is proud, you will have a downfall – not maybe, not possibly, not if. You *will* fall down if you are proud. That is a promise from God, but because He loves you, He will also be there to pick you up. Bob Dylan once wrote "I've been broken, shattered like an empty cup and I'm just waiting on the Lord to rebuild and fill me up." God sometimes has to shatter us and break us, so He can pick us up, rebuild us, and fill us up again. If you want glory and honor from God, you need to be humble and submissive. Humility and humbleness come before honor, just like gas goes in the tank before you drive, and the ticket goes to the usher before you get into the stadium. It is a requirement. You can't get into the stadium without your ticket. You can't drive your car without gas. You can't have honor without humility. God is really clear about this.

God tells us again in Proverbs 15:33, "The fear of the Lord teaches a man wisdom, and humility comes before honor." And again in Proverbs 22:4, "Humility and the fear of the Lord bring wealth and honor and life." Okay, let's try this both ways. Which do you want – poverty, disgrace, and death or wealth, honor, and life? No, God, I don't want wealth, honor, and life. Just give me poverty, disgrace, and death. What idiot would think like that? Of course, you'd want wealth and honor and life! And God says that humility and fear of the Lord will bring those things.

But God tells us to fear Him in awesome reverence of His power (Hebrews 12:28). You can fear someone's power but still love him. You can serve that person out of love. I certainly fear God's power because He is awesome, and I know that He has the power to do what He says He will do. I am in awe of that power, and I also fear it, so I would fear being disobedient to God because I believe His Word, but I serve Him out of love and respect and gratitude and humbleness.

Maybe you've had that experience with a coach or a teacher in your life who had great authority or power. You liked the coach, but you also feared him because you knew how great his authority and power was.

When I wanted to learn how to drive harness horses as a hobby, I sought out some experienced trainers and listened to everything they told me. I listened out of fear and respect – fear because I didn't want to get killed (the horses are going really fast), but also out of respect because I knew they knew what they were talking about. There was no doubt in my mind that they knew how to do it. Well, God is telling us the same exact thing. There is a perfect plan for each and every one of our lives. We don't have the plan; God has the plan and the power to make it happen.

And if the Creator of all things has a plan specifically designed for you and for me, then shouldn't that cause us to humble ourselves? In Isaiah 66:2, God says, "'Has not my hand made all these things, so they came into being?' declares the Lord. 'This is the one I esteem: he who is humble and contrite in spirit, and trembles at my word.'" Could He be any clearer? Contrite means to have a repentant heart, to be sorrowful about your mistakes. This is the person God esteems, the person He lifts up, the one He exalts.

Ironic, isn't it? The God who has all power over all things lifts us up when we admit our mistakes, while so often, in our fallen human nature, we, who do not have much power, even over a few things, want to criticize and condemn others for their mistakes. Why? Because we often operate with an inflated sense of our own importance, and as such, we are not humbling ourselves. Paul warns against this in Romans 12:3, "For by the grace given me I say to every one of you: Do not think of yourself more highly than you ought ...." We have a natural ability to compare ourselves with others so that we can look good, no matter what is going on, and yet, that comparison is pointless. We're all sinners. We all fall short of the glory of God (Romans 3:23), and so the only comparison we should be making is between Jesus and ourselves. How am I doing compared to Him? How are you doing compared to Him? God's requirement for admission into heaven is absolute perfection, and the only way any of us meets that requirement is by faith in the perfect work of Jesus Christ. We can't do it on our own. I can't raise my status in God's sight by earning it, by doing more, giving more, sacrificing more. Once I am saved, my status in God's sight is that I am adopted into His family as a son, and He loves me, period.

And if that's true for me, it's true for every believer because we are all His children. Shouldn't that affect the way I live my life? Yes. In Ephesians 4:1–3, Paul says, "As a prisoner for the Lord, then, I urge you to live a life worthy of the calling you have received. Be completely humble and gentle; be patient, bearing with one another in love. Make every effort to keep the unity of the Spirit through the bond of peace." God called you and me to live a life worthy of the calling we received. If we have this free gift of salvation, we are not supposed to chuck it or ignore it. We are supposed to reflect it and glorify God through our lives and spread the Word. How do we do that? Paul says number one on the list is to be completely humble and gentle – not a little bit, not some, but *completely* humble and gentle.

That doesn't come easy for me. I don't always want to be humble or gentle, but I do want to be obedient to God's Word. Sometimes, it helps me deal with it if I get as literal as possible with the issue at hand. For example, I know I struggle with being completely humble and gentle ... how could I force the issue with myself? How about this – I picture myself wearing a sign all day, everywhere I go, a sign that says, "I am completely humble." I really believe that my actions would be different, including inside my own home.

How about you? How would your actions change if you had to wear that sign today? Tomorrow? At the next department meeting or family gathering? Whether it's a literal sign or not, as Christians, we are walking advertisements for Christ. If I asked your spouse or your co-worker or your neighbor to describe you to me, and I wrote their description on a sign that you would wear the next day, what would they say about you? What would be written on that sign you would be wearing?

If we are not completely humble, we are not reflecting Christ. If we are in charge, and we make decisions apart from God's Word, then we are not submissive to God's Spirit, we are not humble, and God won't exalt us. Coming from a business environment, where the goal is to exalt yourself and achieve success in the eyes of other people, the idea that God wants me to be humble so *He* can exalt me and bless me was a huge revelation for me. The longer I've been a Christian, the more I want to realize God's full blessing in my life. I want to be exalted by Him, not by myself or by other people.

And I truly believe that God has the power and the choice to exalt me or not. That really does influence me. I know I'm prideful. There are some things I think I'm good at and some things I'm proud of.

God said to me, "Jack, you do nothing good, and you have nothing to be proud of. Yes, there are things I can accomplish with My power working through you, if you let Me, but it's Me working through you, not you doing it."

So, I have to make some changes in my life. Me, the big shot, the king, the general, the man in charge, has to give up his position, and so do you, regardless of what earthly positions or titles you have. We have a choice to make today, a choice to make about going forward. How are we going to live the rest of our lives?

If we continue to live the same way and don't humble ourselves, if we continue to exalt ourselves, then we miss the prize, we miss the Lord's blessings because we are not following His instructions. We need to make a conscious decision about whether we will feed the spirit or the flesh. The one you feed will live; the one you starve will die. If you wanted to lose weight, you couldn't just think about it; you would have to make a conscious decision. If you wanted to go into the gym and rebuild your muscles, you couldn't just think about it. You would have to decide to go back to the gym and start to work out each and every day.

We have to do the same thing with our spiritual muscles. We have to flex them to build them up, and we have to make a conscious decision today to do it, regardless of the spiritual high or low we're experiencing at the moment. I've been to Promise Keepers conferences (a 2-day gathering of Christian men of all denominations), and I've heard some great sermons, and I have walked out of those events totally fired up. And guess what? I go back to my regular life – and it doesn't take long before the waves of the world come crashing in at me, and I start to be with the world again – and by Tuesday, Wednesday, Thursday, I forget about Promise Keepers. I'm finished, and that rush of inspiration has faded. I have to live in my day to day life, making one choice at a time to humble myself before the Lord so that He will lift me up in due time.

James 4:10 says, "Humble yourselves before the Lord, and he will lift you up." The opposite of that is if you don't humble yourself, He won't lift you up. It's pretty simple. If we are assertive as Christians, if we jump to decisions without consulting God because we think we know best, if we don't seek God's counsel, it means we are acting out of arrogance, and that is always going to turn into a disaster. We want wealth and honor and to be exalted by God, but it's ironic and sad that we are not willing to do what God tells us to do to get it.

It's not like we can pretend that we don't know what He wants from us. Philippians 2:3 says, "Do nothing out of selfish ambition or vain conceit, but in humility consider others better than yourselves." If we are not doing this, we should prayerfully ask God to break us so that we can be obedient. There is a tremendous blessing for brokenness. God broke me at age 36. I had been saved for three years, but I wasn't growing spiritually. It wasn't until He broke me and took everything away that I was able to say, "God, I don't care what happens next. I lost all my money, my marriage, and my friends, but God I don't care what happens next, I'm with you wherever you want to take me. If you want me on the street corner shining shoes, that's fine. I'll go there and let's do that. I just want to be with you." Everything I ever tried to do in my life had just gotten me nowhere except the gutter, beaten and disgusted, but when I said, "Lord, I'm yours," my life changed from that point on in a big way. During that time of brokenness, God gave me a verse to hold on to, and it's still my life verse: Matthew 6:33, "But seek first his kingdom and his righteousness, and all these things will be given to you as well." I put God first, and my life changed.

I'm like the lost sheep in scripture. We don't get the whole sheep and shepherd thing in our culture, so let me give you a quick explanation of why it's significant. The shepherd's job is to take care of the sheep in the field. If the sheep runs away, the shepherd goes after him, catches him, and – ouch – breaks his leg. That might seem cruel. Is he punishing the sheep? Actually no, he does it to protect the animal in the long run. You see, if the shepherd can't watch the sheep, the sheep will wander off and be eaten by a wild animal. Because he loves the sheep and doesn't want that to happen, the shepherd breaks the sheep's leg, and then carries him around on his neck until the leg heals. He carries the sheep for a month, two months, for as long as it takes, and when the leg is finally healed, he puts him down, and the sheep never leaves the shepherd's side again.

That is what God is doing when He breaks us. He is training us to trust Him and to stay close to Him, so we can be safe.

I have no desire to leave God's side again. I've been broken, and I know what it means. It's worthwhile, but it's not fun, and so, as I read scripture and pray and meditate, I try to find those lessons where I can learn the point without having to feel the point piercing my heart. One of those lessons God has been teaching me is to humble myself, and my heart's desire is that you, like my son Ricky, would learn from them so you don't have to learn these lessons the hard way.

Here are some things I've been learning about the characteristics of a humble person. This person doesn't yell, doesn't accuse, doesn't always have to be right (a big problem with me), doesn't curse, and is not quick to point out faults in others. He lives by the serenity prayer. Anybody who has been in A.A. (Alcoholics Anonymous) or N.A. (Narcotics Anonymous) is familiar with it. Here's the serenity prayer: "God, grant me the serenity to accept the things I cannot change, the courage to change the things I can, and the wisdom to know the difference." That's a good prayer to live by, although you won't find it in the Bible. If I'm a humble person and you cut me off in traffic, I don't scream, but I also don't cut you off. A humble person never seeks revenge because he or she trusts God's judgment for everything. A humble person should be soft-spoken and not have to be right about everything. (And yes, I put that one in there twice because it's that important!) There's no gossiping, no spreading or listening to rumors or lies; speak only the truth, let your yes be yes and your no be no. That, to me, would be a humble person.

Can you describe yourself that way? Better yet, would others describe you that way? Do you want others to describe you that way?

My challenge to you today is the same challenge that God gave me – Are you going to continue to live the same way, or are you going to humble yourself? The sooner you humble yourself, the sooner God will begin to bless you. Who wouldn't want that?

When you finish this chapter, I invite you to humble yourself before the Lord by getting on your knees and asking Him to show you, on His terms, the stuff you need to deal with. Little by little, day by day, He will show you things and actions you need to take, and as you continue to grow as a believer in Jesus Christ, He will keep showing you the stuff He wants you to work on. Why? Not because it will make God love you any more, but *because* God loves you and wants to exalt you and bless you in this lifetime, because the more things you can learn here, the more you can access the full blessings God wants to give you, and the fewer things you're going to need to learn the hard way.

The more you humble yourself, the more the God of the universe will exalt you. Who wouldn't want that?

Follow Directions

When all else fails, read the directions. Or stop, and ask for some.

Many of us could have avoided years of frustration with that blinking light on the VCR if we'd just read the directions. Or we could have gotten to that new restaurant an hour sooner if we'd stopped and asked someone how to get there.

Maybe it's pride, maybe it's just that we're in too much of a hurry, but something about the word "directions" makes us run the other way. Reading or asking for directions is an admission of ignorance. It blatantly announces to our ego and anyone in the room that we have no clue and need help from a wiser, better-informed expert, only to find such silly advice as this little gem from a hairdryer manual: "Do not use while sleeping." Or the one on the bottom of a bakery dessert box that says, "Do not turn upside down."

Sometimes, people even ignore the verbal, step-by-step instructions that their GPS is giving them as they are driving. What's up with that? Why buy the GPS if you're going to ignore it?

Just about anything we can buy comes with a set of instructions on how to use and care for the item, and if that little leaflet or label or manual is missing, we can always backtrack to the brand name, the designer, or manufacturer and request the instructions.

Follow directions. How simple is that? You take a drive, you get directions, and you follow the signs, right?

Lately I've been thinking a lot about signs, probably because of all the construction I'm dodging in South Florida. And I'm thinking especially about signs from God and signs of the world. Signs usually communicate a direction to go, an informational message, a safety warning, or an instruction.

For instance, in my usual commute, I see a sign that says "I-95 North." When I need to head north along the east coast of Florida, I follow that sign. If I don't, I won't get where I want to go.

One of my favorite instructional signs is at the gas station, "Do not ignite match while fueling," unless you would like to get to heaven ahead of schedule.

Does God give us signs? Absolutely. Do his signs give directions? Information? Warnings and instructions? Yes, yes, yes, and yes. Scripture abounds with signs from God that are there for our blessing, to guide us in life, to inform us about God's will, to warn us about disobeying Him, and to instruct us in how we should live.

Sometimes, we don't feel like we're heading to heaven. We thought the journey would make us carefree and giddy, but now we I've got a flat tire or a steaming radiator. We're grumpy and annoyed, mad and confused. Been there? I have. What happened? You know for certain that you're a Christian, but are you missing the peace of God in your heart? Are you tense and aggravated? Do you feel a void, as if something's missing in your life? Are you wondering what your purpose is in life?

For example, if I put bread in my toaster and it doesn't work, it's broken. Yes, it's still a toaster, but it's not fulfilling the purpose for which it was designed because something is keeping it from functioning the way it is supposed to. And yes, you can still be a Christian, but you, too, can reach a point where you are not fulfilling the purpose for which God designed you because something is coming between you and God – something that is keeping your spiritual life from functioning the way it is supposed to.

Life can be like that. We are created in the image of God, and He gives us the best set of directions we could ask for, and that's the Bible. It truly is an instruction manual from THE designer of eternity for living an abundant life, whether we're on the highway or the country lane, as long as we stay focused on the road and don't get distracted by the things around us. Otherwise, we can miss the turn or the warning and land in the ditch.

We can cover up the Holy Spirit with things of the world. We can fill ourselves with lust, rage, jealousy, malice, envy, and so on (spend some time in Colossians Chapter 3, and you'll have a pretty good menu of sins to choose from). God tells us to cast these things off. Get rid of them. If you have crap building up on your battery connections, you clean it off to make sure you're getting the best possible connection to the battery, right? Same thing, spiritually speaking.

We can also distort our connection to God by putting worldly things ahead of the Spirit. Just as various obstacles, including harmless ones like tree limbs, can distort or ruin a satellite dish's effectiveness in transmitting its signal to you, so, too, can things like money, career, possessions, or exercise (all innocent enough until they start creeping into the driver's seat of our lives) get between us and God. When other things take priority over our relationship with God, when we start saying things like, "We'll go back to church once the kids' sports schedules settle down," we have put God in the backseat. We will stop seeing the signs of God in our lives, and we will stop being signs for God in our families and communities.

When that happens, we lose our joy, our peace, our contentment, and then we lose our effectiveness as signs to others in the world.

If I was a policeman and I wore my police uniform, you'd know what I do for a living. You'd know I'm a policeman. If you saw me at the airport and I wore my pilot's uniform, you'd know what I do. The greatest sign that you and I can give as Christians to an unbelieving world is to live our lives sold out to Jesus Christ, so people can simply look at our lives and know without a doubt that we are Christians.

Jesus gives us a great piece of information we can use to influence what others would write on a sign about us: "By this all men will know that you are my disciples, if you love one another" (John 13:35). Loving others is one sign that people should be able to see in our lives, every minute of our day. Honestly, if I hung a sign around your neck that said, "Loves other people, especially other Christians," would your church-mates laugh or nod in agreement? What about your family and co-workers and neighbors? Would they be quick to give examples of how you showed Christ's love to them by acts of kindness, or would they roll their eyes and walk away?

I started thinking about how we can get stubborn and screw up the directions because we think we have a better way, even though the directions are typically written by an expert on the topic. And, usually, it's because we have an attitude that exalts our own opinion above anyone else's. Nowhere is this more apparent than in dealing with teenagers.

I want to share the things with you that God's been laying on my heart, and it starts with a trip we took to Boston to take our son Rick up to college in 2006. He was a freshman in the Berklee School of Music, a very prestigious music school. I was a little overwhelmed with emotion, as I remembered some of the times and troubles we'd had with him growing up – times when he so clearly was on a path to something bad, and we had to force him to follow directions to straighten himself out.

One example was years earlier when he was engaging in a behavior that some teenagers do these days. It's called cutting. It's actually a cry for attention. They cut themselves, hopefully not too far in, but still, it can be pretty deep. It's kind of like Russian roulette. They see how deep they can go. When we discovered this, my wife and I talked to Rick and said, "This kind of behavior isn't cool. What's going on?"

He said, "Oh, don't worry about it."

"Not an acceptable answer. If you don't want to talk to us, you're going to have to talk to a counselor."

"I'm not talking to any counselors, no way."

Rick was about 16 at the time, so we still had authority over him. After much refusing on his part, we ultimately forced him to go, and fortunately, that counselor helped him. The cutting didn't become an issue, and we were very thankful.

The point is that he didn't want to follow our directions, even though we knew what was best. He exalted his opinion and judgment above those of his parents, under whose authority he still lived. And so we forced him to go, even though he didn't want to, and even though he fought against us. It's been a pattern in his life, where we've had to demand his obedience and hold him accountable.

About a year before this cutting incident, he decided he'd had enough with the saxophone lessons. He was in high school and had been taking lessons since he was a little boy.

He said, "I want to quit. I don't want to play anymore. I'm done with the sax."

Beth and I looked him dead in the eye, and we said, "No, you're not. You will be taking saxophone lessons until you finish high school, and then if you decide that you don't want to play anymore, fine. But we've invested in that saxophone, and you are taking lessons until you're out of high school." And he did.

And finally, he was preparing to leave for college. He was madly in love with his girlfriend, who was a year younger, meaning she would be a high school senior during his freshman year of college. Because of that, he did not want to go to the Berklee College of Music, which, if you're not aware, is one of the top jazz music schools in the country, so this was the opportunity of a lifetime for him. It's like getting to play baseball with the New York Yankees. Just an unbelievable opportunity. And his response?

"No, I don't want to go. I want to stay here. I'll go to FAU (Florida Atlantic University)," a local university, so he could be closer to his girlfriend.

I said, "Son, there's nothing wrong with FAU. It's a fine school, but it's not the Berklee School of Music."

"I don't care. That's where I want to go. I know best."

Beth and I had already conferred on our position, so I said, "Okay, if you want to go there, you can, but there's just one thing."

"What's that?"

"The only check that we're writing is to the Berklee College of Music. So, if you want to go to FAU, good luck, pal. I'm sure you can round up some student loans." After a dose of Dad's medicine, with an extra helping of financial reality, he went to Berklee.

Granted, neither the sax lessons nor the college choice was a life-threatening decision, but each had life-implications attached to it. Because Beth and I are older and have a longer perspective than Rick, we understood those implications and chose to intervene. Not long after the FAU versus Berklee "discussions," he actually thanked us for not letting him quit the saxophone because now he loves music and jazz, and it brings him great joy and happiness. Beth and I know that, one day, he'll be thanking us for sending him to Berklee. And we also know that whether he says thanks or not, we probably saved his life by insisting that he visit that counselor to deal with the cutting issue.

We had to say no to our son multiple times because we love him. Occasionally, those choices dealt with serious behaviors that were leading him far off of God's instructions for life. And guess what? Rick didn't agree a lot of the time. As a matter of fact he was upset with us on several occasions because of our saying no. And then I thought about the times that God says no to us because He loves us so much, because He knows for sure what's in our best interest, and because even if we don't like it, He loves us too much to let us mess up our lives. I was just overwhelmed with gratitude to God for the times that He said no in my life.

We took Rick to Boston, and I have to tell you it was a big financial sacrifice to send him to that school. It's very expensive. We flew up with him, and he was kind of overwhelmed by the circumstances, but suffice it to say, he didn't say thank you. Hey, he's 18; that's not so unusual.

We didn't send him to Berklee to hear him say thank you. That was okay. I didn't expect that, although considering the amount of money we spent, a thank you might have been nice. I couldn't help but think of all the times that I don't say thank you to God or even to my own parents. When we got home from Boston, I went to my parents' house. My dad was 75, and my mom was 71 at that time. I said "Hey, I don't know if I've ever said this to you, but thank you for the sacrifices you made in my life to give me everything you possibly could."

And then, I thought about God and the sacrifice God made. And you know the sacrifice – Jesus on the cross. What more of a sacrifice could there be? I was overwhelmed with gratitude to God for doing that for us. It makes me want to be completely sold out to God, and it made me wonder, where am I distracted from Him? What am I focused on? Am I focused on my flesh, on my earthly desires and ambitions, or am I focused on the Spirit? If we're focused wrongly, if we are focused on the flesh, the good news is that we can always turn around and come back to God, and do the right thing by following the directions He gives us in His Word.

God wants us to spend eternity with Him in heaven and His

Word, the Bible, gives us directions to follow, so we'll end up in the right place. According to the "Original Manufacturer" (God himself) the road to heaven is through Jesus Christ. That's probably the most important direction of all.

Does the Bible also give us warnings? Yes, it does. Certainly, there are many warnings that deal with our physical and relational safety, but I'm focusing on our spiritual life. If I choose to ignore the "Spiritual Danger" sign, I also am choosing the consequences of whatever danger comes at me. Is there a consequence for ignoring or not following (disobeying) God's signs?

Absolutely. God tells us that on Judgment Day, we will be accountable for and judged on everything we did (Matthew 12:36, Romans 14:12, Hebrews 4:13). He warns us clearly, several times. Just consider the Parable of the Talents in Matthew 25:14–28: We will be held accountable for making good use of the gifts Jesus gave us. In this sense, "gift" is referring to spiritual gifts (your talents and abilities and the way God wired you as a person, unique and individual and one of a kind ... just like snowflakes). To the servant that pleased the master by the way he used the talents, his master said, "'Well done, good and faithful servant! You have been faithful with a few things; I will put you in charge of many things. Come and share your master's happiness'" (Matthew 25:23).

What are we supposed to do with these gifts God gives us? God specifically tells us how we can put our spiritual gifts and talents to work. "You did not choose me, but I chose you and appointed you to go and bear fruit – fruit that will last" (John 15:16). One way we can quickly be about the business of bearing fruit is to "Live such good lives among the pagans that, though they accuse you of doing wrong, they may see your good deeds and glorify God on the day he visits us" (1 Peter 2:12). A different translation, The Message, puts it this way: "Live an exemplary life among the natives so that your actions will refute their prejudices. Then they'll be won over to God's side and be there to join in the celebration when he arrives." When people are won over to Christ because of the way you lived your life, you are producing fruit that will last for eternity.

God has warned us that He expects us to use our gifts for His glory. Living to bring God glory simply means that what we do causes others to have a favorable view of God and that we give God the credit for our abilities and for the good things that others see in us. What happens when we don't do that? What happens when we ignore His warnings? Listen to how God weeps over those who ignore His sign: "O Jerusalem, Jerusalem, you who kill the prophets and stone those sent to you, how often I have longed to gather your children together, as a hen gathers her chicks under her wings, but you were not willing. Look, your house is left to you desolate" (Matthew 23:37–38).

God is using that verse to speak to every believer today. God says, "I wanted to gather you. I wanted to nurture you and grow you and love you. I wanted to teach you. I wanted to shower every possible blessing on you, but you weren't willing." As a parent, I know how much I love my kids and how much I want to bless them with every possible blessing. I cannot imagine the sorrow and rejection I would feel if they were not willing to receive those blessings from me, if they were indifferent or even hostile to what I had to offer them, and me. If you are not willing to receive what God has to give you, He is very clear: Your house will be left desolate. For Jerusalem, this meant the temple would be spiritually empty, deserted of God's presence. And for us, it means we will be disconnected from God because there is static in our communication line. We will not lose our salvation, but we will lose God's peace and joy and contentment and we will find ourselves once again bouncing across the rough shoulder of the road to heaven, rather than cruising in the paved lane. When you feel void of the Holy Spirit, check your "willingness to receive" gauge. The Holy Spirit is still living in you, but you've been drowning Him out, and as a result, you won't get the benefits and blessings that God wanted you to have.

After almost 20 years as a believer, I still struggle with the things of the world on a daily basis. I have to work at refocusing my life on God's will, refocusing each and every day by praying, "God, how can I serve You better? How can I get closer to You?"

Scripture says, "Come near to God and he will come near to you" (James 4:8). It doesn't say, "Go get yourself lost back in the world." And how easily I can do just that, lose myself back in the world because of anger, unwholesome talk, bitterness and more, and when I do that, I grieve the Holy Spirit (Ephesians 4:17–32). I'll interrupt the blessings that God has for my life. God longs for us to heed His signs, so we can go in the right direction with our lives. When we don't, there are consequences. Remember the Parable of the Barren Fig Tree in Luke 13:6–9 – "If it bears fruit next year, fine! If not, then cut it down."

How long will God have to look for the fruit in your life and mine? I believe God is telling me, "I've looked at your life, and I want to see fruit, Jack – real fruit. You're a mature Christian now. It's not as if you got saved yesterday. You have talents. You have gifts I've given you. I want to see you using them for My kingdom because, otherwise, you're useless."

Are we like that fig tree? We're in God's kingdom being cared for, but we're not producing fruit for God.

This isn't new. In the Old Testament, God had to use signs and miracles to get the attention of Pharaoh as well as his own people. And in the New Testament times, many people demanded a sign from Jesus, and many demand a sign from Him today. Well, guess what? God was upset with those demands in the past, and He's upset with those demands today. Why? Because asking for a sign shows a lack of faith. It really means, "I don't believe you. Prove it to me."

An example of this is found in Matthew 12:38–39. "Then some of the Pharisees and teachers of the law said to [Jesus], 'Teacher, we want to see a miraculous sign from you.' He answered, 'A wicked and adulterous generation asks for a miraculous sign! But none will be given it except the sign of the prophet Jonah.'" Basically they were daring Him to prove He was God. Not a good idea.

The Bible says (Luke 11:30), "For as Jonah became a sign to the Ninevites, so also the Son of Man will be [a sign] to this generation." God says, "No sign for you, folks, other than Christ. That's all the sign you need. You have your sign and you don't see it and you don't get it and you don't understand it. Are you blind?"

Why are they wicked if they ask for a sign? They are wicked because asking God to "prove it" after He's already done so much shows a lack of faith and reveals the unbelief in their hearts. You remember the story of Thomas in John 20:19–28? The resurrected Jesus appears to some of the disciples, and they are overcome with joy. They run back to tell everybody else, "Jesus is back, just like He promised. It's the greatest thing ever. Our Lord is risen." And Thomas doesn't believe.

"What do you mean you don't believe it, Thomas? We saw the Lord. He is risen. He's back."

And Thomas says nope, "Unless I see the nail marks in His hands and put my finger where the nails were, and put my hand into His side, I will not believe it" (John 20:25). Do you hear the "Prove it to me" underneath Thomas' statement?

Shortly after that, Jesus appears smack in the middle of the room with the disciples and there's Thomas. Jesus calls him out, saying, "Put your finger here; see my hands. Reach out your hand and put it into my side. Stop doubting and believe" (John 20:27). Thomas touches Him, and falls down to his knees on the floor, and says in verse 28, "My Lord and my God!"

And Jesus says, in verse 29, "... 'Because you have seen me, you have believed; blessed are those who have not seen and yet have believed.'"

Jesus' response to those who were still looking for signs, for proof, was very clear. Even if I gave you a sign, you still wouldn't believe Me because it's not about the signs; it's about your lack of faith. He presents a great example of this in Luke 16:19–31 about the rich man and Lazarus. In the story, a rich man dies and a poor beggar named Lazarus dies, and they both go their separate ways. As God would have it, the rich man goes to hell. Lazarus, who was poor all his life, is up with Abraham in heaven. Here's the passage:

> So he (the rich man) called to him, "Father Abraham, have pity on me and send Lazarus to dip the tip of his finger in water and cool my tongue, because I am in agony in this fire." But Abraham replied, "Son, remember that in your lifetime you received your good things, while Lazarus received bad things, but now he is comforted here and you are in agony. And besides all this, between us and you a great chasm has been fixed, so that those who want to go from here to you cannot, nor can anyone cross over from there to us." He answered, "Then I beg you, father, send Lazarus to my father's house, for I have five brothers. Let him warn them, so that they will not also come to this place of torment." Abraham replied, "They have Moses and the Prophets; let them listen to them." "No, father Abraham," he said, "but if someone from the dead

goes to them, they will repent." He said to him, "If they do not listen to Moses and the Prophets, they will not be convinced even if someone rises from the dead."

Jesus is pointing out that, even if Lazarus had appeared from the dead, the brothers wouldn't have believed Him because of the hardness of their hearts. What about you? Will God condemn you for your lack of faith or for your lack of belief in all that He is? I'm not talking about whether you're saved; I'm talking about what you did with your faith. Did you live, fully believing God and taking Him at His word or not? Or are you waiting for your own sign, your personal telegram if you will, to tell you what to do? If so, why? You already know what God wants you to do with your life. He wants you to go and make disciples. He wants you to bear fruit, fruit that will last (John 15:16).

You have your instructions. You don't need to pray about that. If you asked me, "What time is church?" and I said, "10:30," and you said, "What time is church?" and I said, "10:30," and you said, "Yeah, but what time is church?" and I said, "10:30," what part of 10:30 wasn't clear? God says you're to go and bear fruit. You're to go and make disciples. Go! Get going. Just do it!

Obedient Christians have no excuse to sit at home waiting and praying for a sign from God about what they are to do with their gifts and talents.

On the other hand, disobedient Christians are, sadly, prone to procrastination ... is that really what You want me to do, Lord? If it's really Your desire for me to share my faith with the guy next door, then give me a sign ... have him walk over here and ask me point blank how to become a Christian.

The religious leaders of Jesus' day were like that. In spite of all they'd witnessed, the Pharisees and Sadducees didn't see who Jesus was, and so they asked for a sign. Jesus admonished them, and He admonishes you and me. Look at Matthew 16:1–4: "The Pharisees and Sadducees came to Jesus and tested him by asking him to show them a sign from heaven. He replied, 'When evening comes, you say, 'It will be fair weather, for the sky is red,' and in the morning, 'Today it will be stormy, for the sky is red and overcast.' You know how to interpret the appearance of the sky, but you cannot interpret the signs of the times."

I can imagine Jesus shaking His head, disgusted with these scholars, the ones who studied the scriptures and should have known, should have recognized all the signs that had accompanied his life on Earth. It's as if He's saying, hey, guys, you know when it's going to rain, you know how to interpret the signs of the world, but you can't interpret spiritual signs? Come on! You're the religious leaders here. You know about the feeding of the 5,000, the raising of Lazarus from the dead, the healings, the blind being given their sight, and on and on, but still, you want more signs? How many more will it take? What's the magic number, so you'll believe?

Are you like that? Do you need some magic number of signs before you'll take Jesus at His word?

The Bible says, "Jesus did many other things as well. If every one of them were written down, I suppose that even the whole world would not have room for the books that would be written" (John 21:25).

Jesus says to us, "Don't you get it? If you don't believe based on My word, then at least believe based on what you see."

Now really, what kind of idiot would I be if you were holding a microphone, and you said to me, "This is a microphone," and I said, "I don't believe you"?

"OK," you say, "we'll turn it on. Testing, testing, yeah it works. See? It's a microphone."

And still, I say, "But I don't believe you."

"What do you mean you don't believe me? It's a microphone. Put it up to your mouth, and talk! If you're not going to believe me at this point, you're just an idiot, or else, you're the most stubborn person alive."

Jesus is saying, "If you don't want to believe Me based on faith," which is what all our belief should be based on, "then believe Me based on what you see." Do you dare deny God when the signs are right there in plain sight?

Don't Get Lost!

So, what other sign do we need? We have everything. God has given us His Holy Spirit to guide and teach us. He has given us His Word, the signs He wants us to follow, including directions, information, warnings, and instructions for how to live the life He has called us to live, so we can be signs for the lost, signs that will point them to the right road.

God gives us lots of signs, but the ultimate sign was Jesus on the cross, making a way, a road, for us to go to heaven. I don't mean to sound harsh, but I believe God is saying to every one of us today, just like the parable of the fig tree, which I translate to mean, "I want to see some fruit. I want to see you living out what you say you believe, so you can be a sign for others to follow."

Listen to the warning God gave His disciples because this warning applies to us today. In Mark 13, Jesus begins warning the disciples about the Great Tribulation to come. He's telling them to be prepared. Based on what we're seeing in the world right now, many people believe that the Tribulation is closer than ever. Listen to what Jesus says in verse 15:

> Let no one on the roof of his house go down or enter the house to take anything out... How dreadful it will be

in those days for pregnant women and nursing mothers! Pray that this will not take place in winter, because those will be days of distress unequaled from the beginning, when God created the world, until now – and never to be equaled again. If the Lord had not cut short those days, no one would survive. But for the sake of the elect, whom he has chosen, he has shortened them.

The elect are you and I, the children of God. And for our sake, God shortened those days.

So, here's Jesus warning of this worst situation you can ever imagine. He continues His warning in verse 23, "So be on your guard; I have told you everything ahead of time." Do you see? God loves us so much that He told us everything ahead of time. We have nothing to worry about. We know exactly how the story ends, and that's with us in heaven with God.

Have you ever seen the Jimmy Stewart movie, *It's a Wonderful Life*? It's one of my favorites. I watch it every Christmas, and you know what? When the cops come to arrest Jimmy Stewart because they think he embezzled the money from the bank, I don't worry. I laugh. I laugh because I know, at the end of the movie, I'm going to hear him say, "I'm the richest man alive because I have friends." I know how the movie ends. I don't panic. Jimmy doesn't go to jail; instead, he lives happily ever after.

It's like Batman or Superman when you were a kid. There's Batman, Mr. Freeze has him, and there's a chainsaw about to cut him in half. You know he's not dying and you know he's getting out. You might not know how, but there's got to be a show next week. Of course, he's getting out. You know how it ends.

And that's the point. We know how it ends. We should have no concern, no worries, and no cares. We should be leaping and rejoicing. Our salvation is assured. Our place in heaven is assured. God has defeated Satan. God has defeated death, and we're going to reign with Him forever because we know the end of the story.

But Jesus gives us a warning about the end. He gives us an instruction and directions to follow. "I tell you the truth, anyone who will not receive the kingdom of God like a little child will never enter it" (Mark

10:15). What does it mean to receive the kingdom of God like a little child? Well, let me tell you.

It became clear to me in 2006 when my son Jackson was four, and my daughter Talia was two. Things will change at some point, but at that time, Daddy was the king of the world. Whatever Daddy says goes. If I say it, it's so. No question, no concern, no worry. For example, we come home from church, and I say, "Kids, we're going to Chuck E. Cheese."

And they respond, "Yay, Daddy's the greatest, we're going to Chuck E. Cheese." Not one question such as, "Dad, is there enough gas in the car to get us there? Dad, do you have enough money in your pocket to pay for the pizza? Dad, you better call ahead and make sure they're open." No. No worry, no concern, no care. Why? Their father told them so and they believe right now that whatever their father says is true, and it is. I have no motivation to lie to them.

God says the same thing to us. "I'm your father. I love you, and you're to believe Me and trust Me, even if you don't understand how things happen. Just trust Me, and believe Me." We get so concerned sometimes about *how* God is going to do things that we often lose our faith and our trust and allow the anxieties and worries of the world to come in and knock us down because we flinched. We got scared. We doubted God, and so we couldn't follow His directions to trust and believe.

The way you get the full benefit of God and the full blessing is you believe Him fully. It's called faith, "... being sure of what we hope for and certain of what we do not see" (Hebrews 11:1). It's easy to say I have faith, until I have a problem, and I can't see how it's going to be resolved. Will I be certain of what I do not see? Will I be certain that God, who is all-powerful and all-knowing and who has my eternal best interest in mind at all times, will handle it even if I can't see how? If I doubt my God, then I have to wonder if my faith is real.

Doubting God prevents us from experiencing God's work in our lives. He said so Himself in James 1:5–8: "If any of you lacks wisdom, he should ask God, who gives generously to all without finding fault, and it will be given to him. But when he asks, he must believe and not doubt, because he who doubts is like a wave of the sea, blown and tossed by the wind. That man should not think he will receive anything from the Lord; he is a double minded man, unstable in all he does."

The man who doubts should not expect to receive anything from the Lord. Why? Because "... without faith, it is impossible to please God ...." Which man are you? And I ask myself, "Which man am I?"

Am I the man who believes God like a little child, or am I the man who doubts? There's no in-between. You're either one or the other. And in my life, I want to make sure that I have surrendered all, that I have completely trusted God as innocently as those little children.

If you have doubt, if you are not sure, then go to God and admit it. Don't try to hide it. Go to God, and say, "Dad, I have a problem. I'm confused, and I have doubt." He already knows anyway, so the sooner you confess that to Him, the sooner He can help you deal with it. You see, when we became believers, God placed His Holy Spirit inside of us, and that Spirit came with a promise, a promise that the Spirit would teach us all things. "But the Counselor, the Holy Spirit, whom the Father will send in my name, will teach you all things and will remind you of everything I have said to you" (John 14:26). That includes teaching us how we can overcome our doubts.

If and when doubt rises, go to God and His Word and pray because, rest assured, God will make it clear to you. And if you need more reassurance as I sometimes do, check out Luke 12:32, one of my favorite verses: "Do not be afraid, little flock, for your Father has been pleased to give you the kingdom...."

Don't be afraid. We have nothing to worry about. Why? Why shouldn't I be afraid? Because my Father is pleased to give me the kingdom. Don't you want the best for your kids? I do. Maybe we all didn't have great parents. Maybe we had terrible parents, but we all have the one same God. We all have a wonderful, infallible, amazing God who loves us so much and says He is pleased to give us the kingdom. He wants us to have it.

Do you understand we are co-heirs to the throne of heaven with Jesus? Picture this: the lawyers for Warren Buffett track you down and say, "Great news. You didn't know it, but you're being adopted by the Buffetts. You're Warren Buffett's kid, and you're heir to his fortune." Or if you prefer, maybe it's Bill Gates. Either way, you'd be dancing as if you'd just won the biggest lottery of all time. The thing is, if you're a believer in Jesus Christ, you're God's kid, and trust me here, God is richer than Buffett and Gates combined times a million, and as an heir, that makes you part of the richest family ever. You have heaven. You have God. God wants to give you His kingdom. He goes on to say in Luke 12:33-34, "Provide purses for yourselves that will not wear out, a treasure in heaven that will not be exhausted, where no thief comes near and no moth destroys. For where your treasure is, there your heart will be also."

Where is my heart? Where is yours? Is it with God or with the world? What do I value? Is my treasure the things of the world, or is my treasure the things of heaven? It's a pretty simple instruction, isn't it? Focus on heaven, and you will treasure the things of God. Don't focus on heaven, and you will not treasure the things of God. I don't like the outcome of the "don't-focus-on-things-of-heaven" option. It has way too much downside risk to it.

And even though I know that risk, my stubborn streak still shows up on occasion, and God has to deal with me like he did with Peter. I love Peter because he's like me – stubborn and sometimes stupid – which is a great recipe for trouble. Peter is also like me because he learned his lessons the hard way, but God still taught him.

I give Peter and the disciples credit. At least after they saw the miracle of Peter walking on water (Matthew 14), they finally said, "Okay, you really are the Son of God. We're done. We believe you. No problem." Do we do the same thing, or do we continually doubt God, putting Him to the test? I would like to think that every believer reading this today has seen God in action in his or her own life; has walked with the Holy Spirit; has known without a doubt that there is a God; that at the moment of salvation, God came to live inside your heart and is with you. So why would you doubt? Why would you still need a sign? At least the disciples said, "Truly you are the Son of God," and then they followed Him.

It was after they believed who He was and followed Him – obeyed His directions – that God worked through them. Scripture says that all things are possible with God (Matthew 19:26, Mark 10:27). God wants to use you to accomplish great things for His kingdom. All you have to do is say "Yes, Lord" and be obedient wherever God places you.

It's not a competition. It's not Jack versus Billy Graham and I don't measure myself against any other believer. My job is to get up in the morning and love the Lord with all my heart and say "Yes, Lord." That's all I have to do. Yes, Lord. And I am blessed based on my obedience to God, not my accomplishments, and the same is true for you. And Yes, God will use your obedience to accomplish wonderful things through you.

If you're not obedient, however, you can rest assured that He will raise up somebody else to accomplish what He wants to do. God does not need Jack to write a book. And God does not need me to preach a sermon. He can use you or someone else to do His work, but He will only use someone who is obedient, so wherever God has placed you in your life, your only job is to say "Yes, Lord."

It seems so simple, and yet, we screw it up all the time. I couldn't help wondering what prevents us from accomplishing God's purpose in our lives. What prevents us from living an abundant, joy-filled Christian life?

Let's look at Martha and Mary in Luke 10:38–42:

> As Jesus and his disciples were on their way, he came to a village where a woman named Martha opened her home to him. She had a sister called Mary, who sat at the Lord's feet listening to what he said. But Martha was distracted by all the preparations that had to be made. She came to him and asked, "Lord, don't you care that my sister has left me to do the work by myself? Tell her to help me!"
>
> "Martha, Martha," the Lord answered, "you are worried and upset about many things, but only one thing is needed. Mary has chosen what is better, and it will not be taken away from her."

Picture this: Martha's there. Mary's there. They're sisters. They know Jesus is coming over for the big dinner, and Martha is working her butt off. You know what it's like to prepare a dinner for guests, and they didn't have your kitchen, did they? It takes work. Martha's working, and Mary isn't. Instead, she's kind of praying, maybe reading her Bible, and having a quiet time with God. Martha's complaining, "Hey, Mary, this is not the best time for that. There's work to be done. Come on, and help me."

Sure enough, Jesus comes in, and you can see it, Mary's sitting at Jesus' feet and Martha's getting everything ready, and now, she's getting mad because this is just not fair – her working so hard, and Mary sitting over there, doing nothing. Finally, she can't take it anymore.

Have you ever been at that stage in your life where finally you're just so angry, so frustrated over something, that it just comes out?

She's at her wits' end, pulls Jesus aside, and unloads. "Hey, this isn't fair. There's so much work to be done, and Mary's sticking it all on me. You're a rabbi. You're a teacher. You tell Mary that she needs to come help me, right now."

And Jesus, obviously seeing the condition of Martha's heart and the condition of Mary's heart, says "Martha, Martha, you are worried about many things."

Is that you and me? Are we worried about the many things of this world that come between us and God and prevent us from doing what we're supposed to do, which is saying "Yes, Lord"? There is a time and place for the work that needs doing, but how often do we let the work overtake the most important thing, which is worshipping God and living for Him? There was Mary doing the right thing, and Jesus basically says, "Hey, Martha, I know there's a lot to do, but right now, only one thing is needed, just one. Just love me. Worship me. Be obedient to me." And notice that He also tells Martha, "This will not be taken from her." You see, Jesus isn't going to take Himself out of our picture. No, He wants to be in the picture with us. The problem that most of us have is that we take Him out of the picture. And even if we don't, the world wants to take our faith, our worship, and our God out of the picture.

By "the world," I mean our everyday lives and what fills them up – things like schedules, jobs, TV, neighbors. Everyone, including our own nature, tells us there's stuff we have to do, and we have to do it before we sit still with God. And absolutely, there is stuff to do. I have to work. I have to take care of my family. I want to love my wife. I want to be a good father to my kids. I want to do everything I can possibly do, but first and foremost, I want to worship my God, because when I put Him first, all the rest of that stuff falls into its proper place.

How can I do that? I follow His directions. What are they? Seek God and His kingdom first (Matthew 6:33).

Where are the directions? In the Bible. It's God's Word and our instruction manual for the abundant life. Jesus warns us not to be distracted by the things of the world, but to keep our eyes on Him. Otherwise, we'll be like Peter, who started out well (walking on water) but got distracted and scared by the wind such that he took his eyes off Jesus and began to sink. We must be careful and prepared and on guard for whatever will distract us from Jesus and scare us off. Some of those things are matters of simple discipline, like choosing to set time aside to read and study the Bible, choosing to turn off the TV because Jesus sure wouldn't watch that show. They are not life-threatening choices, but they do have life implications, just as we saw with my son Ricky.

On the other hand, we do have an enemy, Satan, who will do whatever it takes to keep us from God. In fact he's bent on our destruction. "Your enemy the devil prowls around like a roaring lion looking for someone to devour" (1 Peter 5:8). How can we protect ourselves from our enemy?

God tells us in Ephesians 6:10–18, where He explains all the weapons He has provided for us – the weapons of truth, faith, righteousness, prayer, and the Bible. He completes His instructions for using these weapons by telling us:

> Finally, be strong in the Lord and in his mighty power. Put on the full armor of God so that you can take your stand against the devil's schemes. For our struggle is not against flesh and blood, but against the rulers, against the authorities, against the powers of this dark world and against the spiritual forces of evil in the heavenly realms. Therefore put on the full armor of God, so that when the day of evil comes, you may be able to stand your ground, and after you have done everything, to stand.

We can't be prepared for an attack unless we follow the directions so as to minimize our vulnerability to our enemy.

One of the greatest areas of vulnerability for us is money. God knows it, and there are more than 2,000 verses in scripture that address money and possessions and give warnings or guidance on how to avoid troubles associated with them. One of the clearest is 1 Timothy 6:6–10:

> But godliness with contentment is great gain. For we brought nothing into the world, and we can take nothing out of it. But if we have food and clothing, we will be content with that. People who want to get rich fall into temptation and a trap and into many foolish and harmful desires that plunge men into ruin and destruction. For the love of money is a root of all kinds of evil. Some people, eager for money, have wandered from the faith and pierced themselves with many griefs.

Why do people who want to get rich fall into traps and temptations? It's simple; they take their focus off of God, and they put it on money. They don't follow God's instructions about finances. When that happens, people are prone to foolish and sometimes less-than-ethical choices, activities, and strategies to obtain the wealth they crave. We don't have to look too far in our culture for proof. Can you say "Enron" (one of the greatest stock scandals of all time)? The greed of Wall Street, bankers, and Americans came to a head in 2008, and it has been the cause for one of the greatest times of volatility and portfolio value loss in history. Notice that God didn't say that we would not be faced with those desires, issues, and problems. As a matter of fact He said we would be. And that's why we have to be on guard and follow directions so that we can avoid those pitfalls and temptations that can cause us to wander from our faith and bring many griefs upon ourselves and our families.

So, what are God's directions for dealing with the desire to get rich? Let's pick it up in 1 Timothy 6:11–12: "But you, man of God, flee from all this, and pursue righteousness, godliness, faith, love, endurance and gentleness. Fight the good fight of the faith. Take hold of the eternal life to which you were called when you made your good confession in the presence of many witnesses."

It couldn't be any clearer than that, could it? Are you a man or woman of God or not? It's just that simple. If you are, God has told you what to do. He didn't say you wouldn't be tempted by all this. He said when you are tempted, flee from it, and pursue the things of God.

Our Father wants us to have all the blessings, and He tells us how to get them. Seek first His kingdom and His righteousness, flee the temptations of greed, and pursue righteousness, faith, love, endurance, and gentleness.

God makes it easy for us to read the directions. Are we so foolish that we won't listen? Or are we like the teenage son? I love my son dearly, and I know that he loves me, but when he turned 18, you know what? He still thought he had all the answers to all the questions. It's amazing how absurd his thinking was.

His mother and I fantasize about having a logical discussion with him: "What are you basing your knowledge on, son? You have no life experience. You've done nothing but live in this house. We have the life experience of the world. I've gone down every path you're going to go through. I know where it leads. I know where it goes. And I could tell you how to avoid the dead ends."

It's a fantasy that most parents have, I'm sure, that the child would see the logic and admit his lack of knowledge and ignorance on certain subjects . But no, somehow, based on nothing, based on pride, based on a limited perspective, Rick, at age 18, had this belief that he already knew it all, even though he's never seen, experienced, or had to overcome. And He knows a lot about my past, but completely disregards the lessons it offers.

Aren't we prone to doing the same thing with God? God clearly tells us everything. He's told us the end of the story. His Word is full of others' life experiences that are recorded for us, so we will learn from them. In fact they are directions for us to follow: "For everything that was written in the past was written to teach us, so that through endurance and the encouragement of the Scriptures we might have hope" (Romans 15:4).

God has given us the directions we need to live a life full of the blessings He wants to give us. He has also given us free will to choose whether to follow those directions or not. "But if serving the Lord seems undesirable to you, then choose for yourselves this day whom you will serve ... But as for me and my household, we will serve the Lord" (Joshua 24:15).

It's all right there for the taking, God's promises of blessings for obedience and curses for disobedience (Deuteronomy 28). How easily we overlook the whole consequences-of-our-choices thing. When I think about how that has played out in Rick's life, it's incredible. He didn't want to obey by discussing the reasons for cutting himself, but when he did, he was healed of that issue. He didn't want to keep taking saxophone lessons, but when he did, he discovered great joy in using the talent God has given him. He didn't want to leave town for college, but when he did, he had access to one of the greatest musical schools in the country. When he let go of his will and his preferences and submitted to his earthly father, he eventually received blessings he hadn't expected.

Ideally, the more that happens in each of our lives, the easier it becomes to exchange our I-don't-want-to for "Yes, Lord" and the blessings that follow. The more we read the map, the easier it is to follow directions.

Now, here's what every believer should say and do. It's Psalm 119:59–60: "I have considered my ways and have turned my steps to your statutes, I will hasten and not delay to obey your commands." That's what we're supposed to do – evaluate our ways and then quickly turn and obey God's Word. Proverbs 16:25 says, "There is a way that seems right to a man, but in the end it leads to death." I think about Rick cutting himself, a way that seemed right to him but in the end could lead to death, and I thank God that didn't happen. God's way is the only way. God says, "I am the way and the truth and the life. No one comes to the Father except through me" (John 14:6).

Is there some behavior or thought pattern in your life that might lead to the death of a dream, a relationship, or a goal? Are you cutting yourself out of the blessings that God wants to give you because you aren't willing to follow His directions?

It's time to live for God so that when you finally get to heaven, you will hear Him say, "Well done, good and faithful servant ... Come and share your master's happiness!" (Matthew 25:21, 23). That's what I want to hear.

What I don't want to hear is God saying, "Hey, Jack, welcome home ... you know, there was so much more I could have done in your life. I had such great plans for you. I wanted to work in you. I wanted to mature you and teach you and bless you, but you were not willing. You let the things of the world get in the way. Look at the things I had in store for you, Jack! Look what could have been, if only you'd been willing to give Me more than just two hours on Sunday morning.

Imagine if you'd given Me the other 166 hours a week to work with. If only you'd been willing ..."

Are you willing to say, "I have considered my ways and have turned my steps to your ways"?

Take God's way. Make the turn to His road.

You can hear God saying, "Come. Trust Me. With Me, you can do this." It's so simple, and yet, people make it so complicated. All you have to do is take the next step: Ask Him for directions and follow them! Then you won't have to worry about getting lost.

Are You In or Out?

I can tell you from personal experience that, without God in your life, you will never get the results you want. Nothing else satisfies – not money, power, sex, prestige, or possessions, fame, great looks, lovers, or friends. I tried them all.

Now, think about it this way. Think about traveling to a specific destination rather than to "nowhere." Say you got on a bus, and you knew for an absolute fact that the bus was going to Baltimore. That's what the ticket and the schedule said, and the driver confirmed it, so you're 100 percent certain that the bus is going to Baltimore. If so, then it shouldn't bother you how many times the bus stops along the way. You could let whatever happened during the journey just roll off your back because you knew that, at some point, you'd reach your destination. You could relax and enjoy the trip, especially because you don't even have to drive the bus! The driver is in control. All you have to do is kick back and be the best passenger you can be.

Now, let's zoom out to the spiritual level. What is the destination of your life, and how can you make sense of the road trip? What will happen to you when the trip of life ends, and you die?

If you don't know, then all the stops and layovers and potholes along the road of life create stress, fear, and doubt about what tomorrow will bring. As a Christian, however, I know what my life is supposed to be about, and I know with absolute certainty what's going to happen when I die. I'm going to spend eternity with Jesus Christ in heaven, and so are you, if you are saved. If you're not saved, then you don't know where this bus called "life" is going. Of course, you are scared and panicked. Every turn, every stop, or delay makes you wonder what's going to happen next and if you'll ever get anywhere. You can't enjoy the journey or find satisfaction in it.

Some of you might think that's easy for me to say. You look at what I have going for me at this moment – I'm married to a beautiful woman, I drive a nice car, sold a successful business, got some savings in the bank, get to preach God's Word, and even wrote this book. So, what have you got to complain about, Jack? Your life is good.

It is now, but it sure didn't used to be. Just before God really got hold of my heart, I was as close to bankruptcy as you can be without filing the papers. I had no relationships, no job, and I was literally one month away from being homeless, so when God got my attention and said, "Put Me first, Jack," I said, "Okay." I decided to go for whatever God was offering, and now, nearly 20 years later, I'm here to tell you that it's worth it. Putting God first was the best thing then, and it still is today.

Don't you want to be able to say that same thing? Don't you want to know that, no matter what happens on this Earth, you can have a guaranteed home in heaven for all eternity, where there are no mortgages, no potholes, no pain, no tears, no hamster wheels, and no death?

To be blunt, we're all prone to taking the easy way out and blaming everyone else for how miserable we are. I've had people tell me, "Jack, it's the world's fault, the bank's fault, the government's fault. It's easy for you to talk about your good life, but you don't have my problems. The waves of the world have come in and drowned me. If you had my marriage, my job, my financial responsibilities, my physical infirmities ... Jack, you don't know what the world has done to me. And by the way, yeah, Jack, I too had great dreams for my future when I was a kid, but I never realized them, and now, I couldn't if I wanted to because I'm trapped in this life that I am living now. I couldn't get out if I wanted to."

Hear me clearly. The people who rest on those excuses do not understand that they are sinners, just like every other person in the world. I can say that because I lived that way for years. We are sinners because we are descended from Adam, the first guy on Earth. His sin? Most of us spout off that he disobeyed and ate the fruit, but the real original sin was his motive for chomping down on that fruit in the first place – He wanted to be like God. And that desire to discard the real God and take His place is the sin nature that has been passed down from generation to generation. We inherited that desire to be our own gods, but the irony is that we can barely control our own actions, much less those of other people. Think about it! If I am my own god, how come I can't snap my fingers and get perfect vision, so I can see past the traffic light without my glasses? If I am my own god, why, years ago when I needed to, couldn't I muster up enough discipline to keep myself sober and enjoying life? If I can't do something that simple, how can I expect to exercise godly power over anything or anyone beyond me? Would you want a god that small?

Or would you want a God that is all-powerful, all-knowing – a God who knows you from the inside out because He designed you in your mother's womb (Psalm 139:15–16), a God who tells us flat out that He has great plans for us? "'For I know the plans I have for you,' declares the Lord, 'plans to prosper you and not to harm you, plans to give you hope and a future'" (Jeremiah 29:11). God wants to give you peace and joy and blessings, and He knows how to give them to you because He knows you through and through and loves you anyway, in spite of your sin nature. Why? Because you are His child. He wants a relationship with you now and wants you to be with Him in heaven once this Earthly life is over. But to have those things, we have to do something. We have to call out to Him and believe in Him. In Romans 10:13, God says, "... 'Everyone who calls on the name of the Lord will be saved.'" God isn't going to chase you down, grab you by the neck, and force you to believe Him! But He is always there, waiting for you to call on Him. If you will sincerely look for Him and reach out for Him, you will find Him, and He will respond. That's a promise from God.

God says in Luke 11:9–10, "So I say to you: Ask and it will be given to you; seek and you will find; knock and the door will be opened to you. For everyone who asks receives; he who seeks finds; and to him

who knocks, the door will be opened." There it is. Ask, and you'll receive. Seek, and you'll find. Knock, and the door will be opened. When
you do that, God will deposit His Holy Spirit in you, and His job is
to teach you all things, but you have to take that first step. It's like going to a concert. You have the tickets, but you still have to go inside to
hear the music. Don't worry about what notes are going to be played
in every song or how many songs are going to be played; just enjoy the
music. Accept God into your life, and let Him start to work.

You say, "Jack, I'm nervous, I'm scared; what are people going to
think?" Who cares what other people think? It's your life, your joy, and
your happiness. And it's all about where YOU are going to spend eternity. That's what we are talking about! God is inviting YOU to enjoy
the full benefits of a love relationship with Him.

In Ephesians 2:4–6, God's Word says, "... because of his great love
for us, God, who is rich in mercy, made us alive in Christ even when we
were dead in transgressions – it is by grace you have been saved. And
God raised us up with Christ and seated us with him in the heavenly
realms ...." Maybe you're asking, "How can God love me? I screwed up
so badly, I don't deserve His love. I'm selfish, I'm egotistical, and I can't
do what God wants me to do. I'll never be able to do it."

I can't do it, either, but it's not about us doing it. It's about allowing God to work through us. Trying to "do it" or "do life" on my own
for all those years is why I was so miserable in the first place. My way
couldn't change a thing.

If you're going to be fulfilled in life, there's a big question you're
going to have to settle first – Why am I here? Unless you know the
reason you're here, you'll never be satisfied because you won't be doing what you were designed for. If you're a Phillips-head screwdriver,
you're going to be pretty useless if you spend your life trying to tighten
standard-head screws. And if you're a human being, then you're going
to feel useless or adrift if you're trying to make yourself happy by doing
things you were not really created for.

To find your purpose, which is the only way you'll ever be able to
live the life you imagined, you have to consult the One who created you,
and that's God. Let's see what He has to say. "For he [God] chose us in
him before the creation of the world to be holy and blameless in his
sight. In love he predestined us to be adopted as his sons through Jesus
Christ, in accordance with his pleasure and will ...." (Ephesians 1:4–5).

So, remember what I said at the beginning? God has a perfect plan for each of us, and it's always better than the one we imagine or devise, but until we deal with the God thing, we can't get the benefits of that plan. It's time to deal with the God thing. God is pure, 100% pure. In order for us to get into heaven, then, we also have to be perfectly pure, with no sin in us.

Easy, right? You've never murdered anyone, you haven't told any big lies, you haven't robbed a bank, and everyone says you're the nicest coach in Little League.

Wrong. It doesn't matter how nice you are or how much you've given to the Red Cross. God simply says that we have to be absolutely perfect from day one. Why? Because God is pure and holy and cannot tolerate sin. Don't forget, we are descended from Adam, the one who started this whole "I'll be my own god, thank you very much" issue, and as a result, we've inherited that tainted nature. Being penalized for what an ancestor did might not seem fair, but we're comfortable with the concept. When one guy on the football team commits a foul, the whole team is penalized, right? It's just not fun when that policy is being applied to us individually, but it is what it is. Now, don't throw the book across the room. I know it sounds like a set-up for failure. God knows we're imperfect, and yet still holds us to an impossible standard, so where does that leave us?

With a choice. To understand what God is doing in our lives, we have to understand God's standard. His standard in heaven is endless perfection and complete purity. You can't take one drop of red dye and put it in a big pitcher of water without the whole thing changing color. That's what sin is like in our lives. If I had two glasses of water, and in one glass, I put a little tiny piece of my dog's doody (That's right, dog doody... now tell me this isn't a great book. Where else are you going to get analogies like this?), and in the other glass, I put a big chunk of dog doody in it, which one would you drink? Neither, I hope! Of course, we wouldn't want either one of them because they are both polluted. That's how sin is to God. It doesn't matter if it's a little or a lot; it contaminates the whole glass. Heaven is pure, and any sin, no matter how small or insignificant *we* think it is, would contaminate it.

And no, I'm not saying we are all pieces of dog doody. But we are sinful, impure humans, because we are descended from Adam, the original sinner, and so by the very natural process of being descended from an impure, sinful man, we cannot be pure. An impure ingredient cannot produce a pure product. We needed a way to be made pure and perfect, and God did that in the form of Jesus.

Ephesians 2:4–9 explains it this way:

> But because of his great love for us, God, who is rich in mercy, made us alive with Christ even when we were dead in transgressions – it is by grace you have been saved. And God raised us up with Christ and seated us with him in the heavenly realms in Christ Jesus, in order that in the coming ages he might show the incomparable riches of his grace, expressed in his kindness to us in Christ Jesus. For it is by grace you have been saved, through faith-and this not from yourselves, it is the gift of God – not by works, so that no one can boast.

Impurity cannot be allowed in heaven, but God loves us so much and wants a relationship with us so badly that He made a way for that gap between us to be bridged. He made a way for that "I-god" nature and all the garbage it accumulates to be washed away. He made a way for us to be able to come to Him and be holy, even while we are still alive. We don't have to wait, and we should not wait any longer, for if we do, we will miss God's blessing of abundant life now and eternal life forever. You must decide now, while you are alive. If you die without deciding, then you have decided "NO." Not accepting Him now is the same thing as denying Him. It's that simple.

Even if I tried to deny my connection to Adam, I still had to face my sins and call them what they were. Garbage! And what do I mean by garbage? Jealousy, anger, fear, gossip, sexual immorality, lying, cheating, pornography, drugs, alcohol, lust ... how long a list do I have to make?

Will you pause here for a moment and face your sins? If you're having a little trouble with that word, then think about the signs over your hamster wheels. Greed – did you take money that wasn't yours? Or maybe you "only" cheated on your taxes. Selfishness – what did you choose to keep for yourself that could have been used to help someone in need? Sexual immorality – are you hiding any magazines or Internet sites or relationships from your family?

We might fool other people and even ourselves, but we're sure not putting anything over on God. The incredible thing about God is that He has already seen all that stuff in our lives that we don't want to look at or admit, and He loves us anyway. The Bible tells us that He loved us first, before we even knew Him, and He loves us so much that He took the first step to reconcile us with Him. He sent His son, Jesus, to clean the garbage out of our lives. How did Jesus do that?

Jesus came to Earth, lived a perfect, sin-free life, and because He is descended from God and not Adam, He was also free from Adam's nature. Jesus then died in our place. Why does that matter?

We already said that in order to get into heaven, we have to be perfect. We are not perfect, and we know it. Nobody really has to spell it out for us. What's cool, though, is that we can exchange our garbage record for Jesus' perfect record. In Hebrews 10:14, it says that "... by one sacrifice he [Jesus] has made perfect forever those who are being made holy." That's you and I who are being made holy. If we believe in Jesus and repent of our sins, then we are holy forever – not for a week, month, or year, but forever. Elsewhere in the Bible, God says, "This is the covenant I will make with them. I will put my laws in their hearts and I'll write them on their minds. Their sins and lawless acts I will remember no more" (Hebrews 10:16–17). God will forgive your sin and lawless acts, and He'll never bring them up again. *Ever.* There is no transcript, no personnel file, no record down at police headquarters. It doesn't matter what you've done. God will forgive it and not hold it against you. He goes so far as to say, "... as far as the east is from the west, so far has he removed our transgressions from us" (Psalm 103:12).

If you want that kind of deal, then this exchange of your record for Jesus' record is the first and most important step and cannot be skipped. It's called getting "saved" or being "born again" or "salvation," but all those words mean is that we agree with God. We repent of our sin (meaning we are sorry for it, and we turn away from it), and we believe that Jesus is who He says He is (the living son of God), and we accept Him as our Lord and Savior. We call out to God, believing in Jesus, and when we do, God adopts us as His children, and we are part of His family and heirs to His kingdom!

You might be shaking your head saying, "No way, Jack. I am not going there."

That's your choice. God doesn't force Himself on anyone, but if you reject salvation, what you're really saying is you'd rather keep going nowhere with your tiny "I-god" philosophy when you could have Jesus and all His blessings on Earth and eternity in heaven. You could live a life as a friend and child of God, with the God who created everything, including you. The choice is yours, but come on, at least take a look. If I told you I had gold buried in my backyard, and every day, I went out there and dug more of it up, you might not believe me, but I'll bet you would come and take a look to see for yourself if I was telling the truth, because if I was, you would want some! You wouldn't want to miss out on the riches. So wouldn't you want to take a look for yourself and see whether or not I was lying about Jesus? Jesus is the treasure, not in the money sense, but in the priceless, personal sense.

I understand your hesitation. I knew about Jesus for a long time but never bothered to take a look for myself. I finally did, but as I told you, I came to God the hard way, when my life came crashing down. You don't have to. And absolutely, if this whole Jesus thing were a scam, well, I am reasonably intelligent; I believe I would have figured it out in less than a year. It's not a scam. It's almost 20 years later for me. It's real and it keeps getting better every day. What do you have to lose?

Okay, I'm moving on. So, how do you get saved? It's easy. You can say a simple prayer, right now! Here's how it goes: "Lord, I know I'm a sinner. I repent of my sin. I know You died for my sins on the cross. Come into my heart and live inside me. I accept you as my Lord and Savior."

That's it. The moment you say that prayer, believing in your heart that Jesus really is the Son of God and that He died for your sins, He comes into your heart to live. He takes out your old heart, puts in your new heart, and deposits His Holy Spirit into you, so a part of God is now living inside you! That's what being saved is.

Let's recap what just happened. You recognize that all the stuff you do and have cannot satisfy something deeper inside your heart and soul. You see that the status quo, doing the same thing over and over, isn't working, because you are trying to be your own little god when your godly abilities are severely hampered by human weaknesses and limitations. What do you do? You call out to God to save you, but that means acknowledging that He's in charge and that in order to have a relationship with Him and receive the benefits of it, you have to admit that you are not perfect (you are a sinner) and, therefore, incapable of meeting the one requirement God has – perfection. And so, you agree that Jesus, God's Son, lived a perfect life and died in your place to pay the price for your sins, and you prayed to God and told Him that. You repented of your sins, which means you turned away from them, and you asked God to come inside of your heart and be Lord of your life.

If you went through all that and just prayed that simple prayer, believing without a doubt that Jesus IS the Son of God, welcome to the family of God! I can assure you that your place in heaven is secure, and you will begin to get the benefits of that relationship with Jesus Christ immediately. If for any reason, you haven't yet said that prayer, then I pray that the Holy Spirit of God will work on your heart, and you will come to the point in your life that you will realize that you want Jesus to be God in your life and Lord of your life. Don't delay. You don't know what the future holds. You don't know when you are going to be called to go to heaven or, unfortunately, to go to hell, but right now, you can choose the final, eternal destination of your life's ticket.

In 1 Thessalonians 5:2 (and in 2 Peter 3:10), we are told that "the day of the Lord will come like a thief in the night." You don't know when your time on this planet will be over. You can't say, as some do about the hurricane forecasts, "Death never comes here; I'll be fine." Well, I guess you could say that, but you would be wrong. The reality is that 10 out of 10 people will die. Still, God allows you the freedom to reject His warnings. People ignore storm warnings all the time, and some of them don't live to tell about it.

So, is that it? Do you just get saved, and life keeps on going as it did before?

No! May it never be so, because you would miss all the blessings God has in store for you in this life now (that's the abundant life "now" God promises every believer). If you want the peace and joy that God offers for this Earthly life and the comfort God gives as you go through struggles, then you'll make more room for God in your life, and the more room you make for Him, the more your life will change for the better.

So, what about you? Are you in or out?

Ending Notes

Well, there you have it. Was I right? Do you think now you have the roadmap to the ultimate Christian Life? I hope so. Now, make sure you DON'T BLOW IT WITH GOD!

But remember one thing, the most important thing. Yes, God has provided us a roadmap, but the best part of the ultimate Christian life is walking through your life on Earth with Jesus as your guide, traveling the road and making the journey WITH God, your loving Father, with you and guiding you every step of the way. You are not alone ... God is with YOU. The Holy Spirit of God living inside of you will be with you to guide you, direct you, comfort you, teach you, and love you every step of the way. The only way you can blow it is if you don't do it with Jesus.

There is no better journey than one shared with a friend. Jesus is your friend, and He loves you. So enough of the reading ... time to start living!

Enjoy it all.
Jack

Acknowledgments

Where do I even start? So many people have touched a part of this project, whether directly or through their influence over the years. Whether it was showing me unconditional love when I needed it or simply giving me a pat on the back, meaning, "Keep on going, don't give up," it's all important to me. How can mere words truly acknowledge your impact on my life and on the writing of this book? Well, let me give it my best shot ...

First, to Jesus Christ, my Lord and Savior, for the great gift of salvation He has given me. I am so grateful and comforted by the knowledge I will spend all eternity with God in heaven. Right now, though, of equal value to me has been God's gift of His Holy Spirit, which He deposits in every believer on our accepting Him as Lord and Savior. To have the privilege and joy of God's Holy Spirit living inside me – guiding me, helping me, loving me, teaching me, praying for me, walking with me every step of the way – has been the most valuable thing I have ever received in my life. It truly is my treasure. I think that is why each day (since 1991, when I came to know the Lord) just keeps getting better and better – because I am living it with God. Thank you, Jesus. Thank you, God. Thank you, Father.

To my wonderful wife, Beth, who has stood by my side throughout every day of our lives together – who prayerfully, lovingly, and faithfully supports me in everything I do, whether I am right or wrong.

(Now, that is devotion, for which I am grateful, and love, which I do not deserve, but appreciate so much). Thank you for loving me through thick and thin pizza. God truly blessed me the day He gave you to me as my lifemate.

To my wonderful three children: Ricky (21), Jackson (7), and Talia (5). Oh, how much I love each one of you! God has shown me just a glimpse of how much He loves us, His children, by giving me the three of you to love. The unique love I have for you each is amazing; it just encompasses all of my heart, so much so that after I met you, Ricky, I never thought I'd have room in my heart to love any more children. I loved you so much, and yet in God's power, I am able to love all three of you with ALL my heart. Now, that is awesome!

Ricky, I've taught you everything I know, yet I know that is not enough. I promise you this – everything you will ever need or want comes from God, so make sure you take the time to learn from Him.

Jackson, you are my son, through and through. I know all the junk that comes with that (sorry, I'm not perfect) but with God's power and Spirit inside you, I pray you will maximize the good traits I have been able to pass along to you and completely reject and discard that which is garbage! I love you, son.

Talia, where do I even begin – your sweet smile, your loving face, the kindness and sweetness of God expressed in your little heart and smile. You are truly my angel. I have said it to you kids over and over again, but I want to say it here where you can always see it, where it never goes away. "Daddy loves you, and thanks Jesus for you every single day of my life." I truly must be the luckiest and most blessed man alive.

To my mom and dad for giving me physical life and a lifelong love and friendship that is unmatched. I've met a lot of people, but none have been so blessed as I in the parent department. I got all the aces in this game! Thank you, God. Thanks, Mom and Dad, for always loving me, no matter what. Your unconditional love for me has taught me and blessed me more than you will ever know.

To my wonderful brother Mike, my supporter, friend, and protector all my life. I have learned so much from you. I thank God we have the opportunity to share so many memories, not just from childhood, but also by creating new ones as we go, with each other and with our families. Boy, I love you. To Leslie, my sister-in-law, thank you for taking time to understand me and for loving me. You are not just a family member to me, but also a loved and valued friend.

To my nephews, Zac and Dylan. You guys are the greatest. Thank you for always believing in me and always loving me no matter what I thought or what I did. Watching you guys grow and getting to be a part of your lives is a blessing I cherish. Zac, those Springsteen concerts will never be forgotten. Dylan, watching you pitch and play high school baseball recently was one of the most thrilling moments of my life. It just made me so happy to see you carrying on the Levine tradition, which you know always includes baseball!

To Aunt Bunny, my best friend for so many years. If not for you, I might not have made it down to paradise (Florida). I miss you so much. You are gone, but not forgotten. Love you.

To Beth, George, Jake and Alexa, what a long strange trip it's been! You've got to love America (and chairs and croissants, among other things). Thank you, my wonderful cousins, who love us so much. See you in Disney!

To the Big H, Uncle Herb. Thanks for your help and advice over the years. You are always willing to help my family and me and always have been. We are lucky to be blessed with such a great uncle as you – the smartest man I know and a great guy!

Lots of love and special thanks to my aunts, uncles and cousins who loved me and encouraged me all my life, no matter what, especially Aunt Mick, Uncle Sy, Uncle Hank and Kalliope. To my cousins Renee and Phyllis, Bonnie and Al, Randy and Cory, Robbie, Kelly, Quinn and Kayla. Susie, John and the Max man. Adam, Jordan and Vanessa. A special thanks to the Hammers – that would be Cousin Cliff and Cousin Glenn (with whom I have had some of the happiest times in my life ... Tahoe, anyone?) To Pam, Taylor, Carly, and Jonah, I love you all.

To Sean Legasse (and his wonderful family), you are my brother in life. Thanks for being my sounding board and for saving my life. I don't recall ever having a friend like you who was always so giving of himself and so supportive of me in everything I did. I am so happy to know you and the singing voice-mail messages I get. Well, how can you put a price on that! Move home already, man, I miss you. Haven't I let you have enough "roof time" yet?

To Wayne and Sharon Gill, faithful friends to the end. Wayne, my brother and accountability partner, my teacher and mentor, but most importantly, my friend, thanks for being there for me every step of the journey. We know God brought our families together, and I am so glad He has kept us together as we continue to seek and serve Him with our lives.

To Dr. David Morgan and his family (Eileen, his beautiful wife; Edmund and Lance; Pat and the rest of the wonderful Morgan family). Even though you went home to be with the Lord long ago, it was in you (and your family) that I saw the joy of the Lord, the peace of the Lord, the comfort of the Lord, reflected through your sweet beautiful smiling face. I heard such passion in your booming voice as you would close in prayer, your powerful prayers reaching to God's throne in heaven. Yet, your humble, loving, peaceful heart and the actions of your life lived for Jesus spoke louder than a thousand prayers. In you, I saw what I wanted, what I had to have, because you had the treasure – you had everything. Even though you were never wealthy by the world's standards, you were definitely the richest man I ever met. Even though we did not spend much time together, the short time in which I got to know you moved me, so I had to imitate your life ... and then, of course, I learned and realized that you were simply imitating Jesus. Thanks for doing such a great job. See you at the Lord's table, my friend.

To Scott Stevens. Outlaw, you are the man. When Bruce said, "You'll need a good companion now for this part of the ride," he was not fooling. I am very grateful that God gave you to me. Your advice has been invaluable, but your friendship is worth even more. If not for you, I would not know how to salute!

To Scott Sakoff. You are like a brother to me. Thanks for loving me unconditionally. Great dinners, great nights at Pompano and a great friendship. My prayer for you is that God will bless you with all the desires of your heart and that you bless God with the desire of His heart, which is an even closer relationship with you.

To Wayne Bostain, I think you are my oldest and closest Florida friend, buddy. It's been a lot of years since we played softball at Loggers Run. You are a true friend and a great guy. I love you. We've been through it all together, and I wouldn't have it any other way. You are a true blessing to me.

To Ron and Christie Secreto and family (including my godson Rocco ... go get 'em Rock!). What a ride, buddy boy. I am so glad you are back on top where you deserve to be. Thanks for pitching me batting practice, and who will ever forget Rathburns (simply known as "Kevin's") in Atlanta (and, of course, the accompanying trip to the Pit). There is so much more than I could thank you for, but loyalty and friendship like yours is hard to find, and I am lucky to have found it.

To Andy Brief. Buddy boy, Jake Brief wanting to see Bruce on his ninth birthday, Rachael's drawing from years ago, that ferry ride I took one time in Miami to see you on vacation, Adclub, Whit Hobbs (swim trunks), Al Feldman (cigars), Fred Stern, Stan Turk, Kenmore Emerson, Henry, The Glaze, Glenn Greenberg, all the Kornhauser kids (especially Edie), Lauren Roberts, Harry Fox, and NW Ayer, and now you want me to talk about the Bruce years ... and the recent culmination of all things in Fort Lauderdale where we got to share life with our buddy after the show. Come on, you've got to be kidding! Blood brothers! No retreat, no surrender! I can honestly say some of the best hours of my life were spent with you. I cherish your lifelong friendship and look forward to many more ridiculously insane hours at Bruce shows and other worthy events, even if it's a French fry, a quick meeting with the "gentleman" or a Flower Drum lunch, I'll take it. And remember, don't walk under the scaffolding.

To Joe and Carmen Zappoli and their family. God blessed me so richly when all of you came into my life. But you already knew that! Remember Lance (that cowboy), and I'll always remember the phone call with the Doc in the car and all the rides while sharing each other's innermost thoughts and feelings. Thanks for always making me feel special and important. You are a great friend and a true man of God with one of the most loving and tender hearts toward others I have ever seen. I know and pray God will continue to bless you and your family, but no matter what happens, just remember one thing – "We'll figure it out!"

To Rene Kageff (and family). Rene, my brother, I am so proud of you. Watching you trust and grow in the Lord has been one of my great joys. Many are called, but so few respond as God truly desires. Your faithfulness, love, and living for God are an inspiration to me. I am blessed to know you and watch you grow in the Lord, and I can't wait to see what God is going to do with the rest of your surrendered life. Thank you for being my true brother in Christ.

To Al Ott. Hey, big guy, I still see you lying face down in the grass at softball practice, but you always got back up – a lesson I live by. You are such a dear friend. I am so sorry that we are separated by distance, but not by our hearts. Thanks for all your love and support over the years. Hurry up, and move back to Florida.

To Dave Shaner. Thanks, buddy, for loving me and for being such a true follower of the Lord. I know we both struggle, but you have sharpened me as iron sharpens iron, and I pray I have been able to repay the favor.

To Josh Shaner. Buddy boy, you are a good student. You listened and did what you had to. I love you and thank you for allowing me to be a part of your life. I hope I can continue to be a blessing to you and to guide you in any way you need. A lot of people talk about it, but YOU DID IT! I am very proud of you.

To Pat Sheehan. My brother, thanks for covering my back all these years, especially the wild ones before I got married. I love you, and I am so glad God brought you into my life. We have gotten to share so many things – God, TMS, and a lot of great conversations on many rides home. I am praying that God richly blesses you, and thank you for the brother, friend, and protector you have been to me.

To all my brothers at Boca Glades Baptist Church Men's Ministry. Thank you for showing me what true brotherhood means. I have been molded and changed by the bonds that have been forged over years of sharing and caring for each other, by the transparency, the tough love, the truth, and the guiding hand of our Lord and Savior Jesus Christ that has permeated this group. Thanks to each and every one of you for being a part of it, for making it so easy for me, and for being such a blessing and a constant in my life. I have been blessed by all those wonderful Saturday mornings more than I could ever describe to anyone. God has used them to mold me and shape me into being a better man. Thanks, guys, for the love!

To Truman Herring, my first pastor, and still my pastor today almost 20 years later. You are my spiritual father, a gift from God, and the man who is more like Jesus than anyone I know, in every area of his life. Your patience and love in answering my questions gently guided me always back to Jesus and His Word. I know God's providence and hand put me in your office that Tuesday morning back in 1991 and I keep giving thanks for that every day. You, Connie, and your family have been a tremendous blessing to me. There aren't words to properly express my gratitude for all you have done for me, for believing in me, trusting me, encouraging me to start to preach when I came to you with that crazy idea, and using your contacts and network to get me opportunities to do what I felt God calling me to do. I hope I can repay you by pouring into the lives of other young men and trying to be a role model and mentor to them. If I can do half the job for them that you have done for me, they will be the luckiest men in the world. Thank you, Truman; you are a Godsend.

To all the pastors who have helped me and encouraged me so much, who have become my friends and mentors and allowed me the privilege of sharing their pulpits. I am honored, guys. Thank you, Bob Dyshuk, Dale Faircloth, Mike Butzberger, Rob Taylor, Paul Luis, Jason Bland, Don Karpinen, Sandy Huntsman, and Scott Opalsky.

David Hughes, thanks for the encouragement, brother, for sharing ideas, and for loving my kids so much! You could do nothing better for me than that.

To Michele Chin. What a wonderful, loving, kind, Godly woman you are. You inspire me so much, and I appreciate your dedication to your profession and more importantly to God. Thank you for allowing me the privilege of sharing some of God's Word with you and for the continued encouragement you give me to do just that.

To Shawn Bombaro (Ranger, Bomber, Lester). You know I love you, and I know God has great plans for your life. I am proud of you for seeking His will and His face above all things. Keep the faith. Pillar out.

To Chris Hammond. You walk the walk all the way. Thanks for your inspiration and your friendship. I know God has knit us together for a reason. Keep living for the Lord; people see it, and it is inspirational!

To Claudia and Meyer Pinnachow. Thank you for your love and friendship. What a long way we've come, and how great is our God to bless our families as He has. I love you guys and am so happy you have followed God and His call on your lives. I look forward to being able to spend quality time with you again soon.

To Nelson Ortega, my brother, my brother, my brother. What a long time it's been. All I can say is "Wow! How the Lord has taken hold of your life." You are living proof of God's power and a changed life. May you always stay close to God, walk in His Word, and live abundantly for Him. I cherish the time we have spent together over these last 15 years and delight in the fact there is more to come.

To Dave Belson. We met in 1977 when you were just a kid. You're a special guy, and God used you to witness to me, even when you were just a boy. I am so proud of the man you have become, of your family, and your walk with God. I know it's not easy, but it's all about staying faithful to God and not compromising. You made your choice to follow Jesus when you were still a boy. You have never wavered, and I know God's reward for that kind of faith will be greater than you can ever imagine. Thank you for letting me be a part of your life.

To Willie Aragon. I love you, man. You are the sweetest, kindest guy I know and a true friend. I am so glad our friendship has moved beyond our business introduction. You have the most wonderful gifts a man can have, which is kindness for others and a love for the Lord. Thank you. Blessings to you and your family.

To Ruben "Hurricane" Garcia. Thanks for everything. Thanks for giving me an ear to talk to and for listening and encouraging me in everything I do. I am blessed to have a Christian friend and brother such as you!

Sal "The Promoter" Delfino. Thanks for all your hard work, support and faithfulness to God and to me. I am so lucky to have you as a friend and co-laborer for Christ.

To Larry Haynes. Buddy boy, did you get your humor yet? You got out on top, kid; you won the game. Now, enjoy the spoils of victory!

To Shane Rimer. Thanks for all your editing help with all my sermon CDs over the years. Hot newsflash, kid – hang on! God's not done with you yet!

To Keith and Milt Hitson. It's hard to believe there is still a place in this world where a man's word is his bond. In Hamilton County, you have shown me that truth is still valued above all, and you guys are living proof of that! Thank you for all your help and friendship. Keith, you are right, the dinners were the best part of everything! I believe we'll be having them again soon! Thanks for helping me in any and every way you possibly could. I treasure our friendship.

To Mark and Renee Harding. I will never forget the trust and faith you both had in me and were willing to put in me. I will forever be grateful for that show of support and encouragement. You will never know just how much it meant to me. Thanks.

To Steven DeSisto, aka Max. I love you. Thanks for showing me Babe Ruth's grave and a lifetime of friendship. If we keep remembering driving around in your Mustang all those years, then we can stay young forever.

To Leo Harmonay. Remember, "Time is an ocean, but it ends at the shore!" Make the most of it NOW!

To John Walchli. Long may you run!

To Gerry Poole, if there was one man I'd want in the foxhole with me, it's you. Thanks for never, never giving up on me, no matter how hard the battle.

To David Rice. Brother, seeing the miracle God has done in your life, how He has restored you and showered His love upon you, and how you have accepted it brings me greater joy then I can describe. It is my pleasure and privilege to be a part of your life.

To everyone else I love and forgot to mention ... I'm sorry. Please e-mail me, and I'll put you in the next book.

Special Thanks

Lee Owen of WritePointMedia, Inc., my editor, coach, and sister in the Lord. Thank you for your wisdom, guidance, friendship, and advice. I could not have written this book without you. You kept my head straight and focused when I thought it was too tough, and I wanted to quit. Thanks for taking me through step by step. Thanks for letting me call and vent and then sending me back to work. I hope you are as pleased and satisfied with this book as I am. I know the prayer of your heart is that God be glorified and uplifted through our work together. Our prayer from the beginning has been that God would use this book to reach and grow people for His kingdom, so they may bear fruit and fruit that will last. Thanks for the pruning sessions and the fruit! Your editing skills were of tremendous value to me, but your friendship, guidance, and encouragement are worth even more.

John Rabe, buddy, it was you and me in the beginning. Thank you for your friendship and hard work. You were the first one I talked to about the idea for this book, and your insight and advice proved invaluable. Your feedback allowed me to see where I truly wanted to go with the book; I know it took a long time, but I'll trust God on his timing, as always. I am so grateful you are in my life as a friend and brother in Christ. Any guy who loves lunch and Springsteen as much as you is all right in my book.

Bob Zuccaro, you know how much you helped me, your technical expertise in fact-checking and proofing and undying loyalty to me and the Lord are so appreciated. I pray you are satisfied with the result. You were the greatest Felix Unger ever and a great friend and brother in the Lord. Thanks!

And to Carl Foster, you know this is just the beginning. I believe God has brought us together for this project, and I knew the first time I met you that you were the man for the job. After all, what good is having a book if no one reads it. So, my friend... the bat's in your hands. Start swinging!

FREE INSIDE-THE-BOOK EXCLUSIVE OFFER!

The *Don't Blow It with God* Messages

FREE- 3 different audios of Jack Alan Levine's relevant and dynamic messages. Each one will teach you first hand another principle of "Don't Blow it With God"

You can download for free by logging into our website
www.DontBlowItWithGod.com

or have all 3 CD's mailed directly to you for just a total of $2.95 for shipping and handling.

| **Download and listen from your computer...** | **...which works with Apple iPod, iPhone and most other MP3 devices...** | **...or, order a CD and have it shipped right to your door!** |

GO NOW TO: DontBlowItWithGod.com

www.DontBlowItWithGod.com

Coming Soon!

Jack Levine's New Book
**Where the Rubber Meets the Road
with God**

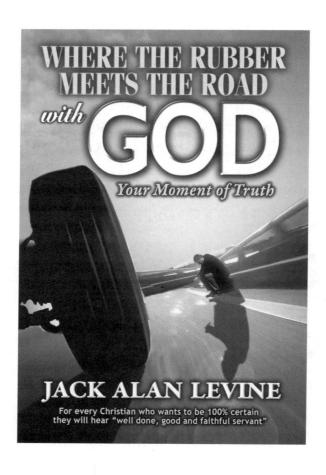